3rd Workshop on Issues in Teaching Computational Linguistics 2008

(TeachCL 08)

Held in conjunction with ACL-HLT 2008

Columbus, Ohio, USA
19-20 June 2008

ISBN: 978-1-61738-551-3

Printed from e-media with permission by:

Curran Associates, Inc.
57 Morehouse Lane
Red Hook, NY 12571

proceedings.com

Some format issues inherent in the e-media version may also appear in this print version.

Printed by Curran Associates, Inc. (2010)

Association for Computational Linguistics
209 N. Eighth Street
Stroudsburg, Pennsylvania 18360

Phone: 1-570-476-8006
Fax: 1-570-476-0860

acl@aclweb.org

Additional copies of this publication are available from:

Curran Associates, Inc.
57 Morehouse Lane
Red Hook, NY 12571 USA
Phone: 845-758-0400
Fax: 845-758-2634
Email: curran@proceedings.com
Web: www.proceedings.com

Introduction

Many of us in this field face the daily challenge of trying to teach computer scientists, linguists and/or psychologists together. Following the success of the two previous ACL workshops (2002 and 2005, `http://www.eecs.umich.edu/~radev/TeachingNLP`) on this theme, we held this 2-day workshop associated with ACL-HLT 2008 to carefully examine the advantages and disadvantages of an interdisciplinary approach, and to explore techniques specifically aimed at teaching programming to social scientists and linguistics to computer scientists. As computational linguistics (hopefully) becomes of more and more relevance to industrial applications, we must ensure that our students (both undergraduate and graduate) are given adequate preparation for functioning in a practical industrial environment as well as an academic research environment. We need to exchange views on appropriate curriculum for both undergraduate students and graduate students, and linguists, psychologists and computer scientists. There are many questions to be addressed about the necessary background for linguists, psychologists and computer scientists before they can communicate effectively with each other and learn at the same pace.

How much math is necessary? Is it possible to teach linguists Natural Language Processing techniques without first teaching them how to program? Can undergraduates hold their own in graduate courses? Can linguists and computer scientists make separate but equal contributions to term projects? How can linguistics students get ACL publications? What is the relevance of psycholinguistics?

In addition to fifteen high quality reviewed papers and an invited talk by Lori Levin and Drago Radev on the recent very successful American Computational Linguistics Olympiad, the program includes three panels: a panel on industry expectations for computational linguists organized by Chris Brew; a panel on essential curriculum for computational linguistics organized by Emily Bender and Fei Xia; and a panel on techniques for teaching extremely interdisciplinary classes organized by Gina Levow.

The specific goals of this workshop build upon the goals of past CL teaching workshops:

- To provide a setting for mutual feedback on participants' instructional approaches as well as guidance on future directions.
- To identify and separate from the general teaching aspirations of host departments the key features of an elective undergraduate and graduate curriculum in computational linguistics.
- To determine a curriculum that embraces diversity of background as an opportunity rather than shies from it as a problem.
- To generally promote visibility for the study of CL teaching as a bona fide scholarly activity
- In the case of the industrial panel, to set up a situation in which those responsible for education and training in CL-using industry become more aware of the diversity of backgrounds available in the ACL world.

We are especially grateful to the panel organizers, the presenters who submitted excellent papers and to our hard working program committee. Particular thanks go to Richard Wicentowski for being Publications Chair.

Martha Palmer, Chris Brew, Fei Xia

Organizers:

Martha Palmer, University of Colorado, USA
Chris Brew, The Ohio State University, USA
Fei Xia, University of Washington, USA

Program Committee:

Steven Bird, Melbourne University, Australia
Robert Dale, Macquarie University, Australia
Jason Eisner, Johns Hopkins University, USA
Tomaz Erjavec, Josef Stefan Institute, Slovenia
Mary Harper, University of Maryland, USA
Julia Hirschberg, Columbia University, USA
Graeme Hirst, University of Toronto, Canada
Julia Hockenmaier, University of Illinois - UIUC, USA
Ewan Klein, University of Edinburgh, UK
Lillian Lee, Cornell University, USA
Lori Levin, Carnegie Mellon University, USA
Gina-Anne Levow, University of Chicago, USA
Liz Liddy, Syracuse University, USA
Edward Loper, University of Pennsylvania, USA
Detmar Meurers, Universität Tübingen, Germany
Ani Nenkova, University of Pennsylvania, USA
James Pustejovksy, Brandeis University, USA
Massimo Poesio, University of Trento, Italy / University of Essex, UK
Dragomir Radev, University of Michigan, USA
Anoop Sarkar, Simon Fraser University, Canada,
Harold Somers, University of Manchester, UK
Matthew Stone, Rutgers University, USA
Richard Wicentowski (Publications Chair), Swarthmore College, USA
Dekai Wu, Hong Kong University of Science and Technology, China

Invited Speakers:

Dragomir Radev, University of Michigan, USA
Lori Levin, Carnegie-Mellon University, USA

Panel Organizers:

Emily Bender, University of Washington, USA
Chris Brew, The Ohio State University, USA
Gina-Anne Levow, University of Chicago, USA
Fei Xia, University of Washington, USA

Table of Contents

Teaching Computational Linguistics to a Large, Diverse Student Body: Courses, Tools, and Interdepartmental Interaction
Jason Baldridge and Katrin Erk 1

Building a Flexible, Collaborative, Intensive Master's Program in Computational Linguistics
Emily M. Bender, Fei Xia and Erik Bansleben 10

Freshmen's CL Curriculum: The Benefits of Redundancy
Heike Zinsmeister 19

Defining a Core Body of Knowledge for the Introductory Computational Linguistics Curriculum
Steven Bird 27

Strategies for Teaching "Mixed" Computational Linguistics Classes
Eric Fosler-Lussier 36

The Evolution of a Statistical NLP Course
Fei Xia 45

Exploring Large-Data Issues in the Curriculum: A Case Study with MapReduce
Jimmy Lin 54

Multidisciplinary Instruction with the Natural Language Toolkit
Steven Bird, Ewan Klein, Edward Loper and Jason Baldridge 62

Combining Open-Source with Research to Re-engineer a Hands-on Introductory NLP Course
Nitin Madnani and Bonnie J. Dorr 71

Zero to Spoken Dialogue System in One Quarter: Teaching Computational Linguistics to Linguists Using Regulus
Beth Ann Hockey and Gwen Christian 80

The North American Computational Linguistics Olympiad (NACLO)
Dragomir R. Radev, Lori Levin and Thomas E. Payne 87

Competitive Grammar Writing
Jason Eisner and Noah A. Smith 97

Studying Discourse and Dialogue with SIDGrid
Gina-Anne Levow 106

Teaching NLP to Computer Science Majors via Applications and Experiments
Reva Freedman 114

Psychocomputational Linguistics: A Gateway to the Computational Linguistics Curriculum
William Gregory Sakas 120

Support Collaboration by Teaching Fundamentals
Matthew Stone 129

Workshop Program

Thursday, June 19, 2008

8:55–9:00 Welcome

Paper Presentation I: Curriculum Design

9:00–9:30 *Teaching Computational Linguistics to a Large, Diverse Student Body: Courses, Tools, and Interdepartmental Interaction*
Jason Baldridge and Katrin Erk

9:30–10:00 *Building a Flexible, Collaborative, Intensive Master's Program in Computational Linguistics*
Emily M. Bender, Fei Xia and Erik Bansleben

10:00–10:30 *Freshmen's CL Curriculum: The Benefits of Redundancy*
Heike Zinsmeister

10:30–11:00 Coffee Break

Paper Presentation II and Panel I: Curriculum Design

11:00–11:30 *Defining a Core Body of Knowledge for the Introductory Computational Linguistics Curriculum*
Steven Bird

11:30–12:30 Panel Discussion I: Curriculum Design (organized by Fei Xia and Emily Bender)

12:30–2:00 Lunch Break

Thursday, June 19, 2008 (continued)

Paper Presentation III: Course Design

2:00–2:30 *Strategies for Teaching "Mixed" Computational Linguistics Classes*
Eric Fosler-Lussier

2:30–3:00 *The Evolution of a Statistical NLP Course*
Fei Xia

3:00–3:30 *Exploring Large-Data Issues in the Curriculum: A Case Study with MapReduce*
Jimmy Lin

3:30–4:00 Coffee Break

Paper Presentation IV: Using NLP Tools

4:00–4:30 *Multidisciplinary Instruction with the Natural Language Toolkit*
Steven Bird, Ewan Klein, Edward Loper and Jason Baldridge

4:30–5:00 *Combining Open-Source with Research to Re-engineer a Hands-on Introductory NLP Course*
Nitin Madnani and Bonnie J. Dorr

Panel II: Industry Panel

5:00–6:00 Panel Discussion II: Industry Panel (organized by Chris Brew)

Friday, June 20, 2008

Friday, June 20, 2008 (continued)

Paper Presentation V and Invited Talk

9:00–9:30 *Zero to Spoken Dialogue System in One Quarter: Teaching Computational Linguistics to Linguists Using Regulus*
Beth Ann Hockey and Gwen Christian

9:30–10:30 *The North American Computational Linguistics Olympiad (NACLO)*
Dragomir R. Radev, Lori Levin and Thomas E. Payne

10:30–11:00 Coffee Break

Paper Presentation VI: Course Design

11:00–11:30 *Competitive Grammar Writing*
Jason Eisner and Noah A. Smith

11:30–12:00 *Studying Discourse and Dialogue with SIDGrid*
Gina-Anne Levow

12:00–12:30 *Teaching NLP to Computer Science Majors via Applications and Experiments*
Reva Freedman

12:30–1:30 Lunch Break

Paper Presentation VII: Course Design

1:30–2:00 *Psychocomputational Linguistics: A Gateway to the Computational Linguistics Curriculum*
William Gregory Sakas

2:00–2:30 *Support Collaboration by Teaching Fundamentals*
Matthew Stone

Friday, June 20, 2008 (continued)

Panel III: Course Design

2:30–3:30	Panel Discussion III: Course Design (organized by Gina-Anne Levow)
3:30–4:00	Coffee Break
4:00–5:00	General Discussion and Closing

Teaching computational linguistics to a large, diverse student body: courses, tools, and interdepartmental interaction

Jason Baldridge and Katrin Erk
Department of Linguistics
The University of Texas at Austin
{jbaldrid,erk}@mail.utexas.edu

Abstract

We describe course adaptation and development for teaching computational linguistics for the diverse body of undergraduate and graduate students the Department of Linguistics at the University of Texas at Austin. We also discuss classroom tools and teaching aids we have used and created, and we mention our efforts to develop a campus-wide computational linguistics program.

1 Introduction

We teach computational linguistics courses in the linguistics department of the University of Texas at Austin, one of the largest American universities. This presents many challenges and opportunities; in this paper, we discuss issues and strategies for designing courses in our context and building a campus-wide program.[1] The main theme of our experience is that courses should be targeted toward specific groups of students whenever possible. This means identifying specific needs and designing the course around them rather than trying to satisfy a diverse set of students in each course. To this end, we have split general computational linguistics courses into more specific ones, e.g., working with corpora, a non-technical overview of language technology applications, and natural language processing. In section 2, we outline how we have stratified our courses at both the graduate and undergraduate levels.

As part of this strategy, it is crucial to ensure that the appropriate student populations are reached and that the courses fulfill degree requirements. For example, our *Language and Computers* course fulfills a Liberal Arts science requirement and our *Natural Language Processing* is cross-listed with computer science. This is an excellent way to get students in the door and ensure that courses meet or exceed minimum enrollments. We find that many get hooked and go on to specialize in computational linguistics.

Even for targeted CL courses, there is still usually significant diversity of backgrounds among the students taking them. Thus, it is still important to carefully consider the teaching tools that are used; in section 3, we discuss our experience with several standard tools and two of our own. Finally, we describe our efforts to build a campus-wide CL program that provides visibility for CL across the university and provides coherence in our course offerings.

2 Courses

Our courses are based on those initiated by Jonas Kuhn between 2002 and 2005. Since 2005, we have created several spin-off courses for students with different backgrounds. Our broad goals for these courses are to communicate both the practical utility of computational linguistics and its promise for improving our understanding of human languages.

2.1 Graduate

We started with two primary graduate courses, *Computational Linguistics I and II.* The first introduces central algorithms and data structures in computational linguistics, while the second focuses on learn-

[1] Links to the courses, tools, and resources described in this paper can be found on our main website: http://comp.ling.utexas.edu

Proceedings of the Third Workshop on Issues in Teaching Computational Linguistics (TeachCL-08), pages 1–9,
Columbus, Ohio, USA, June 2008.

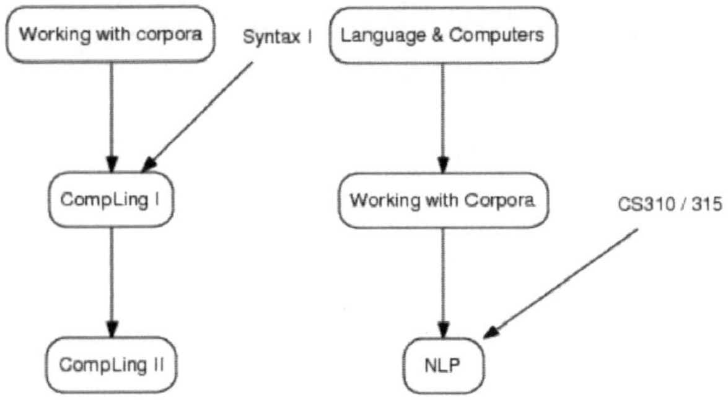

Figure 1: Flow for non-seminar courses. Left: graduate courses, right: undergraduate courses.

ing and disambiguation. This served a computationally savvy segment of the student population quite well. However, we view one of our key teaching contributions as computational linguists in a linguistics department to be providing non-computational students with technical and formal skills useful for their research. We discovered quickly that our first computational linguistics course did not fill these needs, and the second is not even accessible to most students. The graduate linguistics students did put in the effort to learn Python for *Computational Linguistics I*, but many would have preferred a (much) gentler introduction and also more coverage of issues connected to their linguistic concerns. This led us to create a new course, *Working with Corpora.*

Still, there is a need for the primary courses, which receive interest from many students in computer science and also graduate students from other departments such as German and English. One of the great surprises for us in our graduate courses has been the interest from excellent linguistics and computer science undergraduates.

We have sought to encourage our students to be active in the academic community outside of UT Austin. One way we do this is to have a final project for each course (and most seminars) that has four distinct stages: (i) a project proposal halfway through the semester, (ii) a progress report three-quarters of the way through, (iii) a 10-minute presentation during the last week of class, and (iv) a final report at the end. We have found that having course projects done in this staged manner ensures that students think very thoroughly about what their topic is early on, receive significant feedback from us, and then still have enough time to do significant implementation for their project, rather than rushing everything in last minute. Also, by having students do presentations on their work before they hand in the final report, they can incorporate feedback from other students. A useful strategy we have found for scoring these projects is to use standard conference reviews in *Computational Linguistics II.* The final projects have led to several workshops and conference publications for the students so far, as well as honors theses. The topics have been quite varied (in line with our varied student body), including lexicon induction using genetic algorithms (Ponvert, 2007), alignment-and-transfer for bootstrapping taggers (Moon and Baldridge, 2007), lemmatization using parallel corpora (Moon and Erk, 2008), graphical visualization of articles using syntactic dependencies (Jeff Rego, CS honors thesis), and feature extraction for semantic role labeling (Trevor Fountain, CS honors thesis).

Working with corpora. Computational linguistics skills and techniques are tremendously valuable for linguists using corpora. Ideally, a linguist should be able to extract the relevant data, count occurrences of phenomena, and do statistical analyses. The intersection of these skills and needs is the core of this course, which covers corpus formats (XML, bracket formats for syntax, "word/POS" formats for part-of-speech information), query languages and tools (regular expressions, cqp, tregex), and some statistical analysis techniques. It also teaches Python gently for liberal arts students who have *never programmed* and have only *limited or no* knowledge of text processing. Other main topics are the compilation of corpora and corpus annotation, with issues like representativity and what meta-data to include. At the end of this course, students are prepared for our primary computational courses.

We observed the tremendous teaching potential of effective visualization in this course with the R statistics package. It was used for statistical analyses: students loved it because they could produce meaningful results immediately and visualize them. The course includes only a very short two-session introduction to working with R. We were worried that this would overtax students because R is its own programming language. But interestingly they had no problems with learning this second programming language (after Python). This is particularly striking as most of the students had no programming experience prior to the class.

We have not yet used the Natural Language Toolkit (Loper and Bird, 2002) (see Section 3.1) in this course. But as it, too, offers visualization and rapid access to meaningful results, we intend to use it in the future. In particular, the NLTK allows very easy access to Toolbox data (Robinson et al., 2007), which we feel will greatly improve the utility and appeal of the course for the significant number of documentary linguistics students in the department.

Seminars. We also offer several seminars in our areas of interest. These include *Categorial Grammar*, *Computational Syntax*, and *Lexical Acquisition*. These courses have attracted "non-computational" linguistics students with related interests, and have served as the launching point for several qualifying papers and masters theses. It is important to offer these courses so that these students gain a view into computational linguistics from the standpoint of a topic with which they already have some mastery; it also ensures healthier enrollments from students in our own department.

We are currently co-teaching a seminar called *Spinning Straw into Gold: Automated Syntax-Semantics Analysis*, that is designed to overlap with the CoNLL-2008 shared task on joint dependency parsing and semantic role labeling. The entire class is participating in the actual competition, and we have been particularly pleased with how this external facet of the course motivates students to consider the topics we cover very carefully – the papers truly matter for the system we are building. It provides an excellent framework with which to judge the contributions of recent research in both areas and computational linguistics more generally.

2.2 Undergraduate

Our first undergraduate course was *Introduction to Computational Linguistics* in Fall 2006. Our experience with this course, which had to deal with the classic divide in computational linguistics courses between students with liberal arts versus computer science backgrounds, led us to split it into two courses. We briefly outline some of the missteps with this first course (and what worked well) and how we are addressing them with new courses.

Introduction to Computational Linguistics. This course is a boiled-down version of the graduate *Computational Linguistics I* taught in Fall 2006. Topics included Python programming, regular expressions, finite-state transducers, part-of-speech tagging, context-free grammar, categorial grammar, meaning representations, and machine translation.

Overall, the course went well, but enrollment dropped after the mid-term. As many have found teaching such courses, some students truly struggled with the course material while others were ready for it to go much faster. Several students had interpreted "introduction" to mean that it was going to be *about* computational linguistics, but that they would not actually have to *do* computational linguistics. Many stayed with it, but there were still others who could have gone much further if it had not been necessary to slow down to cover basic material like *for* loops. Note that several linguistics majors were among the compationally savvy students.

In fairness to the students who struggled, it was certainly ill-advised to ask students with no previous background to learn Python and XFST in a single semester. One of the key points of confusion was regular expression syntax. The syntax used in the textbook (Jurafsky and Martin, 2000) transfers easily to regular expressions in Python, but is radically different from that of XFST. For students who had never coded anything in their life, this proved extremely frustrating. On the other hand, for computationally savvy students, XFST was great fun, and it was an interesting new challenge after having to sit through very basic Python lectures.

On the other hand, the use of NLTK to drive learning about Python and NLP tasks (like building POS-taggers) significantly eased the burden for new programmers. Many of them were highly satisfied that they could build interesting programs and experiment with their behavior so easily.

Language and Computers. We had fortunately already planned the first replacement course: *Language and Computers*, based on the course designed at the Department of Linguistics at the Ohio State University (Brew et al., 2005). This course introduces computational linguistics to a general audience and is ideal for students who want exposure to computational methods without having to learn to program. We designed and taught it jointly, and added several new aspects to the course. Whereas OSU's course fulfills a Mathematical and Logical Analysis requirement, our course fulfills a Science requirement for liberal arts majors. These requirements were met by course content that requires understanding and thinking about formal methods.

The topics we added to our course were question answering, cryptography,[2] and world knowledge. The course provides ample opportunity to discuss high-level issues in language technology with low-level aspects such as understanding particular algorithms (e.g., computing edit distance with dynamic programming) and fundamental concepts (such as regular languages and frequency distributions).

In addition to its target audience, the course nonetheless attracts students who are already well-versed in many of the low-level concepts. The high-level material plays an important role for such students: while they find the low-level problems quite easy, many find a new challenge in thinking about and communicating clearly the wider role that such technologies play. The high-level material is even more crucial for holding the interest of less formally minded students. It gives them the motivation to work through and understand calculations and computations that might otherwise bore them. Finally, it provides an excellent way to encourage class discussion. For example, this year's class became very animated on the question of "Can a machine think?" that we discussed with respect to dialogue systems.

Though the course does not require students to do any programming, we do show them short programs that accomplish (simplified versions of) some of the tasks discussed in the course; for example, short programs for document retrieval and creating a list of email address from US census data. The goal is to give students a glimpse into such applications, demonstrate that they are not hugely complicated magical systems, and hopefully entice some of them to learn how to do it for themselves.

The 2007 course was quite successful: it filled up (40 students) and received very positive feedback from the students. It filled up again for this year's Spring 2008 offering. The major challenge is the lack of a textbook, which means that students must rely heavily on lecture slides and notes.

Words in a Haystack: Methods and Tools for Working with Corpora. This advanced undergraduate version of *Working with corpora* was offered because we felt that graduate and undergraduate linguistics students were actually on an equal footing in their prior knowledge, and could profit equally from a gentle introduction to programming. Although the undergraduate students were active and engaged in the class, they did not benefit as much from it as the graduate students. This is likely because graduate students had already experienced the need for extracting information from corpora for their research and the consequent frustration when they did not have the skills to do so.

Natural Language Processing. This is an demanding course that will be taught in Fall 2008. It is cross-listed with computer science and assumes knowledge of programming and formal methods in computer science, mathematics, or linguistics. It is designed for the significant number of students who wish to carry on further from the courses described previously. It is also an appropriate course for undergraduates who have ended up taking our graduate courses for lack of such an option.

Much of the material from *Introduction to Computational Linguistics* will be covered in this course, but it will be done at a faster pace and in greater detail since programming and appropriate thinking skills are assumed. A significant portion of the graduate course *Computational Linguistics II* also forms part of the syllabus, including machine learning methods for classification tasks, language modeling, hidden Markov models, and probabilistic parsing.

We see cross-listing the course with computer science as key to its success. Though there are many computationally savvy students in our liberal arts college, we expect cross-listing to encourage significantly more computer science students to try out a course that they would otherwise overlook or be unable to use for fulfilling degree requirements.

[2]The idea to cover cryptography came from a discussion with Chris Brew; he now teaches an entire course on it at OSU.

3 Teaching Tools and Tutorials

We have used a range of external tools and have adapted tools from our own research for various aspects of our courses. In this section, we describe our experience using these as part of our courses.

We have used Python as the common language in our courses. We are pleased with it: it is straightforward for beginning programmers to learn, its interactive prompt facilitates in-class instruction, it is text-processing friendly, and it is useful for gluing together other (e.g., Java and C++) applications.

3.1 External tools and resources

NLTK. We use the Natural Language Toolkit (NLTK) (Loper and Bird, 2002; Bird et al., 2008) in both undergraduate and graduate courses for in-class demos, tutorials, and homework assignments. We use the toolkit and tutorials for several course components, including introductory Python programming, text processing, rule-based part-of-speech tagging and chunking, and grammars and parsing. NLTK is ideal for both novice and advanced programmers. The tutorials and extensive documentation provide novices with plenty of support outside of the classroom, and the toolkit is powerful enough to give plenty of room for advanced students to play. The demos are also very useful in classes and serve to make many of the concepts, e.g. parsing algorithms, much more concrete and apparent. Some students also use NLTK for course projects. In all, NLTK has made course development and execution significantly easier and more effective.

XFST. A core part of several courses is finite-state transducers. FSTs have unique qualities for courses about computational linguistics that are taught in linguistics department. They are an elegant extension of finite-state automata and are simple enough that their core aspects and capabilities can be expressed in just a few lectures. Computer science students immediately get excited about being able to relate string languages rather than just recognizing them. More importantly, they can be used to elegantly solve problems in phonology and morphology that linguistics students can readily appreciate.

We use the Xerox Finite State Toolkit (XFST) (Beesley and Karttunen, 2003) for in-class demonstrations and homeworks for FSTs. A great aspect of using XFST is that it can be used to show that different representations (e.g., two-level rules versus cascaded rules) can be used to define the same regular relation. This exercise injects some healthy skepticism into linguistics students who may have to deal with formalism wars in their own linguistic subfield. Also, XFST allows one to use lenient composition to encode Optimality Theory constraints and in so doing show interesting and direct contrasts and comparisons between paper-and-pencil linguistics and rigorous computational implementations.

As with other implementation-oriented activities in our classes, we created a wiki page for XFST tutorials.[3] These were adapted and expanded from Xerox PARC materials and Mark Gawron's examples.

Eisner's HMM Materials. Simply put: the spreadsheet designed by Jason Eisner (Eisner, 2002) for teaching hidden Markov models is fantastic. We used that plus Eisner's HMM homework assignment for *Computational Linguistics II* in Fall 2007. The spreadsheet is great for interactive classroom exploration of HMMs—students were very engaged. The homework allows students to implement an HMM from scratch, giving enough detail to alleviate much of the needless frustration that could occur with this task while ensuring that students need to put in significant effort and understand the concepts in order to make it work. It also helps that the new edition of Jurafsky and Martin's textbook discusses Eisner's ice cream scenario as part of its much improved explanation of HMMs. Students had very positive feedback on the use of all these materials.

Unix command line. We feel it is important to make sure students are well aware of the mighty Unix command line and the tools that are available for it. We usually have at least one homework assignment per course that involves doing the same task with a Python script versus a pipeline using command line tools like `tr`, `sort`, `grep` and `awk`. This gives students students an appreciation for the power of these tools and for the fact that they are at times preferable to writing scripts that handle everything, and they can see how scripts they write can form part of such pipelines. As part of this module,

[3] `http://comp.ling.utexas.edu/wiki/doku.php/xfst`

we have students work through the exercises in the draft chapter on command line tools in Chris Brew and Marc Moens' Data-Intensive Linguistics course notes or Ken Church's *Unix for Poets* tutorial.[4]

3.2 Internal tools

Grammar engineering with OpenCCG. The grammar engineering component of *Computational Syntax* in Spring 2006 used OpenCCG,[5] a categorial grammar parsing system that Baldridge created with Gann Bierner and Michael White. The problem with using OpenCCG is that its native grammar specification format is XML designed for machines, not people. Students in the course persevered and managed to complete the assignments; nonetheless, it became glaringly apparent that the non-intuitive XML specification language was a major stumbling block that held students back from more interesting aspects of grammar engineering.

One student, Ben Wing, was unhappy enough using the XML format that he devised a new specification language, DotCCG, and a converter to generate the XML from it. DotCCG is not only simpler—it also uses several interesting devices, including support for regular expressions and string expansions. This expressivity makes it possible to encode a significant amount of morphology in the specification language and reduce redundancy in the grammar.

The DotCCG specification language and converter became the core of a project funded by UT Austin's Liberal Arts Instructional Technology Services to create a web and graphical user interface, VisCCG, and develop instructional materials for grammar engineering. The goal was to provide suitable interfaces and a graduated series of activities and assignments that would allow students to learn very basic grammar engineering and then grow into the full capabilities of an established parsing system.

A web interface provided an initial stage that allowed students in the undergraduate *Introduction to Computational Linguistics* course (Fall 2006) to test their grammars in a grammar writing assignment. This simple interface allows students to first write out a grammar on paper and then implement it and test it on a set of sentences. Students grasped the concepts and seemed to enjoy seeing the grammar's coverage improve as they added more lexical entries or added features to constrain them appropriately. A major advantage of this interface, of course, is that it was not necessary for students to come to the lab or install any software on their own computers.

The second major development was VisCCG, a graphical user interface for writing full-fledged OpenCCG grammars. It has special support for DotCCG, including error checking, and it displays grammatical information at various levels of granularity while still allowing direct *source text* editing of the grammar.

The third component was several online tutorials—written on as publicly available wiki pages—for writing grammars with VisCCG and DotCCG. A pleasant discovery was the tremendous utility of the wiki-based tutorials. It was very easy to quickly create tutorial drafts and improve them with the graduate assistant employed for creating instructional materials for the project, regardless of where we were. More importantly, it was possible to fix bugs or add clarifications while students were following the tutorials in the lab. Furthermore, students could add their own tips for other students and share their grammars on the wiki.

These tools and tutorials were used for two graduate courses in Spring 2007, *Categorial Grammar* and *Computational Linguistics I*. Students caught on quickly to using VisCCG and DotCCG, which was a huge contrast over the previous year. Students were able to create and test grammars of reasonable complexity very quickly and with much greater ease. We are continuing to develop and improve these materials for current courses.

The resources we created have been not only effective for classroom instruction: they are also being used by researchers that use OpenCCG for parsing and realization. The work we did produced several innovations for grammar engineering that we reported at the workshop on Grammar Engineering Across the Frameworks (Baldridge et al., 2007).

3.3 A lexical semantics workbench: Shalmaneser

In the lexical semantics sections of our classes, word sense and predicate-argument structure are core topics. Until now, we had only discussed word sense

[4] `http://research.microsoft.com/users/church/wwwfiles/tutorials/unix_for_poets.ps`

[5] `http://openccg.sf.net`

disambiguation and semantic role labeling theoretically. However, it would be preferable to give the students hands-on experience with the tasks, as well as a sense of what does and does not work, and why the tasks are difficult. So, we are now extending Shalmaneser (Erk and Pado, 2006), a SHALlow seMANtic parSER that does word sense and semantic role assignment using FrameNet frames and roles, to be a teaching tool. Shalmaneser already offers a graphical representation of the assigned predicate-argument structure. Supported by an instructional technology grant from UT Austin, we are extending the system with two graphical interfaces that will allow students to experiment with a variety of features, settings and machine learning paradigms. Courses that only do a short segment on lexical semantic analysis will be able to use the web interface, which does not offer the full functionality of Shalmaneser (in particular, no training of new classifiers), but does not require any setup. In addition, there will be a stand-alone graphical user interface for a more in-depth treatment of lexical semantic analysis. We plan to have the new platform ready for use for Fall 2008.

Besides a GUI and tutorial documents, there is one more component to the new Shalmaneser system, an adaptation of the idea of grammar engineering workbenches to predicate-argument structure. Grammar engineering workbenches allow students to specify grammars declaratively. For semantic role labeling, the only possibility that has been available so far for experimenting with new features is to program. But, since semantic role labeling features typically refer to parts of the syntactic structure, it should be possible to describe them declaratively using a tree description language. We are now developing such a language and workbench as part of Shalmaneser. We aim for a system that will be usable not only in the classroom but also by researchers who develop semantic role labeling systems or who need an automatic predicate-argument structure analysis system.

4 University-wide program

The University of Texas at Austin has a long tradition in the field of computational linguistics that goes back to 1961, when a major machine translation project was undertaken at the university's Linguistics Research Center under the direction of Winfred Lehman. Lauri Karttunen, Stan Peters, and Bob Wall were all on the faculty of the linguistics department in the late 1960's, and Bob Simmons was in the computer science department during this time. Overall activity was quite strong throughout the 1970's and 1980's. After Bob Wall retired in the mid-1990's, there was virtually no computational work in the linguistics department, but Ray Mooney and his students in computer science remained very active during this period.[6]

The linguistics department decided in 2000 to revive computational linguistics in the department, and consequently hired Jonas Kuhn in 2002. His efforts, along with those of Hans Boas in the German department, succeeded in producing a computational linguistics curriculum, funding research, (re)establishing links with computer science, and attracting an enthusiastic group of linguistics students.

Nonetheless, there is still no formal interdepartmental program in computational linguistics at UT Austin. Altogether, we have a sizable group of faculty and students working on topics related to computational linguistics, including many other linguists, computer scientists, psychologists and others who have interests directly related to issues in computational linguistics, including our strong artificial intelligence group. Despite this, it was easy to overlook if one was considering only an individual department. We thus set up a site[7] to improve the visibility of our CL-related faculty and research across the university. There are plans to create an actual program spanning the various departments and drawing on the strengths of UT Austin's language departments. For now, the web site is a low-cost and low-effort but effective starting point.

As part of these efforts, we are working to integrate our course offerings, including the cross-listing of the undergraduate *NLP* course. Our students regularly take Machine Learning and other courses from the computer science department. Ray Mooney will teach a graduate *NLP* course in Fall 2008 that will offer students a different perspective and we hope that it will drum up further interest

[6] For a detailed account, see: `http://comp.ling.utexas.edu/wiki/doku.php/austin_compling_history`

[7] `http://comp.ling.utexas.edu`

in CL in the computer science department and thus lead to further interest in our other courses.

As part of the web page, we also created a wiki.[8] We have already mentioned its use in teaching and tutorials. Other uses include lab information, a repository of programming tips and tricks, list of important NLP papers, collaboration areas for projects, and general information about computational linguistics. We see the wiki as an important repository of knowledge that will accumulate over time and continue to benefit us and our students as it grows. It simplifies our job since we answer many student questions on the wiki: when questions get asked again, we just point to the relevant page.

5 Conclusion

Our experience as computational linguists teaching and doing research in a linguistics department at a large university has given us ample opportunity to learn a number of general lessons for teaching computational linguistics to a diverse audience.

The main lesson is to stratify courses according to the backgrounds different populations of students have with respect to programming and formal thinking. A key component of this is to make expectations about the level of technical difficulty of a course clear before the start of classes and restate this information on the first day of class. This is important not only to ensure students do not take too challenging a course: other reasons include (a) reassuring programming-wary students that a course will introduce them to programming gently, (b) ensuring that programming-savvy students know when there will be little programming involved or formal problem solving they are likely to have already acquired, and (c) providing awareness of other courses students may be more interested in right away or after they have completed the current course.

Another key lesson we have learned is that the formal categorization of a course within a university course schedule and departmental degree program are massive factors in enrollment, both at the undergraduate and graduate level. Computational linguistics is rarely a required course, but when taught in a liberal arts college it can easily satisify undergraduate math and/or science requirements (as *Language and Computers* does at OSU and UT Austin, respectively). However, for highly technical courses taught in a liberal arts college (e.g., *Natural Language Processing*) it is useful to cross-list them with computer science or related areas in order to ensure that the appropriate student population is reached. At the graduate level, it is also important to provide structure and context for each course. We are now coordinating with Ray Mooney to define a core set of computational linguistics courses that we offer regularly and can suggest to incoming graduate students. This will not be part of a formal degree program per se, but will provide necessary structure for students to progress through either the linguistics or computer science program in a timely fashion while taking courses relevant to their research interests.

One of the big questions that hovers over nearly all discussions of teaching computational linguistics is: how do we teach the computer science to the linguistics students and teach the linguistics to the computer science students? Or, rather, the question is how to teach both groups *computational linguistics*. This involves getting students to understand the importance of a strong formal basis, ranging from understanding what a tight syntax-semantics interface really means to how machine learning models relate to questions of actual language acquisition to how corpus data can or should inform linguistic analyses. It also involves revealing the creativity and complexity of language to students who think it should be easy to deal with. And it involves showing linguistics students how familiar concepts from linguistics translate to technical questions (for example, addressing agreement using feature logics), and showing computer science students how familiar friends like finite-state automata and dynamic programming are crucial for analyzing natural language phenomena and managing complexity and ambiguity. The key is to target the courses so that the background needs of each type of student can be met appropriately without needing to skimp on linguistic or computational complexity for those who are ready to learn about it.

Acknowledgments. We would like to thank Hans Boas, Bob Harms, Ray Mooney, Elias Ponvert, Tony Woodbury, and the anonymous reviewers for their help and feedback.

[8] `http://comp.ling.utexas.edu/wiki/doku.php`

References

Jason Baldridge, Sudipta Chatterjee, Alexis Palmer, and Ben Wing. 2007. DotCCG and VisCCG: Wiki and programming paradigms for improved grammar engineering with OpenCCG. In *Proceeings of the GEAF 2007 Workshop*.

Kenneth R. Beesley and Lauri Karttunen. 2003. *Finite State Morphology*. CSLI Publications.

Steven Bird, Ewan Klein, Edward Loper, and Jason Baldridge. 2008. Multidisciplinary instruction with the Natural Language Toolkit. In *Proceedings of the Third Workshop on Issues in Teaching Computational Linguistics*. Association for Computational Linguistics.

C. Brew, M. Dickinson, and W. D. Meurers. 2005. Language and computers: Creating an introduction for a general undergraduate audience. In *Proceedings of the Workshop on Effective Tools and Methodologies for Teaching Natural Language Processing And Computational Linguistics*, Ann Arbor, Michigan.

Jason Eisner. 2002. An interactive spreadsheet for teaching the forward-backward algorithm. In Dragomir Radev and Chris Brew, editors, *Proceedings of the ACL Workshop on Effective Tools and Methodologies for Teaching NLP and CL*, pages 10–18.

Katrin Erk and Sebastian Pado. 2006. Shalmaneser – a flexible toolbox for semantic role assignment. In *Proceedings of LREC-2006*, Genoa, Italy.

D. Jurafsky and J. H. Martin. 2000. *Speech and language processing: An Introduction to Natural Language Processing, Computational Linguistics, and Speech Recognition*. Prentice-Hall, Upper Saddle River, NJ.

Edward Loper and Steven Bird. 2002. NLTK: The natural language toolkit. In *Proceedings of the ACL Workshop on Effective Tools and Methodologies for Teaching Natural Language Processing and Computational Linguistics*, pages 62–69. Somerset, NJ: Association for Computational Linguistics.

Taesun Moon and Jason Baldridge. 2007. Part-of-speech tagging for middle English through alignment and projection of parallel diachronic texts. In *Proceedings of the 2007 Joint Conference on Empirical Methods in Natural Language Processing and Computational Natural Language Learning (EMNLP-CoNLL)*, pages 390–399.

Taesun Moon and Katrin Erk. 2008. Minimally supervised lemmatization scheme induction through bilingual parallel corpora. In *Proceedings of the International Conference on Global Interoperability for Language Resources*.

Elias Ponvert. 2007. Inducing Combinatory Categorial Grammars with genetic algorithms. In *Proceedings of the ACL 2007 Student Research Workshop*, pages 7–12, Prague, Czech Republic, June. Association for Computational Linguistics.

Stuart Robinson, Greg Aumann, and Steven Bird. 2007. Managing fieldwork data with Toolbox and the Natural Language Toolkit. *Language Documentation and Conservation*, 1:44–57.

Building a Flexible, Collaborative, Intensive Master's Program in Computational Linguistics

Emily M. Bender
University of Washington
Department of Linguistics
Box 354340
Seattle WA 98195-4340
ebender@u.washington.edu

Fei Xia
University of Washington
Department of Linguistics
Box 354340
Seattle WA 98195-4340
fxia@u.washington.edu

Erik Bansleben
University of Washington
Educational Outreach
UW Tower, Box 359485
4333 Brooklyn Ave., NE
Seattle, WA 98105-9485
ebansleben@extn.washington.edu

Abstract

We present the design of a professional master's program in Computational Linguistics. This program can be completed in one-year of full-time study, or two-three years of part-time study. Originally designed for CS professionals looking for additional training, the program has evolved in flexibility to accommodate students from more diverse backgrounds and with more diverse goals.

1 Introduction

In the past two decades, there has been tremendous progress in natural language processing and various undergraduate/graduate programs in language technology have been established around the world (Koit et al., 2002; Frederking et al., 2002; Dale et al., 2002; Uszkoreit et al., 2005; Pilon et al., 2005).

This paper introduces the University of Washington's Professional Masters Program in Computational Linguistics (CLMA)—one of the largest programs of its kind in the United States—and highlights unique features that are key to its success. The CLMA program is currently operating in its third year as a fee-based degree program managed jointly by the Department of Linguistics and the Educational Outreach arm of the University. The program is distinguished by its programmatic focus, its flexibility, its format and delivery as well as in the partnerships that are an integral part of this degree.

This paper highlights how these features of our program contribute to effective teaching in our interdisciplinary field as well as making the program relevant to both working professionals and students on the research track. We provide a brief program overview highlighting the people and partnerships involved, course design, practicum and research options, and dealing with student diversity. We then reflect on how we have approached the challenges of setting up the program and our future plans.

2 Program Overview

With working professionals who wanted to return to school to retool for a career change in mind, we designed a curriculum that can be completed in 12 months of intensive full-time study. In this way, students can complete the degree without leaving the working world for too long. In addition, the compactness of the program means that even with part-time study (one-two courses per quarter), the program can be completed within a reasonable time horizon (two-three years). Once the program got underway, we found that we also had strong interest from Linguistics students. The flexibility of the part-time option has allowed us to develop a two-year schedule which accommodates students who need time to get up to speed with key CS concepts.

The curriculum is designed around hands-on and collaborative work which prepares students for industry jobs. At the same time, the courses are structured around fundamental building blocks rather than applications in order to teach students to think like computational linguists, and to provide them with an educational foundation which will remain relevant for years to come.

This section gives an overview of the CLMA program, including its structure and participants.

Proceedings of the Third Workshop on Issues in Teaching Computational Linguistics (TeachCL-08), pages 10–18,
Columbus, Ohio, USA, June 2008.

2.1 Program Structure

The CLMA program comprises three quarters (nine courses) of coursework and a summer master's project, which can take the form of an internship or a master's thesis (§3.5). The courses, described in more detail in §3 below, include three courses in Linguistics and six in Computational Linguistics.

The program also offers a series of talks by computational linguists working at local companies, an informal seminar of the computational Linguistics lab group (which includes PhD students and focuses on research methodology), and career development services as we work with students to place them in internships and post-degree jobs.

2.2 The new certificate program

This summer, the program is branching out with a new Certificate in Natural Language Technology. This three-course Certificate includes two NLP courses from the Masters degree and an introductory course titled "Computational Linguistics Foundations" which serves both this Certificate audience and acts as a refresher course for some degree students. It reinforces the concepts from Linguistics, CS and statistics that students rely on heavily in the core course sequence (see §4). The Certificate is an alternate course of study for those students wanting to study a single topic in depth but who are not yet ready to commit to the entire degree.

2.3 Synchronous online and in-person courses

As part of the certificate summer launch, we will be offering a selection of courses in a synchronous online and in-person format, streaming the content from the classroom to a live remote audience. This will allow us to extend the reach of the program and make study in Computational Linguistics available to students who otherwise would not have access to instruction in this field without relocating.

In the context of current globalization trends, the need for online and distance education is growing (Zondiros, 2008), and indeed we hope that our audience will extend beyond North America. At the same time, we agree with Neal and Miller's (2004) position that even with remote participants, the classroom remains a key part of the educational experience. We have thus adopted an approach that allows students to be part of a virtual classroom where they can engage with other students while still working from a remote location. This surmounts the hurdle of more traditional distance or online education that is primarily text-based and asynchronous.

In a pilot of an online course offering in Autumn 2007 (with Intro to Syntax), we found that most of the pieces were already in place for taking our courses online: Course materials are already disseminated through websites, student programming work is done on a server cluster that is always accessed remotely, and most of the discussion outside of class happens on electronic discussion boards.

2.4 Faculty and Staff

The CLMA program is taught by a group of instructors who combine academic knowledge and practical expertise in the field. The program budget supports two faculty positions, one tenure-track (and guaranteed by the College of Arts and Sciences), and one two-year visiting position.[1] Each of these faculty teach two of the core NLP courses described in §3.1 below and one seminar each year. In addition, they share the work of supervising MA theses and internships over the summer. In recognition of this supervising load, their schedules are arranged so that they each have one non-summer quarter off from teaching. A third faculty member in Computational Linguistics teaches three graduate-level courses in Computational Linguistics per year, and takes on one-two MA students from each CLMA cohort.

The program also includes a part-time administrator and a technical specialist within the Department of Linguistics. In addition, the program includes affiliated instructors and guest lecturers, ranging from faculty members of other departments such as CS and Statistics to researchers from industry.

2.5 Students

A strength of the program is its emphasis on student diversity and allowance for individualized student needs. The program allows for both part-time and full-time enrollment and includes both recent college graduates as well older, more non-traditional students who work in industry. We have students from throughout the US, as well as from

[1] To be converted to tenure-track in the future, once the program has a longer track-record.

Canada, China, Germany, India, Japan, and Russia. Two-year course schedules allow students to begin CLMA course work while simultaneously taking CS and statistics courses in the first year, increasing the diversity of backgrounds of our students. The program is starting to deliver several courses online (see §2.3) which provides additional flexibility to local students while also reaching a wider national and international audience. Lastly, the program seeks to foster both research and industry interests by providing both thesis and internship options.

2.6 Advisory board

The program maintains an advisory board composed of significant industry researchers and practitioners, including representatives from AT&T, Boeing, Google, IBM, Microsoft, Nuance, PARC, and Yahoo!, and faculty from several departments at the University. This board was instrumental in developing the original program focus and curriculum outline, as well as providing input from the perspective of employers as the University decided whether or not to launch the program. It continues to be engaged in guiding the program's content, providing internship opportunities for students, and keeping the content relevant to current industry trends.

2.7 Support from Educational Outreach

Another element of success is a centralized infrastructure of administration and support available through the University's Educational Outreach division (UWEO) which manages the CLMA program, among more than 30 degree offerings.

UWEO provides many benefits, including considerable institutional knowledge in starting a new degree program, providing methods of separating fee-based revenue from that of state-run programs, marketing expertise, fiscal management, registration services and more. As the outreach arm of the University, UWEO works closely with non-traditional students and is able to leverage its industry contacts to assist serving this community most effectively.

Lastly, partnering with UWEO also serves as a method of risk management for all new degree programs. As a state school, the University may have difficulty in getting state approval and funding for new degree programs unless initial need and demand can be demonstrated persuasively. UWEO can assume a certain degree of risk during the start-up phase of new programs allowing for additional flexibility and time to reach financial viability.

3 Curriculum Design

The program curriculum was designed according to the following principles: (1) we should provide students with an educational foundation that is relevant in the long term; (2) we should emphasize hands-on coursework to provide depth of understanding as well as practical experience students can point to when looking for a job; and (3) we should highlight unifying themes in a diverse set of subject matter.

The courses were designed by taking an inventory of the applications and research areas that comprise Computational Linguistics, and then breaking them down into subtasks. These subtasks were then grouped by similarity into coherent courses, and the courses into core and elective sets. Three topics resisted classification into any particular course: ambiguity resolution, evaluation, and multilingualism. These became our cross-cutting themes which are highlighted throughout all of the courses. In addition to understanding each subtask, working computational linguists need to know how to combine the stages of linguistic processing into end-to-end systems. For this reason, we include a capstone "Systems and Applications" course in which students work in groups to create an NLP application.

Key to making the Computational Linguistics curriculum fit into one calendar year was deciding not to include the course "Intro to Computational Linguistics." Such a course serves to expose students to a broad range of topics in the field and get them interested in exploring further. CLMA students are already interested in further studies in Computational Linguistics, and will be exposed to a broad range of topics throughout the curriculum. However, we did still want to give the students an overview of the field so that they could see how the rest of their studies will fit in. This is done through a two-day orientation at the start of each year. The orientation also introduces the three cross-cutting themes mentioned above, gives the students a chance to get to know each other and the CLMA faculty, and provides practical information about the university such as libraries, computing lab facilities, etc.

3.1 Required courses

There are six required courses: The first two are Linguistics courses, and the remaining four form the NLP core courses. Among the four NLP courses, Ling 572 should be taken after Ling 570, and Ling 573 should be taken after Ling 570, 571, and 572.

Ling 450 (Intro to Linguistic Phonetics): Introduction to the articulatory and acoustic correlates of phonological features. Issues covered include the mapping of dynamic events to static representations, phonetic evidence for phonological description, universal constraints on phonological structure, and implications of psychological speech-sound categorization for phonological theory.

Ling 566 (Intro to Syntax for Computational Linguistics): Introduction to syntactic analysis and concepts (e.g., constituent structure, the syntax-semantics interface, and long-distance dependencies). Emphasis is placed on formally precise encoding of linguistic hypotheses and designing grammars so that they can be scaled up for practical applications. Through the course we progressively build up a consistent grammar for a fragment of English. Problem sets introduce data and phenomena from other languages.

Ling 570 (Shallow Processing Techniques for NLP): Techniques and algorithms for associating relatively surface-level structures and information with natural language data, including tasks such as tokenization, POS tagging, morphological analysis, language modeling, named entity recognition, shallow parsing, and word sense disambiguation.

Ling 571 (Deep Processing Techniques for NLP): Techniques and algorithms for associating deep or elaborated linguistic structures with natural language data (e.g., parsing, semantics, and discourse) and for associating natural language strings with input semantic representations (generation).

Ling 572 (Advanced Statistical Methods in NLP): Major machine learning algorithms for NLP, including Decision Tree, Naive Bayes, kNN, Maximum Entropy, Support Vector Machine, Transformation-Based Learning, and the like. Students implement many of these algorithms and use them to solve classification and sequence labeling problems.

Ling 573 (NLP Systems and Applications): Design and implementation of coherent systems for practical applications, with topics varying year to year. Sample topics: machine translation, question answering, information retrieval, information extraction, dialogue systems, and spell/grammar checking. In 2006, the students collectively built a question answering system, which was further developed into a submission to the TREC competition (Jinguji et al., 2006). This year's class is developing a chatbot to submit to the Loebner Prize competition, an implementation of the Turing Test.

Among the required courses, Ling 566 was created a year before the CLMA program started, and has been taught four times. Ling 450 is an established course from our Linguistics curriculum. Ling 570-573 were newly created for this program, and have each been taught three times now. We have put much effort in improving course design, as discussed in (Xia, 2008).

3.2 The prerequisites for the required courses

In order to cover the range of methodologies and tasks that our program does in its core sequence, we need to set as a prerequisite the ability to program, including knowledge of data structures and algorithms, and expertise in C++ or Java.[2] Another prerequisite is a college-level course in probability and statistics. Without such knowledge, it is all but impossible to discuss the sophisticated statistical models covered in the core NLP courses. For the two Linguistics required courses, the only prerequisite is a college-level introductory course in Linguistics or equivalent. Because our students have very diverse backgrounds, we have tried several approaches to help the students meet all these prerequisites, which will be discussed in §4.

3.3 Elective courses

All students must take three electives, including one in Linguistics, one in Computational Linguistics, and one more in Computational Linguistics or a related field. The Linguistics electives are drawn from the broad range of graduate-level Linguistics courses offered in the department. The related fields

[2]Knowing Perl or Python is recommended but not required, as we believe that good C++ or Java programmers can learn Perl or Python quickly.

electives include courses in CS and Electrical Engineering on topics such as Machine Learning, Graphical Models, Artificial Intelligence, and Human-Computer Interaction as well as courses in the Information School on topics such as Information Retrieval. We maintain a list of pre-approved courses, which grows as students find additional courses of interest and petition to have them approved.

The annual elective offerings in Computational Linguistics include Multilingual Grammar Engineering, as well as seminars taught by the Computational Linguistics faculty and by guest experts (including researchers in local industry), covering new topics each year. Recent topics include: Corpus Management, Development and Use, Text-to-Speech, Multimodal Interfaces, Lexical Acquisition for Precision Grammars, Semi-supervised and Unsupervised Learning for NLP, and Information Extraction from Heterogeneous Resources. There are four-five such seminars per year, three from the Computational Linguistics faculty and one-two from guest experts.

We ask students to present their choices of electives for approval, and require that they articulate reasons why their range of choices constitutes a coherent course of study.

3.4 Hands on, interactive courses

All of the courses in the curriculum are hands-on, emphasizing learning through doing as well as collaboration between the students. Theoretical concepts introduced in lecture are put into practice with problem sets (e.g., in Intro to Syntax), programming assignments (in the core sequence) and opened-ended projects (in the Systems and Applications course and the seminars). Student collaboration is promoted through group projects as well as active online discussion boards where students and faculty together solve problems as they arise.

3.5 The master's project

In addition to nine courses, the students need to complete a master's project, either through an internship or through completing a master's thesis.

The internship option: Internships counting towards the MA degree must be relevant to Computational Linguistics or human language technology more broadly. Students develop a pre-internship proposal, including a statement of the area of interest and proposed contributions, a discussion of why the company targeted is a relevant place to do this work, and a list of relevant references. Once the students have been offered and accepted an internship, they write a literature review on existing approaches to the task in question.

At the end of the internship, students write a self-evaluation which they present to the internship supervisor for approval and then to the faculty advisor. In addition, we require a confidential, written evaluation from the intern's supervisor which references the self-evaluation. If this evaluation does not indicate satisfactory work, the internship will not count.

Students also write a post-internship report, including a description of the activities undertaken during the internship and their results, a discussion of how the program course work related to and/or prepared the student for the internship work, and a second version of the literature review. We expect the second review to be different from the initial version in incorporating the additional perspective gained in the course of the internship as well as any additional key papers that the student discovered in the course of internship work.

The thesis option: This option is recommended for students who wish to petition for admission to the Department's PhD program, and encouraged for students who wish to apply to other PhD programs in the near future. An MA thesis typically involves the implementation of working systems (or extensions or experimental evaluations thereof). In some cases, they may provide theoretical contributions instead. MA theses require a thorough literature review, are typically longer (30-50 pages), and represent the kind of research which could be presented at major conferences in our field.

The milestones: While the internship and a significant portion of the thesis work are conducted in the summer for full-time students, we start monthly graduation planning meetings as early as the preceding October to help students decide which option they should take. For those seeking internships, we will help them identify the companies that match their interests and make the contact if possible.

Students who choose the thesis option are required to turn in an initial thesis proposal that includes a thesis topic, a summary of major existing approaches, the students' proposed approach, and a plan for evaluation. With the feedback from the faculty, the students will revise their proposals several times before finalizing the thesis topic. Students are encouraged to take elective courses relevant to their topic. Because the amount of research is required for a good master's thesis, we expect students with this option to take one or two additional quarters to finish than the ones who choose the internship option.

4 Challenges

In this section, we address several challenges that we encountered while establishing the new program.

Students enrolling in our program have varied backgrounds in Linguistics, CS and other undergraduate majors. In addition, some students come to us straight from undergraduate studies, while others are re-entry students. To better prepare students for the program, starting this year we offer an eight-week summer refresher course, which reinforces the most important skills from contributing disciplines to prepare students for the CLMA core courses. The course covers the following topics: (1) formal grammars and formal languages, (2) finite-state automata and transducers, (3) review of main concepts from probability and statistics, (4) review of major data structures and algorithms, and (5) using Unix and computer clusters.

After students are admitted to the program, they are asked to take an online placement test to identify the areas that they need to strengthen before entering the program. They can then choose to take the summer course or study on their own.

While some of our students, typically fresh out of college or stepping out of the workforce for retraining to switch careers, are eager to complete the degree in one year, others wish to complete the program while continuing their current employment or simply need more time. We offer various options to accommodate different needs:

Part-time vs. full-time Students can complete the program in one year, taking three classes each quarter and completing the master's project in the summer. At this pace, the program is very intense. The program also offers part-time options, allowing students to take courses one or two at a time. This works well for students who are currently employed and also leaves time for students coming from a Linguistics background to take CS and Statistics courses before approaching the Computational Linguistics core sequence. While full-time students must start in Autumn quarter, part-time students can start in any academic quarter.

Curriculum flexibility Students who come to us with an extensive background in Linguistics (e.g., a prior MA), can waive one or more of the Linguistics requirements, giving them more time in their schedule for Computational Linguistics or related fields courses, such as CS.

Program options Our courses are open to qualified students for single-course enrollment, allowing people who don't have the time or financial resources to commit to the whole master's program to benefit from the course offerings. In addition, the three-course certificate provides more continuity than single-course enrollment (though less than the full master's program) as well as the recognition of a certificate. In either case, graduate non-matriculated status allows such students to apply their coursework to the master's program at a later date.

Master's project options In providing for both internships and master's theses, the program can accommodate students seeking training for positions in industry as well as those seeking to continue graduate studies. In the former case, the practical experience of an internship together with the industry connections it can provide are most valuable. In the latter case, a chance to do independent research is more appropriate. Students who spread the program out over more than one year can do internships in the summer between years one and two in addition to the master's project (internship or thesis) in the second summer. Finally, the "internship option" can also be fulfilled by ordinary full-time employment: when students begin full-time positions in the summer after they complete coursework or apply the knowledge gained in the master's program to new projects at their current places of employment.

In class or online By offering our courses in a hybrid, synchronous in-person and online format, we add the flexibility to attend our program from anywhere in the world while still benefiting from the same courses, lectures, online discussions and collaborative work. The online option is also beneficial to local students, allowing them to tune in, for example, when home caring for a sick child, to review lectures previously attended, to attend online on days without other on-campus obligations and to avoid the commute. In the 2008-2009 school year, three of our courses will be offered in this format, and we plan to extend the offerings going forward.

5 Outcomes

5.1 Enrollment, graduation rate and placement

In years 1-3, 70 students have enrolled, and about 30 of them enrolled as full-time students.[3] To data 13 have completed the program, and at least nine of them are currently in jobs related to Computational Linguistics. Another 12 are projected to graduate this year. Out of these 25 students, 15 chose the internship option and 10 chose the thesis option. We have placed students in internships with companies such as Amazon.com, Google, Microsoft, PARC, Tegic (Nuance), and VoiceBox, and have graduates working at companies such as Cataphora, Cisco, Google, InXight, Tegic (Nuance), and VoiceBox. Among the 10 students who took the thesis option, four received RAships from CLMA faculty's research grants, and at least two will enroll in our Ph.D. program after receiving their MAs.

Recent internal research completed by UWEO identified a total of 34 CL programs, 23 in the US and 11 in Western Europe. These programs vary from named degrees in Computational Linguistics or a similar variant, to concentrations in other degrees and to loose courses of study. It appears that there is one other university in the US that has enrollment as high or higher than our own, but all other programs typically have at least 50% fewer students enrolling as of 2007. Given that this program is only in its third year, we consider this level of high comparative enrollment a strong measure of success. Additionally, during this 3 year period, there has been an upward trend in applications which may be a reflection on the growth and awareness of the discipline, but may also be a reflection on the growing reputation of the program.

5.2 Student feedback

We sent an anonymous survey to all alumni and current students (N=70) asking them about the effectiveness of the overall CLMA program, individual courses, the curriculum, success in getting a job as well as for some qualitative feedback about the strengths and weaknesses of the program. We received 31 responses (44% response rate). For the sake of brevity, we will provide a selection of questions and categorize the results as follows: positive (1=very well, 2=fairly well), neutral (3=so so); negative (4=not very well, 5=poorly).

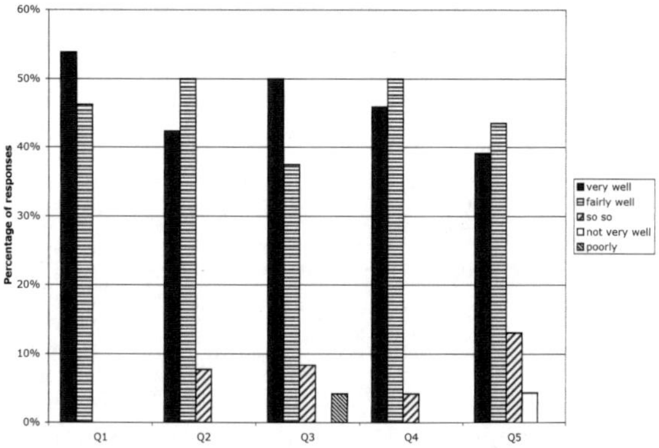

Figure 1: Student and alumni responses

As shown in Figure 1, the responses were overwhelmingly positive. The first four questions ask how well the program as a whole helped the students achieve the goals of learning to think like a computational linguist (Q1), understanding the state of the art in Computational Linguistics (Q2), understanding the potential contributions of both machine learning and knowledge engineering (Q3), and preparation for a job in industry (Q4). The fifth question asks how helpful the CLMA experience has been/will be in finding a job.[4] There were a number of other questions, but the results are all very similar to the ones above. These same questions were also asked with respect to individual courses. The results were again similar, although slightly lower. Positive responses were in the range of 80%-95%, neutral in the range

[3] Some of them later switched to part-time status due to various reasons (e.g., the intensity of the program, financial consideration).

[4] Each of these questions was answered by 24-27 students.

of 5-20% and negative responses were usually limited to no more than 5%. For the question of how well the program has prepared students for their current job (alumni only, N=5), 100% answered positively. For the question about how important the program was in attaining their current job, again 100% felt that the program was crucial.

We also received valuable qualitative feedback on this survey. The majority of students (67%) felt that the program was very intense, but very much worthwhile. The faculty consistently receives high praise; students enjoy the small hard-working community; and comments indicate that the coursework is relevant for their future career. When asked about suggestions for improvement, students provided a number of logistical suggestions, would like to see some degree of student mentoring, and seek to find ways to reduce the intensity of the program, especially for part-time students who are working. It is clear, though, from the overall survey results, that students feel very positive about the program as a whole, and its relevance for their professional future.

While we at first thought the program to be primarily a one-year program, the intensity of the curriculum has resulted in a number students taking longer than one year to complete the program which has impacted the number of students who have thus far completed. Consequently, we will consider student feedback from the survey which—in conjunction with the new preparatory course—should lead us to find methods of reducing the intensity but maintaining the high quality.

6 Conclusion and future directions

6.1 Lessons learned

In starting this program, we had the privilege of designing the curriculum first and then hiring faculty to teach the required courses. We worked closely with our advisory board to develop a course of study well-suited to training students for industry jobs, while also striving to design a program that will remain relevant to graduates many years down the line.

Financial support from UWEO allowed us to jump in with both feet, offering the full curriculum from year one. This was critical in attracting a strong and reasonably large student body. It also provided the freedom to design a curriculum that goes in-depth into Computational Linguistics.

Other facets of our curriculum which contribute to its success include: (1) We combine in-depth exploration of particular topics with cross-cutting themes that tie the courses together. (2) The courses emphasize hands-on work, providing immediate motivation to delve deeper into the theoretical concepts presented. (3) The program combines high intensity with high levels of support: We ask the students to attempt real-world scale projects and then assist them in achieving these goals through providing software to work from, offering high levels of online interaction to answer questions, and facilitating collaboration. By working together, the students can build more interesting systems than anyone could alone, and therefore explore a broader territory. In addition, collaborative projects help students benefit from each other's diverse backgrounds.

At the same time, we've found providing multiple ways of completing program requirements to be key to allowing students from different backgrounds to succeed. Exceptional students coming from Linguistics can get up to speed quickly enough to complete the program on a full-time schedule (and some have), but many others benefit from being able to take it more slowly, as do some students from a CS background. We also find that having expertise in Linguistics among the students significantly benefits the overall cohort.

6.2 Future directions

In the near future, we plan to expand our online offerings, which directly expands our audience and benefits local students as described above. We have found connecting course work to faculty research and/or external competitions such as TREC and the Loebner Prize to be extremely motivating and rewarding for students, and plan to seek more opportunities for doing so. We are also expanding out interdisciplinary reach within the university. The TREC submission was done jointly with faculty from the Information School. This year's guest faculty course will be offered jointly with a course in the School of Art on interface design. In pursuing all of these directions, we will benefit from input from our advisory board as well as feedback from current students and alumni.

References

Robert Dale, Diego Molla Aliod, and Rolf Schwitter. 2002. Evangelising Language Technology: A Practically-Focussed Undergraduate Program. In *Proceedings of the First ACL Workshop on Effective Tools and Methodologies for Teaching NLP and CL.*

Robert Frederking, Eric H. Nyberg, Teruko Mitamura, and Jaime G. Carbonell. 2002. Design and Evolution of a Language Technologies Curriculum. In *Proceedings of the First ACL Workshop on Effective Tools and Methodologies for Teaching NLP and CL.*

Dan Jinguji, William D. Lewis, Efthimis N. Efthimiadis, Joshua Minor, Albert Bertram, Shauna Eggers, Joshua Johanson, Brian Nisonger, Ping Yu, and Zhengbo Zhou. 2006. The University of Washington's UW-CLMAQA system. In *Proceedings of the Text Retrieval Conference (TREC) 2006*, Gaithersburg, Maryland.

Mare Koit, Tiit Roosmaa, and Haldur Oim. 2002. Teaching Computational Linguistics at the University of Tartu: Experience, Perspectives and Challenges. In *Proceedings of the First ACL Workshop on Effective Tools and Methodologies for Teaching NLP and CL.*

Diane Neal, Lisa nad Miller. 2004. Distance education. In Robert W. Proctor and Kim-Phuong L. Vu, editors, *Handbook of Human Factors in Web Design.* Lawrence Erlbaum Associates.

Suléne Pilon, Gerhard B Van Huyssteen, and Bertus Van Rooy. 2005. Teaching language technology at the North-West University. In *Proceedings of the Second ACL Workshop on Effective Tools and Methodologies for Teaching NLP and CL.*

Hans Uszkoreit, Valia Kordoni, Vladislav Kubon, Michael Rosner, and Sabine Kirchmeier-Andersen. 2005. Language technology from a European perspective. In *Proceedings of the Second ACL Workshop on Effective Tools and Methodologies for Teaching NLP and CL.*

Fei Xia. 2008. The evolution of a statistical nlp course. In *Proceedings of the Third ACL Workshop on Effective Tools and Methodologies for Teaching NLP and CL*, Columbus, Ohio, June.

Dimitris Zondiros. 2008. Online, distance education and globalization: Its impact on educational access, inequality and exclusion. *European Journal of Open, Distance and E-Learning*, Volume I.

Freshmen's CL curriculum: the benefits of redundancy *

Heike Zinsmeister
Department of Linguistics
University of Konstanz
78457 Konstanz, Germany
Heike.Zinsmeister@uni-konstanz.de

Abstract

In the course of the European Bologna accord on higher education, German universities have been reorganizing their traditional "Magister" and "Diplom" studies into modularized bachelor's and master's programs. This revision provides a chance to update the programs. In this paper we introduce the curriculum of a first semester B.A. program in Computational Linguistics which was taught for the first time last semester. In addition, we analyze the syllabi of four mandatory courses of the first semester to identify overlapping content which led to redundancies. We suggest for future semesters to reorganize the schedules in a way that students encounter recurring topics iteratively in a constructive way.

1 Introduction

We present the first semester curriculum of a newly revised bachelor's program in Computational Linguistics at the University of Heidelberg, Germany, which was taught for the first time at the Department of Computational Linguistics last winter semester. Four courses are mandatory for the students in the first semester: a comprehensive Introduction to Computational Linguistics, backed up with a course on Formal Foundations that emphasizes mathematical topics, and a general introduction to linguistic core modules in Foundations of Linguistic Analysis, the set up is completed by an Introduction to Programming that introduces core concepts of programming employing the programming language Python.

The parallel design leads to a situation in which related topics are introduced in the same semester in parallel fashion. Redundant duplication per se is to be avoided given that lecture time is always too sparse and should be used most efficiently such that there is enough room for examples, short in-course exercises, questions and discussions.

We analyzed the syllabi for common topics and plotted these topics to see whether they are dealt with in a constructive way across the curriculum. For future semesters we suggest some reorganization to optimize the courses' interactions. Since all courses are taught in the department of Computational Linguistics, decisions on both the courses' subtopics as well as their temporal sequencing is in full control of the local department.

We think that it is reasonable to keep the common topics and even the redundancy of introducing them in more than one course only. Iterative reintroduction could be helpful for the students if it is accompanied by a reference to the earlier mention as well as a motivation of the specific relevance for the course at hand. We expect that such an iterative approach reinforces understanding since it allows the students to build upon their prior knowledge and, furthermore, to approach the very same concept from different perspectives. This iterative method is inspired by the idea of spiral learning in the sense of Jerome S. Bruner (Bruner, 1960) which builds on a constructivist view on learning. It assumes that learning is an active process in which learners construct new ideas or concepts based upon

* This paper is about the curriculum taught at the Department of Computational Linguistics at the University of Heidelberg, where the author used to work.

Proceedings of the Third Workshop on Issues in Teaching Computational Linguistics (TeachCL-08), pages 19–26,
Columbus, Ohio, USA, June 2008.

their prior knowledge. A curriculum can support this process if it revisits its basic ideas repeatedly: "the spiral curriculum [..] turns back on itself at higher levels" (Bruner, 1960, p.53).

The rest of this paper is organized as follows. First, we briefly sketch the Bologna Process, an effort of harmonizing higher education in Europe and also the special situation in Heidelberg being the background against which the bachelor's program described is created. Then, we introduce the bachelor's program of Computational Linguistics at the University of Heidelberg in Germany and describe its four mandatory courses of the first semester. We analyze the syllabi for common topics, and, finally, present a re-organized schedule for future semesters which is inspired by an iterative learning approach.

2 Background

The European Bologna Process is an effort of European countries to establish a common higher education area by the year 2010. Its central element is the introduction of a two-cycle study system consisting of bachelor's and master's degrees with comparable qualifications throughout Europe based on a common credit transfer system which allows for comparing the workload of individual courses.[1]

In the course of this international harmonizing effort, German universities are reorganizing their programs from traditional "Magister" or "Diplom" programs to modular bachelor's and master's programs. Previously "Magister" or "Diplom" was first degree in Germany, i.e. a bachelor's degree did not exist. A characteristic of the traditional programs was the freedom of choice they offered to their students, more pronounced in the "Magister" programs than in the "Diplom" programs the latter of which were traditionally realized in more technically oriented disciplines and the former in the humanities. Both type of programs were set up with a standard period of study of nine to ten semesters but the average student required more than this. European bachelor's programs predetermine a highly structured curriculum and offer a first university degree after six or seven semester of study.

The Computational Linguistics department in Heidelberg was pioneering with an early bachelor's program devised by Peter Hellwig at the beginning of the Bologna Process. Adaptions of the original bachelor's program became necessary due to general developments in the international Bologna policy and finally the need for a revised program emerged. This was realized in 2007 by Anette Frank who had filled the by then vacant chair in Computational Linguistics. The change of the departmental head brought a change from a more vocationally oriented program that prepared students to take jobs in the local language technology industry to a more academically oriented one, which is reflected in the revised syllabus. We will point to differences between the original program and the revised program where relevant.

3 The Study of Computational Linguistics in Heidelberg

> Computational linguistics (CL) is a discipline between linguistics and computer science which is concerned with the computational aspects of the human language faculty. [...] The applied component of CL is more interested in the practical outcome of modeling human language use. The goal is to create software products that have some knowledge of human language. [...] Theoretical CL takes up issues in formal theories. [...] Computational linguists develop formal models simulating aspects of the human language faculty and implement them as computer programs. (www.aclweb.org/nlpfaq.txt, credited to Hans Uszkoreit)

This quote from Hans Uszkoreit outlines the knowledge and skills that a study of CL should equip its students with: programming skills, handling of formal models, algorithmic thinking and last but not least an explicit knowledge of linguistic analysis.

All four areas are covered in our freshmen's classes which are introduced in more detail in subsequent subsections after the presentation of the overall program.

[1] One European Credit Transfer System point corresponds to 25-30 hours workload on the student cf. http://www.uni-heidelberg.de/studium/bologna/materialien/diploma/ECTSUsersGuide05.pdf. For the Bologna Process in general see http://ec.europa.eu/education/policies/educ/bologna/bologna_en.html.

In Heidelberg, B.A. students have to collect 180 credit points to complete their study. They normally enroll in two or three subjects which means that they take Computational Linguistics as main subject (in which it provides 75% of the overall workload), secondary main subject (50%) or minor subject (25%) [2] in combination with complementary subjects in the areas of computer science[3], humanities, psychology, economics, or law. Table 1 gives an overview of the courses in a 75% B.A. The first semester requirements are the same in all B.A. options involving Computational Linguistics.[4] In addition to the courses depicted in Table 1 students need to gain credits in Generic Competences ('übergreifende Kompetenzen' aka soft skills and courses from other departments of the faculty).[5]

3.1 The Curriculum

We thought it relevant for the students to get acquainted with Computational Linguistics proper as early as the first semester. Therefore, in addition to an introduction to formal foundations and programming a comprehensive introduction to algorithms and analysis in computational linguistics is mandatory. It was the first time that this combination of courses was taught. Before that, the Introduction to Computational Linguistics also introduced students to core linguistic topics which were spread across the whole course. The motivation for an independent introduction to linguistics was that students should get a profound background knowledge in linguistic analysis such that further courses could build on them. Before that, even basic concepts such as morpheme had to be reintroduced. Introduction to Programming and Formal Foundations used to be in complementary distribution due to the fact that they used to be taught by the one and the same person. An additional lecturer position in the department allowed us to to offer both courses in parallel.

The Freshmen's curriculum consists of four mandatory courses which are described in the following.

3.1.1 Introduction to Computational Linguistics

The core lecture of the first semester is the Introduction to Computational Linguistics. It is held four hours a week and is worth six credit points. It introduces the foundations of Computational Linguistics, its research objectives and research methods. It provides an overall survey of the field: the levels of language description, formal-mathematical and logical models as well as algorithmic approaches for processing such formal models. Specific topics are: dealing with ambiguities, approximation of linguistic regularities, and the relation of language and knowledge; some applications of Computational Linguistics are also introduced. Mandatory readings are selected sections from Jurafsky & Martin (2000), complemented by chapters from Carstensen et al. (2004) and Bird et al. (forthcoming).

This course is seen as the backbone of the first semester curriculum. We therefore list the lectures in detail. The content of the other three courses is only briefly described below and will be discussed in Section 4.

The first part of the schedule was strongly inspired by Jurafsky & Martin (2000):

- Sub-token level (3 lectures): computing morphology by means of regular expressions, automata, and transducers.
- Token level and context (4 lectures): identifying tokens and computing them by means of tokenizing, edit distance, n-grams, and part-of-speech tagging.
- Syntactic level (6 lectures): syntactic analysis in terms of constituency, dependency, phrase structure grammars and probabilistic context free grammars; formal grammar types: computation of syntactic structure by means of parsing strategies and parsing algorithms, and syntactic resources in terms of treebanks.

The second part of the schedule built more on Carstensen et al. (2004). It mainly dealt with semantic issues in term of analysis, computation, and resources.

[2]The minor subject option had to be introduced due to formal requirements. It is likely to be dispensed with in the future.

[3]Computer science can only be taken as minor subject.

[4]In the 25% B.A. the workload on students is reduced. They only need to attend one of the two courses on formal foundations either Mathematical Foundations in the first semester or Logical Foundations in the second one.

[5]In the 75% B.A. students need to collect 20 credit points in Generic Competences during their three-year study.

<table>
<tr><th>Semester</th><th colspan="2">Computational Linguistics Modules</th><th>Linguistic Modules</th><th colspan="2">Computational Modules</th></tr>
<tr><td>6</td><td colspan="5">BA-Thesis, Oral Exam</td></tr>
<tr><td>5</td><td colspan="3" rowspan="2">Advanced Studies (Computational Linguistics or Formal Linguistics)
Core Studies in Computational Linguistics</td><td rowspan="3">Core Studies in Theoretical or Applied Computer Science</td><td rowspan="3">Software Project</td></tr>
<tr><td>4</td></tr>
<tr><td>3</td><td>Statistical Methods for CL</td><td>Algorithmic CL</td><td>Formal Semantics</td></tr>
<tr><td>2</td><td></td><td>Logical Foundations</td><td>Formal Syntax</td><td colspan="2">Advanced Programming</td></tr>
<tr><td>1</td><td>Introduction to CL</td><td>Mathematical Foundations</td><td>Foundations of Linguistic Analysis</td><td colspan="2">Introduction to Programming</td></tr>
</table>

Table 1: Modules in B.A. Computational Linguistics (75%)

- predicate logic (2 lectures)
- propositional logic and inferences (2 lectures)
- compositional semantics and Lambda calculus (1 lecture)
- lexical semantics including resources (2 lectures)
- discourse semantics / pragmatics (1 lecture)

The schedule was rounded off by two lectures on applications, in particular information extraction and machine translation.

There were eight assessments during the semester of which students had to pass 60%. Most of them dealt with theoretical comprehension, two more practical assessments involved an introduction to basic UNIX tools, and (probabilistic) parsing with the NLTK tools (Bird et al., forthcoming). We decided to split the written exam into two sub-exams, the first one took place in half time the second one in the final week of the semester. Thus students could better focus on the topics at hand.

3.1.2 Formal Foundations part 1: Mathematical Foundations

Formal Foundations is held two hours a week and is worth six credit points. The theory of formal languages is a prerequisite for e.g. model-theoretic semantics and parsing approaches. This lecture in particular deals with mathematical foundations, formal languages and formal grammars, regular expressions and finite automata, context-free languages, context-sensitive languages and Type-0 languages, Turing machines, and computability theory. The recommended reading includes Schöning (2001), Klabunde (1998), Partee et al. (1990), as well as Hopcroft and Ullman (1979).

There were eight graded assessments and the students had to pass 50% of the overall tasks .

3.1.3 Foundations of Linguistic Analysis

The introduction to linguistics is also held two hours a week and is worth four credit points. Linguistic knowledge is a distinctive property of computational linguistics. In this lecture students get a thorough introduction to the core modules of the language faculty: phonetics and phonology, morphology, syntax, semantics, and pragmatics with a special emphasis on linguistic phenomena of German. The core reading was Meibauer et al. (2002).

There were ten small assessments of which the students had to pass eight.

3.1.4 Introduction to Programming

The fourth mandatory course is held four hours a week and is worth six credit points. In this lecture, students learn to devise algorithmic solutions and implementations for problems related to Natural Language Processing. Moreover, the course introduces basic principles of software engineering in order to equip the students with skills to develop correct and maintainable programs. These capabilities are further facilitated in the Advanced Programming course during the second semester and a comprehensive hands-on software project during the advanced phase of undergraduate studies.

Recommended reading is Demleitner (unpublished), Lutz and Ascher (2007), Martelli (2006), as well as the official Python documentation (van Rossum, 2008).

There were ten programming assessments of which the students had to hand in eight and earn half of the points to be permitted to take the final exam.

3.2 Local Conditions

3.2.1 Students

Students require higher education entrance qualification and no other prerequisites. Language of instruction is German but students come from various countries and speak a diversity of native languages, including Bulgarian, Chinese, English, French, Italian, Japanese, Kurdish, Polish, Russian, Spanish, Turkish, Turkmen and Ukrainian. About 40 students enrolled in Computational Linguistics, about two third of which classified themselves as programming beginners. In general about 20% of the first semester students failed at least one of the courses first time.

3.2.2 Realization of Courses

Three of the four courses under examination are taught by faculty members holding a PhD (or a comparable doctoral degree) and one by a member of the faculty still completing his doctorate. The courses are taught as lectures which are accompanied by optional tutorial sessions. These tutorials were coached by undergraduate student tutors who mainly corrected and discussed the students' assessments. The students had to hand in assessments on a regular basis which could either be solved as a group or individually depending on the course. Passing a substantial portion of the exercises was a prerequisite for being permitted to take the courses' exams. Each course provided its own wiki platform for the students to communicate easily among themselves as well as with student tutors and lecturers. The wikis were also a common platform for publishing example solutions by the tutors and keeping records of answers to students' questions.

4 Analysis of the Syllabi

The individual courses were planned in accordance with the sequence of topics in standard textbooks such as Jurafsky and Martin (2000) and Carstensen et al. (2004) for Introduction to Computational Linguistics, Schöning (2001) for Formal Foundations, and Meibauer et al. (2002) for Foundations of Linguistic Analysis. In Introduction to Programming we used a hands-on manuscript (Demleitner, unpublished).

The following list summarizes the main topics that are dealt with in more than one syllabus. Common topics include:

- modules of linguistics: ICL, FLA
- regular expressions: ICL, FF, IP
- automata: ICL, FF
- grammar types: ICL, FF
- morphology: ICL, FLA
- segmentation, tokenization: ICL, FLA, IP
- n-grams: ICL, IP
- phrase-structure grammars: ICL, FF, FLA
- parsing: ICL, FF, IP
- lexical semantics: ICL, FLA
- model in semantics: ICL, FF
- discourse semantics, pragmatics: ICL, FLA

Before the semester started, the group of lecturers met and arranged the general schedules of the courses. During the semester, the lecturers happened to lose track of the progression of other courses. In some cases explicit cross-references were given, for example in the case of lexical semantics, but most of the time, concepts were (re-)introduced in each course independently. Sometimes lecturers asked students whether they were already familiar with a newly introduced topic from other courses; then there was a short discussion in class and students were reminded of previous mentions of that topic. In general, the didactics of the individual courses were not adapted to take account of such recurrence of topics across the curriculum.

Nevertheless, the parallel fashion of the four courses at hand seemed to be reasonable even in this form. Students deemed the interdependence between the courses as appropriate in the final evaluation of the courses. They gave it an average score of 2.052 with a standard deviation of 1.05 on a scale of 1 (very appropriate) to 6 (non-existent).

Our conclusion is that a slight rescheduling of the courses would improve teaching efficiency in the sense that lecturers could count on already introduced materials and students could benefit from recurring topics by exploring them in the context of different disciplines. Table 2 depicts our proposed schedule.

An important and easily realizable change that we suggest is to ensure that all linguistic modules are dealt with first in Foundation of Linguistic Analysis (FLA) before they are set into a more formal and also computational setting in the Introduction to Computational Linguistics (ICL). This could be realized by starting FLA with morphology right from the beginning, instead of introducing the linguistic modules first which was also part of the introduction in ICL. FLA also entered the areas of lexicography and psycho linguistics (aka the mental lexicon) which could be skipped in future semesters. Lectures on phonetics and phonology which were taught after morphology could be rescheduled to the end of the semester. Both topics are relevant for applications which were introduced in the final sessions of ICL and also for subsequent optional seminars in speech generation or speech synthesis in higher semesters.

In Formal Foundations (FF) lectures on grammars, the Chomsky hierarchy, and decision theory took place in lectures 5 and 6. They could be postponed and lectures on automata moved forward instead. This would ensure that both of these topics are dealt with in FF after they have been introduced in ICL. Formal Foundations provides a more formal and deepened insight into these topics and should, therefore, be encountered last.

In Introduction to Programming (IP) issues of algorithms and analysis are a means to an end: they are used in programming examples and assessments. Therefore, such topics should be referred to in IP only after they have been introduced in ICL. The coordination of this already worked out well with respect to n-grams and phrase structure grammars. Lectures on segmentation and regular expressions took place in the last third of the semester and could be moved forward to have them closer to their introduction in the other courses.

From a student's perspective these changes would result in a kind of spiral curriculum. For example, the first encounter with constituency and syntactic phrase structure would be in FLA, the course which is least formal and relates most to secondary school knowledge. Their second involvement with phrase structure would be in ICL and was more formal and also involved computational aspects of syntactic analysis. Then, they would learn more on the formal characteristics of grammars in FF, and finally, they perceived it as an application in an IP programming task. If these lectures are seen as stages on a common pathway of learning then they conform to the idea of spiral learning: in course of time the students return to the same concepts each time on a more advanced level.

Table 2 gives a contrastive overview of the four course curricula and shows how the individual topics could temporally related to one another to support an iterative leaning approach.

The first column counts the semester's teaching units in the average winter semester (which includes some public holidays). Introduction to Computational Linguistics (ICL) and Introduction to Programming (IP) took place twice a week, Foundations of Linguistic Analysis (FLA) and Formal Foundations (FF) only once. The 25th session is followed by another week of revision and final exams, which is not included here.

5 Conclusion

We proposed an enhanced curriculum for teaching parallel freshman's courses in Computational Linguistics, in the spirit of the newly revised bachelor's program in Computational Linguistics at the University of Heidelberg. In particular, we examined the first semester curriculum of four mandatory courses: Introduction to Computational Linguis-

#	Introduction to Computational Linguistics	Formal Foundations	Foundations of Linguistic Analysis	Introduction to Programming
1		sets, iterations, relations		introduction
2	introduction to Computational Linguistics and linguistic modules		morphology: morphemes inflection, derivation	data types
3	regular expression and automata	equivalence relation function, induction formal languages		functions and methods
4	morphology and finite automata		syntax: PoS, topological fields	strings, data structures, control structures
5	morphology and finite transducers	automata: DFAs and NFAs		sequences
6	tokenizer and spelling editor	NFAs, regular grammars regular expression		data structures: dictionaries
7	tokenizing and n-grams		syntax: phrases chunks, X-bar schema	encodings
8	tagging: rule-based, HMMs, Brill	Pumping lemma, minimizing of automata		modules, packages, tests
9	tagging		syntax: valency, semantic roles, gram. functions	modules
10	syntax and CFGs constituency, dependency	closures		exercise: n-grams
11	grammar types, parsing		syntax: sentential level CP/IP structures	regular expressions
12	parsing: bottom up, top down	grammars, left-right derivation, Chomsky hierarchy		regular expressions
13	parsing: Earley algorithm		semantics: meaning, lexical semantics	PS grammar, recursion
14	midterm exam	decision theory		file handling
15	treebanks and PCFCs	parsing: CYK algorithm		tuple, list comprehensions
16	treebanks: resources		semantics: compositional semantics	object-oriented programming: basics
17	semantics: predicate logic	pushdown automata Turing machines, computability theory		oo programming: techniques
18	Christmas puzzle: predicate logic and model theory		pragmatics: deixis, anaphora, information structure	Christmas lecture
19	semantics: propositional logic and inferences	revision: Pumping lemma		oo programming: techniques
20	semantics: propositional logic and inference		pragmatics: speech acts conversational maxims, presuppositions	exercise: segmentation
21	semantics: compositional semantics and • -calculus	a simple grammar for English		factory functions
22	semantics: lexical semantics		phonetics	blocks and visibility
23	semantics: lexical semantics	revision		exceptions
24	semantics: discourse semantics		phonology	object customization
25	applications	exam	revision	exam

Table 2: Re-organized curriculum of first semester courses

tics, Formal Foundations, Foundations of Linguistic Analysis, and Introduction to Programming, and identified common topics. When the four courses were first held in parallel last semester, it happened that recurring topics were introduced independently without taking into account their previous mention in other courses. For future semesters we suggest a better alignment of recurring topics and sketch rearrangements of the courses' schedules. Instead of pruning recurrent topics, we think that from the perspective of the psychology of learning it is useful for the students if the same concepts and ideas are approached from different angles iteratively.

Acknowledgments

We are indebted to our co-instructors in Heidelberg: Anette Frank, teaching the Introduction to Computational Linguistics, Philipp Cimiano teaching Formal Foundations, as well as Matthias Hartung and Wolodja Wentland, co-teaching Introduction to Programming, for sharing their experiences and commenting on versions of this paper. We would also like to thank Anke Holler for valuable input on the history of the Heidelberg B.A. program, Karin Thumser-Dauth for pointing us to the work of Jerome Bruner, Piklu Gupta for commenting on a pre-final version and also for help with the English. A special thank goes to three anonymous reviewers for their very detailed and constructive comments.

References

Steven Bird, Ewan Klein, and Edward Loper. forthcoming. *Natural Language Processing in Python*.

Jerome S. Bruner. 1960. *The Process of Education*. Harvard University Press, Cambridge, Mass.

Kai-Uwe Carstensen, Christian Ebert, Cornelia Endriss, Susanne Jekat, Ralf Klabunde, Hagen Langer. eds. 2004. *Computerlinguistik und Sprachtechnologie. Eine Einführung*. Spektrum, Akademischer Verlag, Heidelberg.

Markus Demleitner. unpublished. Programmieren I. www.cl.uni-heidelberg.de/kurs/skripte/prog1/html/

John E. Hopcroft and Jeffrey D. Ullman. 1979. *Introduction to Automata Theory, Languages and Computation* Addison Wesley.

Daniel Jurafsky and James H. Martin. 2000. *Speech and Language Processing. An Introduction to Natural Language Processing, Computational Linguistics, and Speech Recognition*. Prentice Hall Series in Artificial Intelligence. Prentice Hall.

Ralf Klabunde. 1998. *Formale Grundlagen der Linguistik* Narr, Tübingen.

Mark Lutz and David Ascher. 2007. *Learning Python*. O'Reilly, 2nd Edition.

Alex Martelli. 2006. *Python in a Nutshell. A Desktop Quick Reference*. O'Reilly, 2nd Edition.

Jörg Meibauer et al. eds. 2007. *Einführung in die germanistische Linguistik*. Metzler, Stuttgart.

Barbara Partee et al.. 1990. *Mathematical Methods in Linguistics*. Kluwer, Dordrecht.

Guido van Rossum. 2008. *Python Tutorial*. Python Software Foundation. docs.python.org/tut/tut.html

Uwe Schöning. 2001. *Theoretische Informatik kurzgefasst*. Spektrum Akademischer Verlag in Elsevier.

Defining a Core Body of Knowledge for the Introductory Computational Linguistics Curriculum

Steven Bird
Department of Computer Science and Software Engineering
University of Melbourne, Victoria 3010, Australia
sb@csse.unimelb.edu.au

Abstract

Discourse in and about computational linguistics depends on a shared body of knowledge. However, little content is shared across the introductory courses in this field. Instead, they typically cover a diverse assortment of topics tailored to the capabilities of the students and the interests of the instructor. If the core body of knowledge could be agreed and incorporated into introductory courses several benefits would ensue, such as the proliferation of instructional materials, software support, and extension modules building on a common foundation. This paper argues that it is worthwhile to articulate a core body of knowledge, and proposes a starting point based on the ACM Computer Science Curriculum. A variety of issues specific to the multidisciplinary nature of computational linguistics are explored.

1 Introduction

Surveys of introductory courses in computational linguistics and natural language processing provide evidence of great diversity.[1] Regional variation is stark: courses may emphasise theory over programming (or vice versa), rule-based approaches over statistical approaches (or vice versa), tagging and parsing over semantic interpretation (or vice versa), and so on. The diversity is hardly surprising given the particular background of a student cohort and the particular expertise of an instructor.

In spite of this variation, the introductory course needs to serve some common, basic needs. For some students, it will be the first step in a pathway leading to specialised courses, graduate research, or employment in this field. These students should receive a solid technical foundation and should come away with an accurate picture of the many opportunities that lie ahead. For students who do not continue, the introductory course will be their main exposure to the field. In addition to the technical content, these students need to understand how the field draws from and contributes back to its parent disciplines of linguistics and computer science, along with technological applications that are helping to shape the future information society. Naturally, this course is also a prime opportunity to promote the field to newcomers and encourage them to pursue advanced studies in this area. In all cases, the introductory course needs to cover a core body of knowledge.

The fact that a core body of knowledge exists in computational linguistics is demonstrated anecdotally: a doctoral student is told to curtail her extended discussions of basic POS tagging and CFG parsing algorithms since they are part of the presumed knowledge of the audience; a researcher presenting work to a general linguistics or computer science audience discovers to his surprise that certain methodologies or algorithms need to be explicated and defended, even though they was uncontroversial when presented at a conference; a keynote speaker at a computational linguistics conference can presume that certain theoretical programs and practical goals of the field are widely accepted. These three areas – terminology, methodology, ideology – constitute

[1] http://aclweb.org/aclwiki/index.php?title=List_of_NLP/CL_courses

Proceedings of the Third Workshop on Issues in Teaching Computational Linguistics (TeachCL-08), pages 27–35,
Columbus, Ohio, USA, June 2008.

part of the core body of knowledge of computational linguistics. They provide us with the starting point for identifying the concepts and skills to be covered in the introductory course.

Identifying a core body of knowledge would bring three major benefits. First, technical support would be consolidated: instructional materials together with implementations of standard algorithms would be available in several programming paradigms and languages. Second, colleagues without a research specialization in computational linguistics would have a non-controversial curriculum with external support, a standard course that could be promoted to a broad range of students as a mainstream option, in both linguistics and computer science. Similarly, new graduates beginning a teaching career would be better equipped to push for the adoption of a new computational linguistics or natural language processing course at institutions where it is not yet established. Third, employers and graduate schools would be able to make assumptions about the knowledge and skills of a new graduate.

The goal of this paper is to advocate the idea of consensus around a body of knowledge as a promising way to coordinate the introductory computational linguistics curriculum, without attempting to mandate the structure of individual courses or the choice of textbooks. The paper is organised as follows: section 2 sets the scene by describing a variety of contexts in which computational linguistics is taught, drawing on the author's first-hand experience; section 3 sets out a possible organization for the introductory topics in computational linguistics, modelled on the ACM Computer Science Curriculum; section 4 explores some implications of this approach for curriculum and assessment. The paper closes with remarks about next steps.

2 Contexts for Teaching and Learning in Computational Linguistics

In this section a variety of scenarios are described in which the author has had direct first-hand experience. All cases involve entry-level courses in computational linguistics. They provide the back-drop to the current proposal, exemplifying a range of contexts in which a core body of knowledge would need to be delivered, contexts imposing different constraints on implementation.

Before embarking on this discussion it is helpful to be reminded of the differing backgrounds and goals of new students. Some want to use computational techniques in the analysis of language, while others want to use linguistic knowledge in the development of language technologies. These backgrounds and goals are orthogonal, leading to the grid shown in Table 1.

I will begin with the most common context of a graduate-level course, before progressing to upper-level undergraduate, lower-level undergraduate, and secondary levels.

2.1 Graduate-Level Courses

Dozens of graduate programs in computer science and in linguistics have an introductory course on computational linguistics or natural language processing. In most cases, this is all the formal training a student will receive, and subsequent training is happens in private study or on the job. In some universities this is the entry point into a suite of more advanced courses in such areas as lexical semantics, statistical parsing, and machine translation. Even so, it is important to consider the shared assumptions of these specialised courses, and the needs of a student who only undertakes the introductory course.

There are two principal challenges faced by instructors at this level. The first is to adequately cover the theoretical and practical sides of the field in a single semester. A popular solution is not to try, i.e. to focus on theory to the exclusion of practical exercises, or to simply teach "programming for linguists." The former deprives students of the challenge and excitement of writing programs to automatically process language. The latter fails to cover any significant domain-specific theories or algorithms.

The second challenge is to address the diverse backgrounds of students, ranging from those with a computer science background to a linguistics background, with a scattering of students who have a background in both or in neither.

The author taught at this level at the University of Pennsylvania over a period of three years. Perhaps the most apt summary of the experience is *triage*. Cohorts fell into three groups: (i) students

	Background: Arts and Humanities	Background: Science and Engineering
Language Analysis	Programming to manage language data, explore linguistic models, and test empirical claims	Language as a source of interesting problems in data modeling, data mining, and knowledge discovery
Language Technology	Knowledge of linguistic algorithms and data structures for high quality, maintainable language processing software	Learning to program, with applications to familiar problems, to work in language technology or other technical field

Table 1: Summary of Students' Backgrounds and Goals, from (Bird et al., 2008a)

who are well prepared in either linguistics or computer science but not both (the majority) who will perform well given appropriate intervention; (ii) students who are well-prepared in both linguistics and computer science, able to complete learning tasks on their own with limited guidance; and (iii) students with minimal preparation in either linguistics or computer science, who lack any foundational knowledge upon which to build. Resources targetted at the first group invariably had the greatest impact.

2.2 Specialised Upper-Level Undergraduate Courses

In contrast with graduate-level courses, a specialised upper-level undergraduate course will typically be an elective, positioned in the later stages of an extended sequence of courses (corresponding to ACM unit *IS7 Natural Language Processing*, see §3). Here it is usually possible to make reliable assumptions about background knowledge and skills, and to provide training that is pitched at exactly the right level.

The author taught at this level in the Computer Science and Linguistics departments at the University of Melbourne during the past five years (five times in Computer Science, once in Linguistics). In the Linguistics department, the course began by teaching programming, with illustrations drawn from linguistic domains, before progressing to topics in text processing (tokenization, tagging), grammars and parsing, and data management. Laboratory sessions focussed on the acquisition of programming skills, and we found that a 1:5 staff-student ratio was insufficient.

In the Computer Science department, the first approach was to introduce linguistics for 2-3 weeks before looking at algorithms for linguistic processing. This was unpopular with many students, who did not see the motivation for learning about such topics as morphology and verb subcategorization in isolation from practical applications. A revised version of the course opened with topics in text processing, including tokenization, extracting text from the web, and moving on to topics in language engineering. (Bird et al. (2008b) provide a more extended discussion of opening topics.)

A third option is to teach computational linguistic topics in the context of a specialised course in an allied field. Thus a course on morphology could include a module on finite-state morphology, and a course on machine learning could include a module on text mining. In the former case, a linguistic domain is presupposed and the instructor needs to teach the linguist audience about a particular corpus to be processed or an algorithm to be implemented or tested. In the latter case, a family of algorithms and data structures is presupposed and the instructor needs to teach a computer science audience about linguistic data, structures, and processes that can serve as a domain of application.

2.3 Cross-Disciplinary Transition

People entering computational linguistics from either a linguistics or computer science background are faced with a daunting challenge of learning the fundamentals of the other field before they can progress very far with the study of the target domain. A major institution with a long history of teaching computational linguistics will have a cadre of graduate students and post-doctoral researchers who can support an instructor in teaching a course. However, one measure of the success of the approach being advocated here are that such institutions will be in the minority of those where computational linguistics is taught. In such contexts, a computational linguistics course will be a lone offering, competing for enrolments with a variety of more established electives. To compound the problem, a newcomer to the field may be faced with taking a course in a department other than their host department, a course which presumes background knowledge they lack. Additional support and self-paced learning materials are crucial. Efforts on filling out the computational linguistics content in Wikipedia – by instructors and students alike – will help the entire community.

2.4 Lower-Level Undergraduate Courses

An intriguing option for delivery of an introduction to computational linguistics is in the context of entry-level courses in linguistics and computer science. In some cases, this may help to address the declining interest of students in these individual disciplines.

As computer science finds a broader role in service teaching, rather than in training only those students doing a major, the curriculum needs to be driven by topics of broad appeal. In the author's current first year teaching, such topics include climate change, population health, social anthropology, and finance. Many fundamental concepts in data structures and algorithms can be taught from such starting points. It is possible to include language processing as one of the drivers for such a course.

Many possibilities for including computational linguistics exist in the second-level computer science curriculum. For example, algorithmic methods involving time-space trade-offs and dynamic programming can be motivated by the task of building a simple web search engine (Bird and Curran, 2006). Concrete tasks involve web crawling, text extraction, stemming, and indexing. Spelling correction can be used as a driver for teaching core computer science concepts in associative arrays, linked lists, and sorting by a secondary key.

An analogous opportunity exists in the context of entry-level courses in linguistics. Linguistics students will readily agree that most human knowledge and communication is represented and expressed using language. But it will come as a surprise that language technologies can process language automatically, leading to more natural human-machine interfaces, and more sophisticated access to stored information. In this context, a linguistics student may grasp a broader vision for his/her role in the multilingual information society of the future.

In both cases, the hope is that students are inspired to do further undergraduate study spanning linguistics and computer science, and to enter industry or graduate school with a solid preparation and a suitable mix of theoretical knowledge and technical skills.

The major obstacle is the lack of resources available to the typical instructor, who is not a specialist in computational linguistics, and who has to deliver the course to a large audience having no prior interest or knowledge in this area. They need simple packages and modules that can be incorporated into a variety of teaching contexts.

2.5 Secondary School

Programming and Information Technology have found a place in the secondary curriculum in many countries. The coursework is typically animated with projects involving games, databases, and dynamic websites. In contrast, the curriculum involving the grammar and literature of a major world language typically only uses information technology skills for such mundane tasks as word processing and web-based research. However, as innovators in the language curriculum look for new ways to enliven their classes with technology, computational linguistics offers a ready-made source of interesting problems and methods.

In Australia, the *English Language* curriculum of the Victorian Certificate of Education is a linguistics program offered as part of the last two years of secondary education (VCAA, 2006; Mulder et al., 2001). This course provides a promising host for computational linguistics content in the Victorian secondary curriculum. The author has delivered an "Electronic Grammar" module[2] in an English class in a Victorian secondary school over a three week period, jointly with a teacher who has a double degree in linguistics and computer science. Students were taught the elements of programming together with some simple applications involving taggers, parsers and annotated corpora. These activities served to reinforce students' understanding of lexical categories, lexical semantics, and syntactic

[2] `http://nltk.org/electronic_grammar.html`

ambiguity (i.e. prepositional phrase attachment). Similar methods could be applied in second language learning classes to locate common words and idioms in corpora.

In this context, key challenges are the installation of specialised software (even a programming language interpreter), overcoming the impenetrable nature of standard part-of-speech tagsets by mapping them to simplified tagsets, and providing suitable training for teachers. A promising solution is to provide a self-paced web-based programming and testing environment, side-stepping issues with school infrastructure and teacher training.[3]

3 Defining the CL Body of Knowledge

A promising approach for identifying the CL body of knowledge is to begin with the ACM *Computing Curricula 2001 Computer Science Volume* (ACM, 2001). In this scheme, the body of knowledge within computer science is organised in a three-level hierarchy: subfields, units and topics. Each subfield has a two-letter designator, such as OS for operating systems. Subfields are divided into several units, each being a coherent theme within that particular area, and each identified with a numeric suffix. Within each unit, individual topics are identified. We can select from this body of knowledge the areas that are commonly assumed in computational linguistics (see the Appendix), and then expect them to be part of the background of an incoming computer science student.

The field of linguistics is less systematised, and no professional linguistics body has attempted to devise an international curriculum standard. Helpful compendia of topics exist, such as the *Language Files* (Stewart and Vaillette, 2008). However, this does not attempt to define the curriculum but to provide supporting materials for introductory courses.

Following the ACM scheme, one could try to establish a list of topics comprising the body of knowledge in computational linguistics. This is not an attempt to create a comprehensive ontology for the field (cf. Cole (1997), Uszkoreit et al. (2003)), but rather a simple practical organization of introductory topics.

CL. Computational Linguistics

- CL1. Goals of computational linguistics
  roots, philosophical underpinnings, ideology, contemporary divides
- CL2. Introduction to Language
  written vs spoken language; linguistic levels; typology, variation and change
- CL3. Words, morphology and the lexicon
  tokenization, lexical categories, POS-tagging, stemming, morphological analysis, FSAs
- CL4. Syntax, grammars and parsing
  grammar formalisms, grammar development, formal complexity of natural language
- CL5. Semantics and discourse
  lexical semantics, multiword expressions, discourse representation
- CL6. Generation
  text planning, syntactic realization
- CL7. Language engineering
  architecture, robustness, evaluation paradigms
- CL8. Language resources
  corpora, web as corpus, data-intensive linguistics, linguistic annotation, Unicode
- CL9. Language technologies
  named entity detection, coreference, IE, QA, summarization, MT, NL interfaces

Following the ACM curriculum, we would expect to designate some of these areas as core (e.g. CL1-3), while expecting some number of additional areas to be taken as electives (e.g. three from the remaining six areas). A given curriculum would then consist of three components: (a) bridging studies so students can access the core knowledge; (b) the core body of knowledge itself; and (c) a selection of electives chosen to give students a balance of linguistic models, computational methodologies, and application domains. These issues involve fleshing out the body of knowledge into a sequential curriculum, the topic of the next section.

4 Implications for the Curriculum

The curriculum of an introductory course builds out from the body of knowledge of the field by linearizing the topic areas and adding bridging studies and electives. The result is a pathway that mediates between students' backgrounds and their goals as already schematised in Table 1. Figure 1 displays two hypothetical pathways, one for students

[3] This is a separate activity of the author and colleagues, available via `ivle.sourceforge.net`

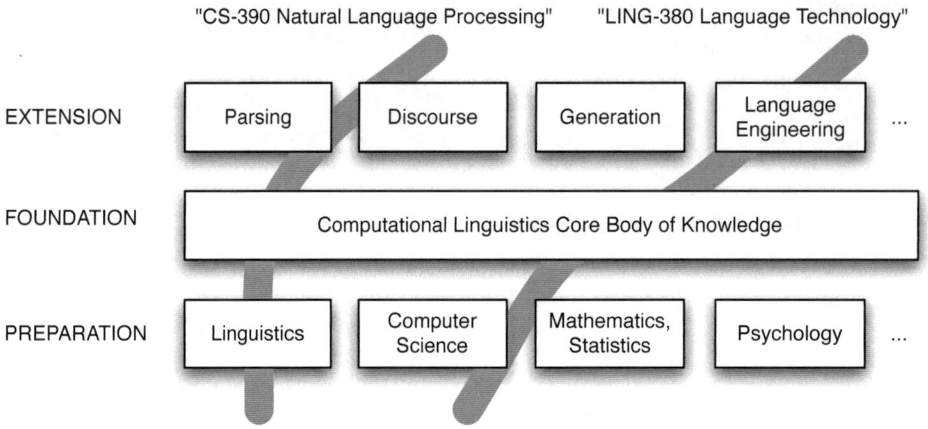

Figure 1: Curriculum as a Pathway Through the Core Body of Knowledge, with Two Hypothetical Courses

from a computer science background wanting to learn about natural language processing, and one for students from a linguistics background wanting to learn about language technology. These could serve as templates for individual advanced undergraduate courses with names that are driven by local marketing needs rather than the need to emphasise the computational linguistics content. However, they could also serve as a guide for a whole series of course selections in the context of a coursework masters program. Clearly, the adoption of a core body of knowledge has rather limited implications for the sequence of an individual curriculum.

This section explores these implications for the curriculum and raises issues for wider discussion and exploration.

4.1 Diverse Entry Points

An identified body of knowledge is not yet a curriculum. It must sit in the context of the background and goals of a particular audience. An analysis of the author's experience in teaching computational linguistics to several types of audience has led to a four-way partitioning of the possible entry points, shown in Figure 2.

The approaches in the top half of the figure are driven by applications and skills, while those in the bottom half are driven by theoretical concerns both inside and outside computational linguistics. The entry points in the top-left and bottom-right of the diagram seem to work best for a computer science audience, while the other two seem to work best for a linguistics audience (though further work is required to put such impressionistic observations on a sound footing).

By definition, all students would have to cover the core curriculum regardless of their entry point. Depending on the entry point and the other courses taken, different amounts of the core curriculum would already be covered. For students with minimal preparation, it might actually take more than one course to cover the core curriculum.

4.2 Bridging Studies

One approach to preparation, especially suitable at the graduate level, is to mandate bridging studies for students who are not adequately prepared for the introductory course. This could range from an individual program of preparatory readings, to a summer intensive course, to a full semester course (e.g. auditing a first or second year undergraduate course such as *Introduction to Language* or *Algorithms and Data Structures*).

It is crucial to take seriously the fact that some students may be learning to program for the first time in their lives. Apart from learning the syntax of a particular programming language, they need to learn a new and quite foreign algorithmic approach to problem solving. Students often report that they understand the language constructs and follow the examples provided by the instructor, but find they are unable to write new programs from scratch.

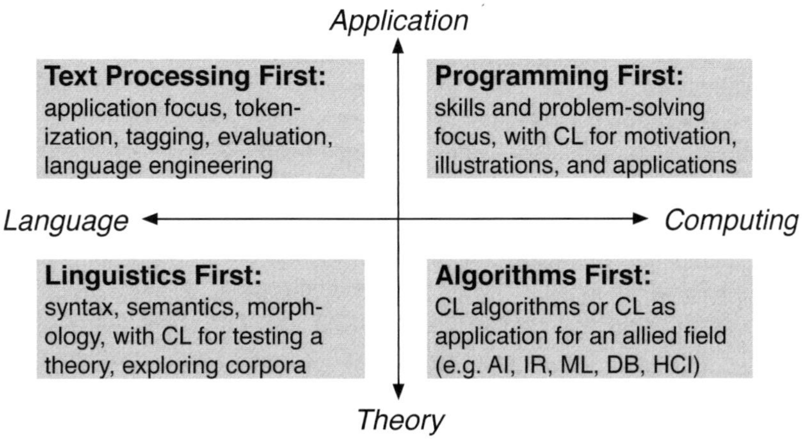

Figure 2: Approaches to Teaching NLP

This accords with the finding that the way in which programmers understand or write programs differs greatly between the novice and the expert (Lister et al., 2006). The issue is independent of the computational linguistics context, and fits the more general pattern that students completing an introductory programming course do not perform as well as expected (McCracken et al., 2001).

Bridging studies can also overlap with the course itself, as already indicated in Figure 1. For example, in the first week of classes one could run a quiz that identifies students who are not sufficiently prepared for the programming component of the course. Such a quiz could include a diagnostic non-programming task, like articulating the search process for looking up a name in a telephone book, which is a predictor of programming skill (Simon et al., 2006). Early intervention could include extra support, readings, classes, and so on. Some students could be alerted to the fact that they will find the course very challenging. Some students in this category may opt to switch to a less demanding course, which might actually be the best outcome for all concerned.

4.3 Organizational Models

Linguistics Model: A natural way to structure the computational linguistics curriculum is to adopt organizational patterns from linguistics courses. This could involve progression up through the linguistic levels from phonology to discourse, or a focus on the analysis of a particular language or language family, the implementation of a particular linguistic theory, or skills development in corpus linguistics or field methods. In this way, content can be packaged to meet local needs, while retaining latitude to enter and exit the core body of knowledge in computational linguistics.

Computer Science Model: The curriculum could adopt organizational patterns from other computer science courses. This could involve progression through families of algorithms, or navigating the processing pipeline of speech understanding, or exploring the pieces of a multi-component system (e.g. question answering). As with the linguistics model, the course would be badged to appeal to students in the local context, while covering the core body of knowledge in computational linguistics.

Vocational Model: In some contexts, established theoretical courses dominate, and there is room to promote a course that is focussed on building programming skills in a new language or for some new application area. This may result in a popular elective that gives students a readily marketable skill.[4] This approach may also work at the secondary level in the form of an after-school club. The course is structured according to the features of a particular programming language, but examples and projects on text processing succeed in covering the core body

[4]The author found this approach to be successful in the case of a database theory course, in which a semester project on building a web database using PHP and MySQL added significant appeal to an otherwise dry subject.

of knowledge in computational linguistics.

Dialectic Model: As discussed above, a major goal for any curriculum is to take students from one of the entry points in Figure 2 into the core body of knowledge. One approach is to consider transitions to topics covered in one of the other entry points: the entry point is a familiar topic, but from there the curriculum goes across to the other side, attempting to span the divide between computer science and linguistics. Thus, a computational linguistics curriculum for a computer science audience could begin with algorithms (bottom-left) before applying these to a range of problems in text processing (top-left) only to discover that richer sources of linguistic knowledge were required (bottom-right). Similarly a curriculum for a linguistics audience could begin with programming (top-right), then seek to apply these skills to corpus processing for a particular linguistic domain (bottom-left).

This last approach to the curriculum criss-crosses the divide between linguistics and computer science. Done well, it will establish a dialectic between the two fields, one in which students reach a mature understanding of the contrasting methodologies and ideologies that exist within computational linguistics including: philosophical assumptions (e.g. rationalism vs empiricism); the measurement of success (e.g. formal evaluation vs linguistic explanation); and the role of observation (e.g. a single datum as a valuable nugget vs massive datasets as ore to be refined).

5 Conclusion

A core body of knowledge is presumed background to just about any communication within the field of computational linguistics, spanning terminology, methodology, and ideology. Consensus on this body of knowledge would serve to underpin a diverse range of introductory curricula, ensuring they cover the core without imposing much restriction on the details of any particular course. Curricula beginning from four very different starting points can progress towards this common core, and thence to specialised topics that maximise the local appeal of the course and its function of attracting newcomers into the field of computational linguistics.

There is enough flexibility in the curriculum of most existing introductory computational linguistics courses to accommodate a core body of knowledge, regardless of the aspirations of students or the research interests of an instructor. If the introductory course is part of a sequence of courses, a larger body of knowledge is in view and there will be scope for switching content into and out of the first course. If the introductory course stands alone as an elective that leads to no other courses, there will also be scope for adding or removing content.

The preliminary discussion of this paper leaves many areas open for discussion and exploration. The analyses and recommendations remain at the level of folk pedagogy and need to be established objectively. The various pathways have only been described schematically, and still need to be fleshed out into complete syllabuses, down to the level of week-by-week topics. Support for skill development is crucial, especially in the case of students learning to program for the first time. Finally, obstacles to conceptual learning and skill development need to be investigated systematically, with the help of more sophisticated and nuanced approaches to assessment.

Acknowledgments

The experiences and ideas discussed in this paper have arisen during my computational linguistics teaching at the Universities of Edinburgh, Pennsylvania and Melbourne. I'm indebted to several co-teachers who have accompanied me on my journey into teaching computational linguistics, including Edward Loper, Ewan Klein, Baden Hughes, and Selina Dennis. I am also grateful to many students who have willingly participated in my explorations of ways to bridge the divide between linguistics and computer science over the past decade. This paper has benefitted from the feedback of several anonymous reviewers.

References

ACM. 2001. *Computing Curricula 2001: Computer Science Volume*. Association for Computing Machinery. http://www.sigcse.org/cc2001/.

Steven Bird and James Curran. 2006. Building a search engine to drive problem-based learning. In *Proceedings of the Eleventh Annual Conference on Innovation and Technology in Computer Science Education*. http://eprints.unimelb.edu.au/archive/00001618/.

Steven Bird, Ewan Klein, and Edward Loper. 2008a. Natural Language Processing in Python. http://nltk.org/book.html.

Steven Bird, Ewan Klein, Edward Loper, and Jason Baldridge. 2008b. Multidisciplinary instruction with the Natural Language Toolkit. In *Proceedings of the Third Workshop on Issues in Teaching Computational Linguistics*. Association for Computational Linguistics.

Ronald Cole, editor. 1997. *Survey of the State of the Art in Human Language Technology*. Studies in Natural Language Processing. Cambridge University Press.

Raymond Lister, Beth Simon, Errol Thompson, Jacqueline L. Whalley, and Christine Prasad. 2006. Not seeing the forest for the trees: novice programmers and the SOLO taxonomy. In *Proceedings of the 11th Annual SIGCSE Conference on Innovation and Technology in Computer Science Education*, pages 118–122.

Michael McCracken, Vicki Almstrum, Danny Diaz, Mark Guzdial, Dianne Hagan, Yifat Ben-David Kolikant, Cary Laxer, Lynda Thomas, Ian Utting, and Tadeusz Wilusz. 2001. A multi-national, multi-institutional study of assessment of programming skills of first-year CS students. *SIGCSE Bulletin*, 33:125–180.

Jean Mulder, Kate Burridge, and Caroline Thomas. 2001. *Macmillan English Language: VCE Units 1 and 2*. Melbourne: Macmillan Education Australia.

Simon Simon, Quintin Cutts, Sally Fincher, Patricia Haden, Anthony Robins, Ken Sutton, Bob Baker, Ilona Box, Michael de Raadt, John Hamer, Margaret Hamilton, Raymond Lister, Marian Petre, Denise Tolhurst, and Jodi Tutty. 2006. The ability to articulate strategy as a predictor of programming skill. In *Proceedings of the 8th Australian Conference on Computing Education*, pages 181–188. Australian Computer Society.

Thomas W. Stewart and Nathan Vaillette, editors. 2008. *Language Files: Materials for an Introduction to Language and Linguistics*. Ohio State University Press.

Hans Uszkoreit, Brigitte Jörg, and Gregor Erbach. 2003. An ontology-based knowledge portal for language technology. In *Proceedings of ENABLER/ELSNET Workshop "International Roadmap for Language Resources"*.

VCAA. 2006. *English Language: Victorian Certicate of Education Study Design*. Victorian Curriculum and Assessment Authority. http://www.vcaa.vic.edu.au/vce/studies/englishlanguage/englangindex.htm%1.

Appendix: Selected Topics from ACM CS Body of Knowledge Related to Computational Linguistics

DS. Discrete Structures
- DS1. Functions, relations and sets
- DS2. Basic logic
- DS5. Graphs and trees
- DS6. Discrete probability

PF. Programming Fundamentals
- PF1. Fundamental programming constructs
- PF2. Algorithms and problem solving
- PF3. Fundamental data structures
- PF4. Recursion

AL. Algorithms and Complexity
- AL1. Basic algorithmic analysis
- AL2. Algorithmic strategies

IS. Intelligent Systems
- IS1. Fundamental issues in intelligent systems
- IS2. Search and constraint satisfaction
- IS3. Knowledge representation and reasoning
- IS7. (Natural language processing)

IM. Information Management
- IM1. Information models and systems
- IM3. Data modeling

SP. Social and Professional Issues
- SP4. Professional and ethical responsibilities
- SP5. Risks and liabilities of computer-based systems

SE. Software Engineering
- SE1. Software design
- SE2. Using application programming interfaces
- SE9. Component-based computing

Strategies for Teaching "Mixed" Computational Linguistics classes

Eric Fosler-Lussier
Dept. of Computer Science and Engineering
Dept. of Linguistics
The Ohio State University
Columbus, OH 43210, USA
fosler@cse.ohio-state.edu

Abstract

Many of the computational linguistics classes at Ohio State draw a diverse crowd of students, who bring different levels of preparation to the classroom. In the same classroom, we often get graduate and undergraduate students from Linguistics, Computer Science, Electrical Engineering and other departments; teaching the same material to all of these students presents an interesting challenge to the instructor. In this paper, I discuss some of the teaching strategies that I have employed to help integrate students in two classes on automatic speech recognition topics; strategies for a graduate seminar class and a standard "lecture" class are presented. Both courses make use of communal, online activities to facilitate interaction between students.

1 Introduction

As one of the themes of the Teach-CL08 workshop suggests, teaching students of many kinds and many levels of preparation within a single course can be an interesting challenge; this situation is much more prevalent in a cross-disciplinary area such as computational linguistics (as well as medical bioinformatics, etc.). At Ohio State, we also define the computational linguistics field relatively broadly, including automatic speech recognition and (more recently) information retrieval as part of the curriculum. Thus, we see three major variations in the preparation of students at OSU:

1. **Home department:** most of the students taking CL courses are either in the Linguistics or Computer Science and Engineering departments, although there have been students from foreign language departments, Electrical Engineering, Psychology, and Philosophy. Although there are exceptions, typically the engineers have stronger mathematical and computational implementation skills and the non-engineers have a stronger background in the theoretical linguistics literature. Bringing these groups together requires a balancing between the strengths of each group.

2. **Specialization (or lack thereof):** Many of the students, particularly in seminar settings, have particular research agendas that are not traditionally aligned with the topic of the class (e.g., students interested in parsing or computer vision taking an ASR-learning course). Furthermore, there are often students who are not senior enough to have a particular research track, but are interested in exploring the area of the course. Our courses need to be designed to reach across areas and draw on other parts of the curriculum in order to both provide connections with the student's current knowledge base, and allow the student to take away useful lessons even they do not plan to pursue the topic of the course further.

3. **Graduate vs. undergraduate students:** in both the CSE and Linguistics departments at Ohio State, CL (and many other) courses are open to both undergraduates and graduate students. These courses fall far enough down the prerequisite chain that the undergraduates who

Proceedings of the Third Workshop on Issues in Teaching Computational Linguistics (TeachCL-08), pages 36–44,
Columbus, Ohio, USA, June 2008.

enroll are usually very motivated (and consequently do well), but one must keep in mind the differences in abilities and time constraints of each type of student. If the graduate students outnumber the undergraduates, introducing mentoring opportunities can provide a rewarding experience for all concerned.

From a practical perspective, this diversity presents a significant challenge – especially in universities where enrollment concerns drive curricular matters to some degree. Inclusiveness is also a reasonable goal from a financial, not just a pedagogical, perspective. CSE enrollments have declined significantly since the dot-com bust (Vegso, 2008), and while the declines are not as sharp as they once were, the current environment makes it more difficult to justify teaching narrow, advanced courses to only a few students (even if this were the practice in the past).

In this paper, I describe a number of strategies that have been successful in bringing all of these diverse populations into two different classes offered at OSU: a graduate seminar and a undergrad/graduate lecture class. The topic of both classes was statistical language processing, with a significant emphasis on ASR. Sample activities are discussed from each class.

While there are significant differences in the way that each class runs, there are several common elements that I try to provide in all of my classes.:

I first establish the golden rule: primary among my self-imposed rules is to make clear to all participants that all points of view are to be respected (although not necessarily agreed with), and that students are coming to this class with different strengths. If possible, an activity that integrates both linguistic and computer science knowledge should be brought in within the first week of the class; in teaching CSE courses, I tend to emphasize the linguistics a bit more in the first week.

I try to help students to engage with each other: a good way to foster inter- and intra-disciplinary respect is to have the students work collaboratively towards some goal. This can be challenging in a diverse student population setting; monitoring progress of students and gently suggesting turn-taking/mentoring strategies as well as designing activities that speak to multiple backgrounds can help ease the disparity between student backgrounds. Preparing the students to engage with each other on the same level by introducing online pre-class activities can also help bring students together.

I try to allow students to build on previous knowledge via processes other than lecturing: a lecture, presented by either a student or a professor, is a "one-size-fits-all" solution that in a diverse population can sometimes either confuse unprepared students, bore prepared students, or both. Interactive in-class and out-of-class activities have the advantage of real-time evaluation of the understanding of students. This is not to say that I never lecture; but as a goal, lecturing should be short in duration and focused on coordinating understanding among the students. Over the years, I am gradually reducing the amount of lecturing I do, replacing it with other activities.

By putting some simple techniques into place, both students and I have noticed a significant improvement in the quality of classes. In Section 2, I describe improvements to a graduate seminar that facilitated interaction among a diverse group of participants. The most recent offering of the 10-week seminar class had 22 participants: 14 from CSE, 7 from Linguistics, and one from another department. In my informal evaluation of background, 13 of the 22 participants were relatively new to the field of computational linguistics ($<$ 2 years experience). Student-directed searching for background materials, pre-posing of questions via a class website, and blind reviewing of extended project abstracts by fellow students were effective strategies for providing common ground.

Section 3 describes improvements in a lecture-style class (Foundations of Spoken Language Processing) which has a similarly diverse participant base: the most recently completed offering had 7 CSE and 3 Linguistics Students, with the undergrad/graduate student ratio 3:7. Devoting one of the two weekly sessions to in-class group practical exercises also bolstered performance of all students.

2 Seminar structure

In developing a graduate seminar on machine learning for language processing, I was faced with a serious challenge: the previous seminar offering (on sequential machine learning) two years prior was not as inspiring as one would hope, with several students not actively participating in the class. This happened in part because students were permitted to suggest papers to read that week, which usually came from their own research area and often had esoteric terminology and mathematics. There was nothing wrong with the papers *per se*, but many of the students were not able to bridge the gap from their own experience to get into the depths of the current paper. While I thought having students partially control the seminar agenda might provide ownership of the material, in practice it gave a few students control of the session each time. In the more recent offering, this problem was likely to be exacerbated: the increased diversity of backgrounds of the students in the class suggested that it would be difficult to find common ground for discussing advanced topics in machine learning.

In previous seminars, students had given computer-projected presentations of papers, which led to rather perfunctory, non-engaged discussions. In the offering two years prior, I had banned computerized presentations, but was faced with the fact that many students still came unprepared for discussions, so the sessions were somewhat hit-and-miss.

In sum, a reorganization of the class seemed desirable that would encourage more student participation, provide students the opportunity to improve their background understanding, and still cover advanced topics.

2.1 A revised seminar structure

The previous instantiation of the seminar met twice weekly for 1 1/2 hours; in the most recent offering the seminar was moved to a single 2 1/2 hour block on Fridays. Each week was assigned a pair of student facilitators who were to lead the discussion for the week. The instructor chose roughly four papers on the topic of the week: one or two were more basic, overview papers (e.g., the Rabiner HMM tutorial (Rabiner, 1989) or Lafferty *et al.*'s Conditional Random Fields paper (Lafferty et al., 2001)), and the remaining were more advanced papers. Students then had varying assigned responsibilities relating to these papers and the topic throughout the week. Out-of-class assignments were completed using discussion boards as part of Ohio State's online course management system.

The first assignment (due Tuesday evening) was to find relevant review articles or resources (such as class or tutorial slides) on the internet relating to the topic of the week. Each student was to write and post a short, one-paragraph summary of the tutorial and its strengths and weaknesses. Asking the students to find their own "catch-up" resources provided a wealth of information for the class to look at, as well as boosting the confidence of many students by letting them find the information that best suited them. I usually picked one (or possibly two) of the tutorials for the class to examine as a whole that would provide additional grounding for class discussions.

The second assignment (due Thursday evening at 8 pm) was for each student to post a series of questions on the readings of the week. At a minimum, each student was required to ask one question per week, but all of the students far exceeded this. Comments such as "I totally don't understand this section" were welcome (and encouraged) by the instructor. Often (but not exclusively) these questions would arise from students whose background knowledge was sparser. In the forum, there was a general air of collegiality in getting everyone up to speed: students often read each others' questions and commented on them inline. Figure 1 shows a sample conversation from the course; many of the small clarifications that students needed were handled in this manner, whereas the bigger discussion topics were typically dealt with in class. Students often pointed out the types of background information that, if discussed in class, could help them better understand the papers.

The facilitators of the week then worked Thursday evening to collate the questions, find the ones that were most common across the attendees or that would lead to good discussion points, and develop an order for the discussion on Friday. Facilitators started each Friday session with a summary of the main points of the papers (10-15 minutes maximum) and then started the discussion by putting the questions up to the group. It was important that the facilitators did not need to know the answers to the questions, but rather how to pose the questions so that a group discussion ensued. Facilitators almost always

Student 1: After reading all of these papers on [topic], astoundingly, a few of the concepts have started to sink in. The formulas are mostly gibberish, but at least they're familiar. Anyhow, I have only mostly dumb questions....

- [Paper 1]:
  - Anyone want to talk about Kullback-Leibler divergence?
  - We've see this before, but I forget. What is an l_2 norm?
  - What's the meaning of an equal symbol with a delta over it?
  - When it talked about the "SI mode", does that mean "speaker independent"?
- [Paper 2]:
  - In multiple places, we see the where we have a vector and a matrix, and they compute the product of the transpose of the vector with the matrix with the vector. Why are they doing that?
- [Paper 3]:
  - I came away from this paper feeling like they gave a vague description of what they did, followed by results. I mean, nice explanation of [topic] in general, but their whole innovation, as far as I can tell, fits into section [section number]. I feel like I'm missing something huge here.
- [Paper 4]:
  - So, they want to maximize $2/|w|$, so they decide instead to minimize $|w|^2/2$. Why? I mean, I get that it's a reciprocal, so you change from max to min, and that squaring it still makes it a minimization problem. But why square it? Is this another instance of making the calculus easier?
  - What are the 'sx' and 'si' training sentences?

Student 2: *But why square it? Is this another instance of making the calculus easier?* I think so. I think it has to do with the fact that we will take its derivative, hence the ^{2} and 1/2 cancel each other. And since they're just getting an argmax, the ^{2} exponent doesn't matter, since the maximum x^2 can be found by finding the maximum x.
Student 3: 'sx' are the phonetically-compact sentences in the TIMIT database and 'si' are the phonetically-diverse sentences.
Student 4: Ah thanks for that; I've wondered the same thing when seeing the phrase "TIMIT si/sx"
Student 5: Oh, so 'si' and 'sx' do not represent the phones they are trying to learn and discern?

Figure 1: Conversation during question posting period in online discussion forum. Participants and papers have been anonymized to protect the students.

had something to contribute to the conversation; releasing them from absolutely needing to be sure of the answer made them (and other participants) able to go out on a limb more in the discussion.

I found that since the instructor usually has more background knowledge with respect to many of the questions asked, it was critical for me to have a sense of timing for when the discussion was faltering or getting off track and needed for me to jump in. I spent roughly a half hour total of each session (in 5-10 minute increments) up at the blackboard quickly sketching some material (such as algorithms unknown to about half of the class) to make a connection. However, it was also important for me to realize when to let the control of the class revert to the facilitators.

The blackboard was a communal workspace: in some of the later classes students also started to get up and use the board to make points, or make points on top of other students drawings. In the future, I will encourage students to use this space from the first session. I suspect that the lack of electronic presentation media contributed to this dynamism.

2.2 Class projects

The seminar required individual or team projects that were developed through the term; presentations took place in the last session and in finals week. Three weeks prior to the end of term, each team submitted a two-page extended abstract describing their

What single aspect of the course did you find most helpful? Why?
Discussions.
Very good papers used.
Style of teaching atmosphere.
Just the discussion style.
Informal, discussion based.
The project.
[Instructor] really explained the intuitions behind the dense math. The pictorial method to explain algorithms.
The breadth of NLP problems addressed.
Instructor's encouragement to get students involved in the classroom discussion.
Interaction between students, sharing questions.
Reading many papers on these topics was good training on how to pull out the important parts of the papers.

What single change in the course would you most like to see? Why?
There are a lot of papers – keeps us busy and focused on the course, but it may be too much to comprehend in a single term.
More background info.
None.
I think it is highly improved from 2 years ago. Good job.
Less emphasis on ASR.
Have some basic optional exercises on some of the math techniques discussed.
Less reading, covered at greater depth.
Make the material slightly less broad in scope.
More quick overviews of the algorithms for those of us who haven't studied them before.

Figure 2: Comments from student evaluation forms for the seminar class

work, as if for a conference submission.

Each abstract was reviewed by three members of the class using a standard conference reviewing form; part of the challenge of the abstract submission is that it needed to be broad enough to be reviewed by non-experts in their area, but also needed to be detailed enough to show that it was a reasonable project. The reviews were collated and provided back to authors; along with the final project writeup the team was required to submit a letter explaining how they handled the criticisms of the reviewers. This proved to be an excellent exercise in perspective-taking (both in reviewing and writing the abstract) and provided experience in tasks that are critical to academic success.

I believe that injecting the tutorial-finding and question-posting activities also positively affected the presentations; many of the students used terminology that was developed/discussed during the course of the term. The project presentations were generally stronger than presentations for other classes that I have run in the past.

2.3 Feedback on new course structure

The student evaluations of the course were quite positive (in terms of numeric scores), but perhaps more telling were the free-form comments on the course itself. Figure 2 shows some of the comments, which basically show that students enjoyed the dynamic, interactive atmosphere; the primary negative comment was about how much material was presented in the course.

After this initial experiment, some of my colleagues adopted the technique of preparing the students for class via electronic discussion boards for their own seminars. This has been used already for two CL seminars (one at Ohio State and another at University of Tübengen), and plans for a third seminar at OSU (in a non-CL setting) are underway. The professors leading those courses have also reported positive experiences in increased interaction in the class.

All in all, while the course was clearly not perfect, it seems that many of the simple strategies that were put into place helped bridge the gap between the backgrounds of students; almost all of the students found the class a rewarding experience. It is not clear how this technique will scale to large classes: there were roughly 20 participants in the seminar (including auditors who came occasionally); doubling the number of postings would probably make facilitation much more difficult, so modifications might be necessary to accommodate larger classes.

3 Group work within a lecture class

I have seen similar issues in diversity of preparation in an undergraduate/graduate lecture class entitled "Foundations of Spoken Language Processing." This class draws students from CSE, ECE, and Linguistics departments, and from both undergraduate and graduate populations.

3.1 Course structure

In early offerings of this class, I had primarily presented the material in lecture format; however, when I taught it most recently, I divided the material into weekly topics. I presented lectures on Tuesday only, whereas on most Thursdays students completed group lab assignments; the remaining Thursdays were for group discussions. For the practical labs, students would bring their laptops to class, connect wirelessly to the departmental servers, and work together to solve some introductory problems.

The course utilizes several technologies for building system components: MATLAB for signal processing, the AT&T Finite State Toolkit (Mohri et al., 2001) for building ASR models and doing text analysis[1], and the SRI Language Modeling Toolkit (Stolcke, 2002) for training n-gram language models. One of the key ideas behind the class is that students learn to build an end-to-end ASR system from the component parts, which helps them identify major research areas (acoustic features, acoustic models, search, pronunciation models, and language models). We also re-use the same FST tools to build the first pieces of a speech synthesis module. Componentized technologies allow the students to take the first step beyond using a black-box system and prepare them to understand the individual components more deeply. The FST formalism helps the Linguistics students, who often come to the class with knowledge of formal language theory.

The group activities that get students of varying backgrounds to interact constitute the heart of the course, and provide a basis for the homework assignments. Figure 3 outlines the practical lab sessions and group discussions that were part of the most recent offering of the course.

Weeks 1 and 3 offer complementary activities that tend to bring the class together early on in the term. In the first week, students are given some speech examples from the TIMIT database; the first example they see is phonetically labeled. Using the Wavesurfer program (Sjölander and Beskow, 2000), students look for characteristics in spectrograms that are indicative of particular phonemes. Students are then presented with a second, unlabeled utterance that they need to phonetically label according to a pronunciation chart. The linguists, who generally have been exposed to this concept previously, tend to lead groups; most students are surprised at how difficult the task is, and this task provokes good discussion about the difference between canonical phonemes versus realized phones.

In the third week, students are asked to recreate the spectrograms by implementing the mel filterbank equations in MATLAB. Engineering students who have seen MATLAB before tend to take the lead in this session, but there has been enough rapport among the students at this point, and there is enough intuition behind the math in the tutorial instructions, that nobody in the previous session had trouble grasping what was going on with the math: almost all of the students completed the follow-on homework, which was to fully compute Mel Frequency Cepstral Coefficients (MFCCs) based on the spectrogram code they developed in class. Because both linguists and engineers have opportunities to take the lead in these activities they help to build groups that trust and rely on each other.

The second week's activity is a tutorial that I had developed for the Johns Hopkins University Summer School on Human Language Technology (supported by NSF and NAACL) based around the Finite State Toolkit; the tutorial acquaints students with

[1] Subsequent offerings of the course will likely use the OpenFST toolkit (Riley et al., 2008).

Week	Lecture topic	Group activity
1	Speech production & perception	Group discussion about spectrograms and phonemes; groups use Wavesurfer (Sjölander and Beskow, 2000) to transcribe speech data.
2	Finite state representations	Use FST tools for a basic language generation task where parts of speech are substituted with words; use FST tools to break a simple letter-substitution cipher probabilistically.
3	Frequency analysis & acoustic features	Use MATLAB to implement Mel filterbanks and draw spectrograms (referring back to Week 1); use spectral representations to develop a "Radio Rex" simulation.
4	Dynamic Time Warping, Acoustic Modeling	Quiz; Group discussion: having read various ASR toolkit manuals, if you were a technical manager who needed to direct someone to implement a system, which would you choose? What features does each toolkit provide?
5	HMMs, EM, and Search	The class acts out the token passing algorithm (Young et al., 1989), with each group acting as a single HMM for a digit word (one, two, three...), and post-it notes being exchanged as tokens.
6	Language models	Build language models using the SRILM toolkit (Stolcke, 2002), and compute the perplexity of Wall Street Journal text.
7	Text Analysis & Speech Synthesis	Use FST tools to turn digit strings like "345" into the corresponding word string ("three hundred and forty five"). This tutorial grants more independence than previous ones; students are expected to figure out that "0" can be problematic, for example.
8	Speech Synthesis Speaker Recognition	Group discussion on a speaker recognition and verification tutorial paper (Campbell, 1997)
9	Spoken Dialogue Systems	Quiz; General discussion of any topic in the class.
10	Project presentations over the course of both sessions	

Week	Homework Task
2	Rank poker hands and develop end-to-end ASR system, both using finite state toolkit.
3	Finish Radio Rex implementation, compute MFCCs.
4	Replace week 2 homework's acoustic model with different classifier/probabilistic model.
5	Implement Viterbi algorithm for isolated words.
6	Lattice rescoring with language models trained by the student.
7	Text normalization of times, dates, money, addresses, phone numbers, course numbers.

Figure 3: Syllabus for Foundations of Spoken Language Processing class with group activities and homeworks.

various finite state operations; the two tasks are a simplified language generation task (convert the sequence "DET N V DET N" into a sentence like "the man bit the dog") and a cryptogram solver (solve a simple substitution cipher by comparing frequencies of crypttext letters versus frequencies of plaintext letters). The students get experience, in particular, with transducer composition (which is novel for almost all of the students); these techniques are used in the first homework, which involves building a transducer-based pronunciation model for digits (converting "w ah n" into "ONE") and implementing a FST composition chain for an ASR system, akin to that of (Mohri et al., 2002). A subsequent homework reuses this chain, but asks students to implement a new acoustic model and replace the acoustic model outputs that are given in the first homework. Similarly, practical tutorials on language models (Week 6) and text analysis (Week 7) feed into homework assignments on rescoring lattices with language models and turning different kinds of numeric strings (addresses, time, course numbers) into word strings.

Using group activities raises the question of how to evaluate individual understanding. Homework assignments in this class are designed to extend the work done in-class, but must be done individually. Because many people will be starting from a group code base, assignments will often look similar. Since the potential for plagiarism is a concern, it is important that the assignments extend the group activities enough that one can distinguish between group and individual effort.

Another group activity that supports a homework assignment is the Token Passing tutorial (Week 5). The Token Passing algorithm (Young et al., 1989) describes how to extend the Viterbi algorithm to continuous speech: each word in the vocabulary is represented by a single HMM, and as the Viterbi algorithm reaches the end of an HMM at a particular timeframe, a token is "emitted" from the HMM recording the ending time, word identity, acoustic score, and pointer to the previous word-token. The students are divided into small groups and each group is assigned a digit word (one, two, ...) with a particular pronunciation. The HMM topology assumes only one, self-looping state per phone for simplicity. The instructor then displays on the projector a likelihood for every phone for the first time frame. The groups work to assign the forward probabilities for the first frame. Once every group is synchronized, the second frame of data likelihoods is displayed, and students then again calculate forward probabilities, and so forth. After the second frame, some groups ("two") start to emit tokens, which are posted on the board; groups then have to also consider starting a new word at the third time step. The activity continues for roughly ten frames, at which point the global best path is found. Including this activity has had a beneficial effect on homework performance: a significantly higher proportion of students across all backgrounds correctly completed an assignment to build an isolated word decoder in this offering of the class compared to the previous offering.

Some of the activities were more conceptual in nature, involving reading papers or manuals and discussing the high-level concepts in small groups (Weeks 4 and 8), with each group reporting back to the class. One of the skills I hope to foster in students is the ability to pick out the main points of papers during the reports back to the main group; I am still thinking about ways to tie these activities into strengthening the project presentations (Week 10).

For the next offering of the class in the upcoming quarter, I would like to reuse the ideas developed in the seminar to reduce the amount of lecturing. The strategy I am considering is to give the students the old lecture slides as well as readings, and have them post questions the evening before class; we can then focus discussion on the points they did not understand. This will likely require the instructor to seed the online pre-discussion with some of the important points from the slides. These changes can be discussed at the workshop.

3.2 Feedback

Student evaluations of the course were very positive; in response to "what single aspect of the course did you find most helpful?," half of the students chose to respond, and all of the responses focused on the utility of the hands-on practicals or homeworks. Anecdotally, I also felt that students were better able to retain the concepts presented in the course in the most recent offering than in previous offerings.

4 Summary

In trying to serve multiple populations of students with different aims and goals, I have found that activities can be designed that foster students' development through team problem-solving and small group work. Online resources such as discussion boards and tutorials using software toolkits can be effectively deployed to minimize the discrepancy in preparations of the students.

Moving away from lecture formats (either in lecture class or seminar presentations) has been helpful in fostering cross-disciplinary interaction for both seminar and lecture classes. I have found that active learning techniques, such as the ones described here, provide more immediate feedback to the instructor as to what material is understood and what material needs extra emphasis.

Acknowledgments

The author would like to thank the anonymous students who agreed to have their conversations published and whose comments appear throughout the paper, as well as Mike White for providing input on the use of the seminar strategies in other contexts. This work was supported in part by NSF CAREER grant IIS-0643901. The opinions and findings expressed here are of the author and not of any funding agency.

References

J.P. Campbell. 1997. Speaker recognition: A tutorial. *Proceedings of IEEE*, 85:1437–1462.

J. Lafferty, A. McCallum, and F. Pereira. 2001. Conditional random fields: Probabilistic models for segmenting and labeling sequence data. In *Proc. 18th International Conference on Machine Learning*.

M. Mohri, F. Pereira, and M. Riley, 2001. *AT&T FSM Library™ – General-Purpose Finite-State Machine Software Tools*. AT&T, Florham Park, New Jersey. Available at http://research.att.com/~fsmtools/fsm.

M. Mohri, F. Pereira, and M. Riley. 2002. Weighted finite-state transducers in speech recognition. *Computer Speech and Language*, 16(1):69–88.

L. Rabiner. 1989. A tutorial on hidden Markov models and selected applications in speech recognition. *Proceedings of the IEEE*, 77(2).

M. Riley, J. Schalkwyk, W. Skut, C. Allauzen, and M. Mohri. 2008. OpenFst library. www.openfst.org.

K. Sjölander and J. Beskow. 2000. Wavesurfer – an open source speech tool. In *Proceedings of ICSLP*, Beijing.

A. Stolcke. 2002. SRILM — an extensible language modeling toolkit. In *Proc. Int'l Conf. on Spoken Language Processing (ICSLP 2002)*, Denver, Colorado.

J. Vegso. 2008. Enrollments and degree production at us cs departments drop further in 2006/2007. http://www.cra.org/wp/index.php?p=139.

S. Young, N. Russell, and J. Thornton. 1989. Token passing: a simple conceptual model for connected speech recognition systems. Technical Report TR-38, Cambridge University Engineering Department, Cambridge, England.

The evolution of a statistical NLP course

Fei Xia
University of Washington
Department of Linguistics
Box 354340
Seattle, WA 98195-4340
fxia@u.washington.edu

Abstract

This paper describes the evolution of a statistical NLP course, which I have been teaching every year for the past three years. The paper will focus on major changes made to the course (including the course design, assignments, and the use of discussion board) and highlight the lessons learned from this experience.

1 Introduction

In the past two decades, there has been tremendous progress in natural language processing (NLP) and NLP techniques have been applied to various real-world applications such as internet/intranet search and information extraction. Consequently, there has been an increasing demand from the industry for people with special training in NLP. To meet the demand, the University of Washington recently launched a new Professional Masters Program in Computational Linguistics (CLMA). To earn the master's degree, students must take nine courses and complete a final project. The detail of the program can be found in (Bender et al., 2008).

One of the required courses is LING572 (Advanced statistical methods in NLP), a course that I have been teaching every year for the past three years. During the process and especially in Year 3, I have made many changes to course content, assignments, and the usage of discussion board. In this paper, I will describe the evolution of the course and highlight the lessons learned from this experience.

2 Background

LING572 is part of the four-course NLP core sequence in the CLMA program. The other three are LING570 (Shallow Processing Techniques for NLP), LING571 (Deep Processing Techniques for NLP), and LING573 (NLP Systems and Applications). LING570 and LING571 are organized by NLP tasks (e.g., language model, POS tagging, Named-entity tagging, chunking for LING570, and parsing, semantics and discourse for LING571); LING572 is organized by machine learning methods; LING573 is the place where students use the knowledge learned in LING570-572 to build NLP systems for some real applications (e.g., question answering and information extraction).

The prerequisites for LING572 are (1) at least one college-level course in probability and statistics, (2) strong programming skills, and (3) LING570. The quarter is ten weeks long, with two 80-minute sessions per week. The class size is relatively small, with ten to twenty students. Most students in LING572 are from the CLMA program and are taking LING571 and other NLP courses at the same time. About a half of the students are from computer science background, and the remaining are from linguistics or other humanity background.

3 Course content

It would be impossible to cover all the major machine learning (ML) algorithms in one quarter; therefore, one of the decisions that I made from the very beginning is that the course would focus on major classification algorithms and spend only one week showing how these algorithms can be applied to sequence labeling problems. I believe that once

Proceedings of the Third Workshop on Issues in Teaching Computational Linguistics (TeachCL-08), pages 45–53,
Columbus, Ohio, USA, June 2008.

students have a solid grasp of these algorithms, it would be easy for them to learn algorithms for other kinds of learning problems (e.g., regression, clustering, and ranking).

The next question is what classification algorithms should be included in the syllabus. Table 1 shows the topics covered each year and the number of sessions spent on each topic. The topics can be roughly divided into three units: (1) supervised learning, (2) semi- and unsupervised learning, and (3) other related topics.

3.1 Year 1

The teaching plan for Year 1 turned out to be too ambitious. For instance, six supervised algorithms were covered in four weeks (i.e., 8 sessions) and four semi-/unsupervised algorithms were covered in 2.5 weeks. Such a tight schedule did not leave sufficient time for students to digest all the important concepts and equations.

3.2 Year 2

In Year 2, I reduced the amount of time spent on Unit (2). For instance, I spent only one session discussing the main ideas in the EM algorithm, without going through the details of the mathematic deduction and special cases of the algorithm such as the backward-forward algorithm and the inside-outside algorithm. Other changes were made to other units, as shown in the second column of Table 1.

3.3 Year 3

In the first two years, my lecturing style was similar to the tutorials given at major NLP conferences (e.g., ACL) in that I covered a lot of material in a short period of time and expected students to digest all the details after class. This approach did not work very well because our students came from very diverse backgrounds (e.g., linguistics, literature, computer science) and many of them were not familiar with mathematic concepts (e.g., Lagrangian, dual problem, quadratic programming, hill climbing) that are commonly used in machine learning. Most of the students were also new to NLP, taking only one quarter of NLP-related courses before taking LING572.

Based on this observation, I made major changes to the syllabus in Year 3: I reduced the lecture material and spent more time on discussion and illustrative examples. For example, on average 1.25 sessions were spent on a supervised algorithm in Year 2 and that number increased to 2.17 sessions in Year 3. I also added one session on information theory, which provides theoretic foundation for many learning methods. Because of this change, some important topics had to be cut, as shown in the last column of Table 1. Fortunately, I was able to incorporate some of the removed topics to two other courses (i.e., LING570 and a seminar on semi- and unsupervised learning) that I was teaching in the same year. The feedback from students indicated that the new course plan for Year 3 was more effective than the ones for the previous two years.

Another change I made was that I divided the teaching material into three types: (1) the essential knowledge that students should fully understand, (2)

Table 1: Content changes over the years (-: topics not covered, *: topics moved to LING570 in the previous quarter, †: topics moved to an NLP seminar)

	Y1	Y2	Y3
(1) Supervised learning:			
kNN	-	1	1
Decision Tree	1	1	1
Decision List	1	1	-
Naive Bayes	-	1	2
Maximum entropy (MaxEnt)	2	2	4
Support vector machine (SVM)	-	-	4
Transformation-based learning (TBL)	2	1	1
Bagging	1	1	-
Boosting	1	2	-
subtotal	**8**	**10**	**13**
(2) Semi-/unsupervised learning:			
Semisupervised	2	1	1†
Unsupervised	3	1	-†
subtotal	**5**	**2**	**1**
(3) Other topics:			
Introduction	1	1	1
Information theory	-	-	1
Feature selection	-	1	1
System combination	1	-	-
Relation between FSA and HMM	1	-	-*
Multiclass → binary	-	1	-*
Beam search	-	1	-*
Student presentation	1	1	-
Recap, summary	3	2	3
subtotal	**7**	**7**	**6**
Total	20	19	20

more advanced topics that students should be aware of but do not have to understand all the details, and (3) related topics that are not covered in class but are available on *additional slides* for people who want to learn more by themselves. Taking MaxEnt as an example, Type (1) includes the maximum entropy principle, the modeling, GIS training, and decoding; Type (2) includes regularization and the mathematic proof that shows the relation between maximum likelihood and maximum entropy as provided in (Ratnaparkhi, 1997), and Type (3) includes L-BFGS training and the similarity between SVM and MaxEnt with regularization (Klein, 2007). Making this distinction helps students focus on the most essential part of the algorithms and at the same time provides additional material for more advanced students.

4 Reading material

One challenge of teaching a statistic NLP course is the lack of good textbooks on the subject; as a result, most of the reading material come from conference and journal papers. The problem is that many of the algorithms covered in class were originally proposed in non-NLP fields such as machine learning and applied mathematics, and the original papers are often heavy in mathematical proofs and rarely refer to the NLP tasks that our students are familiar with. On the other hand, NLP papers that apply these algorithms to NLP tasks often assume that the readers are already familiar with the algorithms and consequently do not explain the algorithms in detail.

Because it is hard to find a suitable paper to cover all the theoretic and application aspects of a learning algorithm, I chose several papers for each algorithm and specified the sections that the students should focus on. For instance, for Maximum Entropy, I picked (Berger et al., 1996; Ratnaparkhi, 1997) for the basic theory, (Ratnaparkhi, 1996) for an application (POS tagging in this case), and (Klein and Manning, 2003) for more advanced topics such as optimization and smoothing.

For the more sophisticated learning methods (e.g., MaxEnt and SVM), it is very important for students to read the assigned papers beforehand. However, some students choose not to do so for various reasons; meanwhile, other students might spend too much time trying to understand everything in the papers. To address this problem, in Year 3 I added five reading assignments, one for each of the following topics: information theory, Naive Bayes, MaxEnt, SVM, and TBL. Each assignment consists of simple questions such as the one in Appendix A. Students were asked to turn in their answers to the questions before class. Although the assignments were very simple, the effect was obvious as students started to ask in-depth questions even before the topics were covered in class.

5 Written and programming assignments

In addition to the reading assignments mentioned above, students also have weekly assignments. For the sake of clarity, we divide the latter into two types, *written* and *programming* assignments, depending on whether programming is required. Significant changes have been made to both types, as explained below.

5.1 Year 1

In Year 1, there were three written and six programming assignments. The written assignments were mainly on mathematic proof, and one example is given in Appendix B. The programming assignments asked students to use the following existing packages to build NLP systems.

1. Carmel, a finite state transducer package written by Jonathan Graehl at USC/ISI.

2. fnTBL (Ngai and Florian, 2001), an efficient implementation of TBL created by Ngai and Florian at JHU.

3. A MaxEnt toolkit written by Le Zhang, available at http://homepages.inf.ed.ac.uk/s0450736.

To complete the assignments, the students needed to study some functions in the source code to understand exactly how the learning algorithms were implemented in the packages. They would then write pre- and post-processing tools, create data files, and build an end-to-end system for a particular NLP task. They would then present their work in class and write a final paper to report their findings.

5.2 Year 2

In Year 2 I made two major changes to the assignments. First, I reduced the number of written assignments on theoretic proof. While such assignments strengthen students' mathematic capability, they were very challenging to many students, especially the ones who lacked mathematics and statistics training. The assignments were also not as effective as programming assignments in understanding the basic concepts for the learning algorithms.

The second major change was to replace the three packages mentioned above with Mallet (McCallum, 2002), a well-known package in the NLP field. Mallet is a well-designed package that contains almost all the learning methods covered in the course such as Naive Bayes, decision tree, MaxEnt, boosting, and bagging; once the training and test data were put into the Mallet data format, it was easy to run all these methods and compared the results.

For the programming assignments, in addition to reading certain Mallet functions to understand how the learning methods were implemented, the students were also asked to extend the package in various ways. For instance, the package includes a text-user-interface (TUI) class called *Vectors2Classify.java*, which produces a classifier from the training data, uses the classifier to classify the test data, compares the results with gold standard, and outputs accuracy and the confusion matrix. In one assignment, students were asked to first separate the code for training and testing, and then add the beam search to the latter module so that the new code would work for sequence labeling tasks.

While using Mallet as a black box is straightforward, extending it with additional functionality is much more difficult. Because the package did not have a detailed document that explained how its main classes should be used, I spent more than a week going through hundreds of classes in Mallet and wrote a 11-page guide based on my findings. While the guide was very helpful, many students still struggled with the assignments, especially the ones who were not used to navigating through other people's code and/or who were not familiar with Java, the language that Mallet was written in.

5.3 Year 3

To address these problems, in Year 3, we changed the focus of the assignments: instead of studying and extending Mallet code, students would create their own package from scratch and use Mallet only as a reference. For instance, in one assignment, students would implement the two Naive Bayes models as described in (McCallum and Nigam, 1998) and compare the classification results with the results produced by the Mallet Naive Bayes learner. In the beam search assignment, students' code would include modules that read in the model produced by Mallet and calculate $P(y \mid x)$ for a test instance x and a class label y. Because the code no longer needed to call Mallet functions, students were free to use whatever language they were comfortable with and could treat Mallet as a black box.

The complete assignments are shown in Appendix C. In summary, students implemented six learners (Naive Bayes, kNN, Decision Tree, MaxEnt, SVM, TBL),[1] beam search, and the code for feature selection. All the coding was completed in eight weeks in total, and the students could choose to either work alone or work with a teammate.

6 Implementation issues

All the programming assignments in Year 3, except the one for MaxEnt, were due in a week, and students were expected to spend between 10 and 20 hours on each assignment. While the workload was demanding, about 90% of students completed the assignments successfully. Several factors contribute to the success:

- All the learners were evaluated on the same classification task.[2] The input and output data format were very similar across different learners; as a result, the code that handled input and output could be reused, and the classification results of different learners could be compared directly.

[1] For SVM, students implemented only the decoder, not the trainer, and they would test their decoder with the models produced by libSVM (Chang and Lin, 2001).

[2] The task is a simplified version of the classic 20-newsgroup text classification task, with only three out of the 20 classes being used. The training data and the test data consist of 900 and 100 examples from each class, respectively.

- I restricted the scope of the assignments so that they were doable in a week. For instance, the complexity of a TBL learner highly depends on the form of the transformations and the type of learning problem. In the TBL assignment, the learner was used to handle classification problems and the transformation had the form *if a feature is present in an instance, change the class label from A to B*. Implementing such a learner was much easier than implementing a learner (e.g., fnTBL) that use more complex transformations to handle sequence labeling problems.

- Efficiency is an important issue, and there are often differences between algorithms on paper and the code that implements the algorithms. To identify those differences and potential pitfalls that students could run into, I completed all the assignments myself at least a week before the assignments were due, and shared some of my findings in class. I also told students the kind of results to be expected, and encouraged students to discuss the results and implementation tricks on the discussion board.

Implementing machine learning algorithms is often an art, as there are many ways to improve efficiency. Two examples are given below. While such tricks are well-known to NLP researchers, they are often new to students and going through them in class can help students to speed up their code significantly.

The trainer for TBL

As described in (Brill, 1995), a TBL trainer picks one transformation in each iteration, applies it to the training data, and repeats the process until no more good transformations can be found. To choose the best transformation, a naive approach would enumerate all the possible transformations, for each transformation go through the data once to calculate the net gain, and choose the transformation with the highest net gain. This approach is very inefficient as the data have to be scanned through multiple times.[3]

A much better implementation would be to go through the training data only once, and for each feature in each training instance, update the net gains of the corresponding transformations accordingly.[4] Students were also encouraged to read (Ngai and Florian, 2001), which proposed another efficient implementation of TBL.

The decoder for Naive Bayes

In the multi-variate Bernoulli event model for the text classification task (McCallum and Nigam, 1998), at the test time the class for a document d is chosen according to Eq (1). If we calculate $P(d|c)$ according to Eq (2), as given in the paper, we have to go through all the features in the feature set F. However, as shown in Eq (3) and (4), the first product in Eq (3), denoted as $Z(c)$ in Eq (4), is a constant with respect to d and can be calculated beforehand and stored with each c. Therefore, to classify d, we only need to go through the features that are present in d. Implementing Eq (4) instead of Eq (2) reduces running time tremendously.[5]

$$c^* = arg\ max_c P(c)P(d|c) \quad (1)$$

$$P(d|c) = \prod_{f \notin d}(1 - P(f|c)) \prod_{f \in d} P(f|c) \quad (2)$$

$$= \prod_{f \in F}(1 - P(f|c)) \prod_{f \in d} \frac{P(f|c)}{1 - P(f|c)} \quad (3)$$

$$= Z(c) \prod_{f \in d} \frac{P(f|c)}{1 - P(f|c)} \quad (4)$$

7 Discussion board

A discussion board is one of the most effective vehicles for outside-class communication and collaboration, as anyone in the class can start a new conversation, read recent posts, or reply to other peo-

[3]Let N_f be the number of features and N_c be the number of classes in a classification task, the number of transformations in the form we specified above is $O(N_f N_c^2)$, which means that the learner has to go through the data $O(N_f N_c^2)$ times.

[4]For each feature t in each training instance x, if x's current label y_c is different from the true label y, there would be only one transformation whose net gain would be affected by this feature in this instance, and the transformation is *if t is present, change class label from y_c to y*. If y_c is the same as y, there would be $N_c - 1$ transformations whose net gain would be affected, where N_c is the number of classes.

[5]This trick was actually pointed out by a student in my class.

ple's posts.[6] Furthermore, some students feel more comfortable posting to a discussion board than raising the questions in class or emailing the instructor. Therefore, I provided a discussion board each time LING572 was offered and the board was linked to the course website. However, the board was not used as much as I had hoped in the first two years.

In Year 3, I took a more pro-active approach: first, I reminded students several times that emails to me should be reserved only for confidential questions and all the non-confidential questions should be posted to the discussion board. They should also check the discussion board at least daily and they were encouraged to reply to their classmates' questions if they knew the answers. Second, if a student emailed me any questions that should go to the discussion board, I would copy the questions to the board and ask the sender to find my answers there. Third, I checked the board several times per day and most of the questions raised there were answered within an hour if not sooner.

As a result, there was a significant increase of the usage of the board, as shown in Table 2. For instance, compared to Year 2, the average number of posts per student in Year 3 more than quadrupled, and at the same time the number of emails I received from the students was cut by 65%. More importantly, more than a half of the questions posted to the board were answered by other students, indicating the board indeed encouraged collaboration among students.

A lesson I learned from this experience is that the success of a discussion board relies on active participation by its members, and strong promotion by the instructor is essential in helping students take advantage of this form of communication.

8 Course evaluation

Students were asked to evaluate the course at the end of the quarter using standard evaluation forms. The results are shown in Table 3.[7] For (1)-(11), students were asked to answer the questions with a 6-point scale: 0 being *Very Poor* and 5 being *Excellent*. The question for (12) is "*on average how many hours per week have you spent on this course?*"; The question for (13) is "*among the total average hours spent on the course, how many do you consider were valuable in advancing your education?*" The values for (1)-(13) in the table are the average of the responses. The last row, Challenge and Engagement Index (CEI), is a score computed from several items on the evaluation form, and reported as a decile rank ranging from 0 (lowest) to 9 (highest). It reflects how challenging students found the course and how engaged they were in it.

Table 2: The usage of the course discussion board

	Y1	Y2	Y3
# of students	15	16	11
# of conversations	13	47	116
Total # of posts	42	149	589
# of posts by the instructor	7	21	158
# of posts by students	35	128	431
Ave # of post/student	2.3	8	39.2

The table shows that the overall evaluation in Year 2 was worse than the one in Year 1, despite much effort put into improving course design. The main problem in Year 2 was the programming assignments, as discussed in Section 5.2 and indicated in Row (11): many students found the task of extending Mallet overwhelming, especially since some of them had never used Java and debugged a large pre-existing package before. As a result, they spent much time on learning Java and trying to figure out how Mallet code worked, and they felt that was not the best way to learn the subjects (cf. the big gap between the values for Row (12) and (13)).

Based on the feedback from the first two years, in Year 3 I made a major overhaul to the course, as discussed in Sections 3-7 and summarized here:

- The lecture material was cut substantially; for instance, the average number of slides used in a session was reduced from over 60 in Year 2 to below 30 in Year 3. The saved time was spent on class discussion and going through examples on the whiteboard.

- Reading assignments were introduced to help students focus on the most relevant part of the

[6]The software we used is called *GoPost*. It is one of the Web-based communication and collaboration applications developed by the Center for Teaching, Learning, and Technology at the University of Washington.

[7]The complete form has thirty questions, the most relevant ones are listed in the table.

Table 3: Student evaluation of instruction (For Item (1)-(11), the scale is between 0 and 5: 0 is *Very Poor* and 5 is *Excellent*; The scale for Item (14) is between 0 and 9, 9 being *most challenging*)

	Y1	Y2	Y3
Number of respondents	14	15	11
(1) The course as a whole	3.9	3.8	5.0
(2) The course content	4.0	3.7	4.9
(3) Course organization	4.0	3.8	4.8
(4) Explanations by instructor	3.7	3.5	4.6
(5) Student confidence in instructor's knowledge	4.5	4.5	4.9
(6) Instructor's enthusiasm	4.5	4.6	4.9
(7) Encouragement given students to express themselves	3.9	4.3	4.6
(8) Instructor's interest in whether students learned	4.5	4.0	4.8
(9) Amount you learned in the course	3.8	3.3	4.8
(10) Relevance and usefulness of course content	4.3	3.9	4.9
(11) Reasonableness of assigned work	3.8	2.0	3.8
(12) Average number of hours/week spent on the course	7.9	21.9	19.8
(13) How many were valuable in advancing your education	6.2	14.5	17.2
(14) Challenge and engagement index (CEI)	7	9	9

reading material.

- Instead of extending Mallet, students were asked to create their own packages from scratch and many implementation issues were addressed in class and in the discussion board.

- Discussion board was highly promoted to encourage outside-class discussion and collaboration, and its usage was increased dramatically.

As shown in the last column of the table, the new strategies worked very well and the feedback from the students was very positive. Interestingly, although the amount of time spent on the course in Y2 and Y3 was about the same, the students in Y3 felt the assigned work was more reasonable than the students in Y2. This highlights the importance of choosing appropriate assignments based on students' background. Also, while the lecture material was cut substantially over the years, students in Y3 felt that they learned more than the students in Y1 and Y2, implying that it is more beneficial to cover a small number of learning methods in depth than to hurry through a large number of topics.

9 Conclusion

Teaching LING572 has been a great learning experience, and significant changes have been made to course content, assignments, and the like. Here are some lessons learned from this experience:

- A common pitfall for course design is being over-ambitious with the course plan. What matters the most is not how much material is covered in class, but how much students actually digest.

- When using journal/conference papers as reading material, it is often better to select multiple papers and specify the sections in the papers that are most relevant. Giving reading assignments would encourage students to read papers before class and provide guidelines as what questions they should focus on.

- Adding new functionality to an existing package is often difficult if the package is very complex and not well-documented. Therefore, this kind of assignments should be avoided if possible. In contrast, students often learn more from implementing the methods from scratch than from reading other people's source code.

- Implementing ML methods is an art, and pointing out various tricks and potential obstacles beforehand would help students tremendously. With careful design of the assignments and in-class/outside-class discussion of implementation issues, it is possible to implement multiple learning methods in a short period of time.

- Discussion board is a great venue for students to share ideas, but it will be successful only if students actively participate. The instructor can play an important role in promoting the usage of the board.

Many of the lessons above are not specific to LING572, and I have made similar changes to other courses that I am teaching. So far, the feedback from the students have been very positive. Compared to the first two years, in Year 3, students were much more active both in and outside class; they were much more satisfied with the assignments; many students said that they really appreciated all the implementation tips and felt that they had a much better understanding of the algorithms after implementing them. Furthermore, several students expressed interest in pursuing a Ph.D. degree in NLP.

In the future, I plan to replace some of the early ML algorithms (e.g., kNN, Decision Tree, TBL) with more recent ones (e.g., conditional random field, Bayesian approach). This adjustment has to be done with special care, because the early algorithms, albeit quite simple, often provide the foundation for understanding more sophisticated algorithms. I will also fine tune the assignments to make them more manageable for students with less CS/math training.

A Reading assignment example

The following is the reading assignment for MaxEnt in Year 3.

(Q1) Let P(X=i) be the probability of getting an i when rolling a dice. What is $P(X)$ according to the maximum entropy principle under the following condition?
(a) P(X=1) + P(X=2) = 0.5
(b) P(X=1) + P(X=2) = 0.5 and P(X=6) = 0.2

(Q2) In the text classification task, $|V|$ is the number of features, $|C|$ is the number of classes. How many feature functions are there?

(Q3) How to calculate the empirical expectation of a feature function?

B Written assignment example

The following is part of a written assignment for Boosting in Year 1: In the basic AdaBoost algorithm, let h_t be the hypothesis created at time t, $D_t(i)$ be the weight of the i-th training instance, and ϵ_t be the training error rate of h_t. Let the hypothesis weight α_t be $\frac{1}{2}ln\frac{1-\alpha_t}{\alpha_t}$ and the normalization factor Z_t be $\sum_i D_t(i)e^{-\alpha_t y_i h_t(x_i)}$. Prove that $Z_t = 2\sqrt{\alpha_t(1-\alpha_t)}$ for any t.

C Programming assignment examples

In Year 3, there were seven programming assignments, as summarized below:

Hw1: Implement the two Naive Bayes models as described in (McCallum and Nigam, 1998).

Hw2: Implement a decision tree learner, assuming all features are *binary* and using information gain as the split function.

Hw3: Implement a kNN learner using cosine and Euclidean distance as similarity/dissimilarity measures. Implement one of feature selection methods covered in class, and test the effect of feature selection on kNN.

Hw4: Implement a MaxEnt learner. For training, use General Iterative scaling (GIS).

Hw5: Run the svm-train command in the libSVM package (Chang and Lin, 2001) to create a SVM model from the training data. Write a decoder that classifies test data with the model.

Hw6: Implement beam search and reduplicate the POS tagger described in (Ratnaparkhi, 1996).

Hw7: Implement a TBL learner for the text classification task, where a transformation has the form *if a feature is present in a document, change the class label from A to B.*

For Hw6, students compared their POS tagging results with the ones reported in (Ratnaparkhi, 1996). For all the other assignments, students tested their learners on a text classification task and compare the results with the ones produced by preexisting packages such as Mallet and libSVM.

Each assignment was due in a week except for Hw4 and Hw6, which were due in 1.5 weeks. Students could choose to work alone or work with a teammate.

References

Emily Bender, Fei Xia, and Erik Bansleben. 2008. Building a flexible, collaborative, intensive master's program in computational linguistics. In *Proceedings of the Third ACL Workshop on Effective Tools and Methodologies for Teaching NLP and CL*, Columbus, Ohio, June.

Adam L. Berger, Stephen A. Della Pietra, and Vincent J. Della Pietra. 1996. A maximum entropy approach to natural language processing. *Computational Linguistics*, 22(1), March.

Eric Brill. 1995. Transformation-based error-driven learning and natural language processing: A case study in part-of-speech tagging. *Computational Linguistics*, 21(4):543–565.

Chih-Chung Chang and Chih-Jen Lin, 2001. *LIBSVM: a library for support vector machines*. Available at http://www.csie.ntu.edu.tw/ cjlin/libsvm.

Dan Klein and Christopher Manning. 2003. Maxent model, conditional estimation, and optimization. ACL 2003 tutorial.

Dan Klein. 2007. Introduction to Classification: Likelihoods, Margins, Features, and Kernels. Tutorial at NAACL-2007.

Andrew McCallum and Kamal Nigam. 1998. A comparison of event models for naive bayes text classification. In *In AAAI/ICML-98 Workshop on Learning for Text Categorization*.

Andrew Kachites McCallum. 2002. Mallet: A machine learning for language toolkit. http://mallet.cs.umass.edu.

Grace Ngai and Radu Florian. 2001. Transformation-based learning in the fast lane. In *Proceedings of North American ACL (NAACL-2001)*, pages 40–47, June.

Adwait Ratnaparkhi. 1996. A Maximum Entropy Model for Part-of-speech Tagging. In *Proc. of Joint SIGDAT Conference on Empirical Methods in Natural Language Processing and Very Large Corpora (EMNLP-1996)*, Philadelphia.

Adwait Ratnaparkhi. 1997. A simple introduction to maximum entropy models for natural language processing. Technical Report Technical Report 97-08, Institute for Research in Cognitive Science, University of Pennsylvania.

Exploring Large-Data Issues in the Curriculum: A Case Study with MapReduce

Jimmy Lin
The iSchool, College of Information Studies
Laboratory for Computational Linguistics and Information Processing
University of Maryland, College Park
jimmylin@umd.edu

Abstract

This paper describes the design of a pilot research and educational effort at the University of Maryland centered around technologies for tackling Web-scale problems. In the context of a "cloud computing" initiative lead by Google and IBM, students and researchers are provided access to a computer cluster running Hadoop, an open-source Java implementation of Google's MapReduce framework. This technology provides an opportunity for students to explore large-data issues in the context of a course organized around teams of graduate and undergraduate students, in which they tackle open research problems in the human language technologies. This design represents one attempt to bridge traditional instruction with real-world, large-data research challenges.

1 Introduction

Over the past couple of decades, the field of computational linguistics, and more broadly, human language technologies, has seen the emergence and later dominance of empirical techniques and data-driven research. Concomitant with this trend is the requirement of systems and algorithms to handle large quantities of data. Banko and Brill (2001) were among the first to demonstrate the importance of dataset size as a significant factor governing prediction accuracy in a supervised machine learning task. In fact, they argue that size of training set is perhaps more important than the choice of machine learning algorithm itself. Similarly, experiments in question answering have shown the effectiveness of simple pattern-matching techniques when applied to large quantities of data (Brill et al., 2001). More recently, this line of argumentation has been echoed in experiments with large-scale language models. Brants et al. (2007) show that for statistical machine translation, a simple smoothing method (dubbed *Stupid Backoff*) approaches the quality of Kneser-Ney Smoothing as the amount of training data increases, and with the simple method one can process significantly more data.

Given these observations, it is important to integrate discussions of large-data issues into any course on human language technology. Most existing courses focus on smaller-sized problems and datasets that can be processed on students' personal computers, making them ill-prepared to cope with the vast quantities of data in operational environments. Even when larger datasets are leveraged in the classroom, they are mostly used as static resources. Thus, students experience a disconnect as they transition from a learning environment to one where they work on real-world problems.

Nevertheless, there are at least two major challenges associated with explicit treatment of large-data issues in an HLT curriculum:

- The first concerns resources: it is unclear where one might acquire the hardware to support educational activities, especially if such activities are in direct competition with research.
- The second involves complexities inherently associated with parallel and distributed processing, currently the only practical solution to large-data problems. For any course, it is diffi-

Proceedings of the Third Workshop on Issues in Teaching Computational Linguistics (TeachCL-08), pages 54–61,
Columbus, Ohio, USA, June 2008.

cult to retain focus on HLT-relevant problems, since the exploration of large-data issues necessitates (time-consuming) forays into parallel and distributed computing.

This paper presents a case study that grapples with the issues outlined above. Building on previous experience with similar courses at the University of Washington (Kimball et al., 2008), I present a pilot "cloud computing" course currently underway at the University of Maryland that leverages a collaboration with Google and IBM, through which students are given access to hardware resources. To further alleviate the first issue, research is brought into alignment with education by structuring a team-oriented, project-focused course. The core idea is to organize teams of graduate and undergraduate students focused on tackling open research problems in natural language processing, information retrieval, and related areas. Ph.D. students serve as leaders on projects related to their research, and are given the opportunity to serve as mentors to undergraduate and masters students.

Google's MapReduce programming framework is an elegant solution to the second issue raised above. By providing a functional abstraction that isolates the programmer from parallel and distributed processing issues, students can focus on solving the actual problem. I first provide the context for this academic–industrial collaboration, and then move on to describe the course setup.

2 Cloud Computing and MapReduce

In October 2007, Google and IBM jointly announced the Academic Cloud Computing Initiative, with the goal of helping both researchers and students address the challenges of "Web-scale" computing. The initiative revolves around Google's MapReduce programming paradigm (Dean and Ghemawat, 2004), which represents a proven approach to tackling data-intensive problems in a distributed manner. Six universities were involved in the collaboration at the outset: Carnegie Mellon University, Massachusetts Institute of Technology, Stanford University, the University of California at Berkeley, the University of Maryland, and University of Washington. I am the lead faculty at the University of Maryland on this project.

As part of this initiative, IBM and Google have dedicated a large cluster of several hundred machines for use by faculty and students at the participating institutions. The cluster takes advantage of Hadoop, an open-source implementation of MapReduce in Java.[1] By making these resources available, Google and IBM hope to encourage faculty adoption of cloud computing in their research and also integration of the technology into the curriculum.

MapReduce builds on the observation that many information processing tasks have the same basic structure: a computation is applied over a large number of records (e.g., Web pages) to generate partial results, which are then aggregated in some fashion. Naturally, the per-record computation and aggregation function vary according to task, but the basic structure remains fixed. Taking inspiration from higher-order functions in functional programming, MapReduce provides an abstraction at the point of these two operations. Specifically, the programmer defines a "mapper" and a "reducer" with the following signatures:

map: $(k_1, v_1) \rightarrow [(k_2, v_2)]$
reduce: $(k_2, [v_2]) \rightarrow [(k_3, v_3)]$

Key/value pairs form the basic data structure in MapReduce. The mapper is applied to every input key/value pair to generate an arbitrary number of intermediate key/value pairs. The reducer is applied to all values associated with the same intermediate key to generate output key/value pairs. This two-stage processing structure is illustrated in Figure 1.

Under the framework, a programmer need only provide implementations of the mapper and reducer. On top of a distributed file system (Ghemawat et al., 2003), the runtime transparently handles all other aspects of execution, on clusters ranging from a few to a few thousand nodes. The runtime is responsible for scheduling map and reduce workers on commodity hardware assumed to be unreliable, and thus is tolerant to various faults through a number of error recovery mechanisms. The runtime also manages data distribution, including splitting the input across multiple map workers and the potentially very large sorting problem between the map and reduce phases whereby intermediate key/value pairs must be grouped by key.

[1] http://hadoop.apache.org/

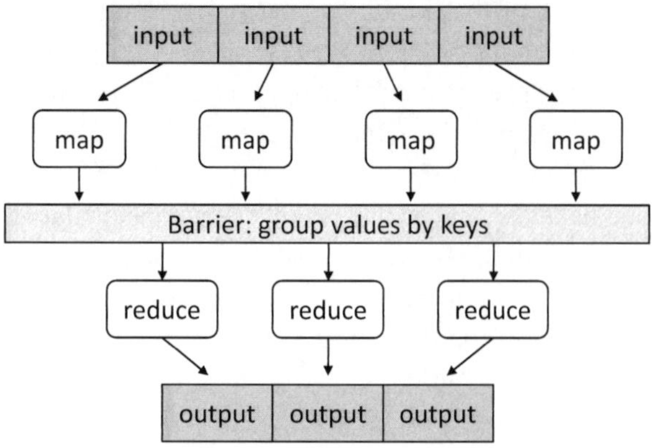

Figure 1: Illustration of the MapReduce framework: the "mapper" is applied to all input records, which generates results that are aggregated by the "reducer".

The biggest advantage of MapReduce from a pedagogical point of view is that it allows an HLT course to retain its focus on applications. Divide-and-conquer algorithms running on multiple machines are currently the only effective strategy for tackling Web-scale problems. However, programming parallel and distributed systems is a difficult topic for students to master. Due to communication and synchronization issues, concurrent operations are notoriously challenging to reason about—unanticipated race conditions are hard to detect and even harder to debug. MapReduce allows the programmer to offload these problems (no doubt important, but irrelevant from the perspective of HLT) onto the runtime, which handles the complexities associated with distributed processing on large clusters. The functional abstraction allows a student to focus on problem solving, not managing the details of error recovery, data distribution, etc.

3 Course Design

This paper describes a "cloud computing" course at the University of Maryland being offered in Spring 2008. The core idea is to assemble small teams of graduate and undergraduate students to tackle research problems, primarily in the areas of information retrieval and natural language processing. Ph.D. students serve as team leaders, overseeing small groups of masters and undergraduates on topics related to their doctoral research. The roles of "team leader" and "team member" are explicitly assigned at the beginning of the semester, and are associated with different expectations and responsibilities. All course material and additional details are available on the course homepage.[2]

3.1 Objectives and Goals

I identified a list of desired competencies for students to acquire and refine throughout the course:

- Understand and be able to articulate the challenges associated with distributed solutions to large-scale problems, e.g., scheduling, load balancing, fault tolerance, memory and bandwidth limitations, etc.
- Understand and be able to explain the concepts behind MapReduce as one framework for addressing the above issues.
- Understand and be able to express well-known algorithms (e.g., PageRank) in the MapReduce framework.
- Understand and be able to reason about engineering tradeoffs in alternative approaches to processing large datasets.
- Gain in-depth experience with one research problem in Web-scale information processing (broadly defined).

With respect to the final bullet point, the students are expected to acquire the following abilities:

- Understand how current solutions to the particular research problem can be cast into the MapReduce framework.
- Be able to explain what advantages the MapReduce framework provides over existing approaches (or disadvantages if a MapReduce formulation turns out to be unsuitable for expressing the problem).
- Articulate how adopting the MapReduce framework can potentially lead to advances in the state of the art by enabling processing not possible before.

I assumed that all students have a strong foundation in computer science, which was operationalized in having completed basic courses in algorithms, data structures, and programming languages

[2]http://www.umiacs.umd.edu/~jimmylin/cloud-computing/

<table>
<tr><th>Week</th><th>Monday</th><th>Wednesday</th></tr>
<tr><td>1</td><td colspan="2" rowspan="3">Hadoop Boot Camp</td></tr>
<tr><td>2</td></tr>
<tr><td>3</td></tr>
<tr><td>4</td><td rowspan="5">Project Meetings: Phase I</td><td></td></tr>
<tr><td>5</td><td>Proposal Presentations</td></tr>
<tr><td>6</td><td rowspan="8">Guest Speakers</td></tr>
<tr><td>7</td></tr>
<tr><td>8</td></tr>
<tr><td>9</td><td rowspan="5">Project Meetings: Phase II</td></tr>
<tr><td>10</td></tr>
<tr><td>11</td></tr>
<tr><td>12</td></tr>
<tr><td>13</td></tr>
<tr><td>14</td><td></td><td rowspan="2">Final Project Presentations</td></tr>
<tr><td>15</td><td></td></tr>
</table>

Figure 2: Overview of course schedule.

(in practice, this was trivially met for the graduate students, who all had undergraduate degrees in computer science). I explicitly made the decision that previous courses in parallel programming, systems, or networks was not required. Finally, prior experience with natural language processing, information retrieval, or related areas was not assumed. However, strong competency in Java programming was a strict requirement, as the Hadoop implementation of MapReduce is based in Java.

In the project-oriented setup, the team leaders (i.e., Ph.D. students) have additional roles to play. One of the goals of the course is to give them experience in mentoring more junior colleagues and managing a team project. As such, they were expected to acquire real-world skills in project organization and management.

3.2 Schedule and Major Components

As designed, the course spans a standard fifteen week semester, meeting twice a week (Monday and Wednesday) for one hour and fifteen minutes each session. The general setup is shown in Figure 2. As this paper goes to press (mid-April), the course just concluded Week 11.

During the first three weeks, all students are immersed in a "Hadoop boot camp", where they are introduced to the MapReduce programming framework. Material was adapted from slides developed by Christophe Bisciglia and his colleagues from Google, who have delivered similar content in various formats.[3] As it was assumed that all students had strong foundations in computer science, the pace of the lectures was brisk. The themes of the five boot camp sessions are listed below:

- Introduction to parallel/distributed processing
- From functional programming to MapReduce and the Google File System (GFS)
- "Hello World" MapReduce lab
- Graph algorithms with MapReduce
- Information retrieval with MapReduce

A brief overview of parallel and distributed processing provides a natural transition into abstractions afforded by functional programming, the inspiration behind MapReduce. That in turn provides the context to introduce MapReduce itself, along with the distributed file system upon which it depends. The final two lectures focus on specific case studies of MapReduce applied to graph analysis and information retrieval. The first covers graph search and PageRank, while the second covers algorithms for information retrieval. With the exception of the "Hello World" lab session, all lecture content was delivered at the conceptual level, without specific reference to the Hadoop API and implementation details (see Section 5 for discussion). The boot camp is capped off with a programming exercise (implementation of PageRank) to ensure that students have a passing knowledge of MapReduce concepts in general and the Hadoop API in particular.

Concurrent with the boot camp, team leaders are expected to develop a detailed plan of research: what they hope to accomplish, specific tasks that would lead to the goals, and possible distribution of those tasks across team members. I recommend that each project be structured into two phases: the first phase focusing on how existing solutions might be recast into the MapReduce framework, the second phase focusing on interesting extensions enabled by MapReduce. In addition to the detailed research

[3]http://code.google.com/edu/parallel/

plan, the leaders are responsible for organizing introductory material (papers, tutorials, etc.) since team members are not expected to have any prior experience with the research topic.

The majority of the course is taken up by the research project itself. The Monday class sessions are devoted to the team project meetings, and the team leader is given discretion on how this is managed. Typical activities include evaluation of deliverables (code, experimental results, etc.) from the previous week and discussions of plans for the upcoming week, but other common uses of the meeting time include whiteboard sessions and code review. During the project meetings I circulate from group to group to track progress, offer helpful suggestions, and contribute substantially if possible.

To the extent practical, the teams adopt standard best practices for software development. Students use Eclipse as the development environment and take advantage of a plug-in that provides a seamless interface to the Hadoop cluster. Code is shared via Subversion, with both project-specific repositories and a course-wide repository for common libraries. A wiki is also provided as a point of collaboration.

Concurrent with the project meetings on Mondays, a speaker series takes place on Wednesdays. Attendance for students is required, but otherwise the talks are open to the public. One of the goals for these invited talks is to build an active community of researchers interested in large datasets and distributed processing. Invited talks can be classified into one of two types: infrastructure-focused and application-focused. Examples of the first include alternative architectures for processing large datasets and dynamic provisioning of computing services. Examples of the second include survey of distributed data mining techniques and Web-scale sentiment analysis. It is not a requirement for the talks to focus on MapReduce *per se*—rather, an emphasis on large-data issues is the thread that weaves all these presentations together.

3.3 Student Evaluation

At the beginning of the course, students are assigned specific roles (team leader or team member) and are evaluated according to different criteria (both in grade components and relative weights).

The team leaders are responsible for producing the detailed research plan at the beginning of the semester. The entire team is responsible for three checkpoint deliverables throughout the course: an initial oral presentation outlining their plans, a short interim progress report at roughly the midpoint of the semester, and a final oral presentation accompanied by a written report at the end of the semester.

On a weekly basis, I request from each student a status report delivered as a concise email: a paragraph-length outline of progress from the previous week and plans for the following week. This, coupled with my observations during each project meeting, provides the basis for continuous evaluation of student performance.

4 Course Implementation

Currently, 13 students (7 Ph.D., 3 masters, 3 undergraduates) are involved in the course, working on six different projects. Last fall, as planning was underway, Ph.D. students from the Laboratory for Computational Linguistics and Information Processing at the University of Maryland were recruited as team leaders. Three of them agreed, developing projects around their doctoral research—these represent cases with maximal alignment of research and educational goals. In addition, the availability of this opportunity was announced on mailing lists, which generated substantial interest. Undergraduates were recruited from the Computer Science honors program; since it is a requirement for those students to complete an honors project, this course provided a suitable vehicle for satisfying that requirement.

Three elements are necessary for a successful project: interested students, an interesting research problem of appropriate scope, and the availability of data to support the work. I served as a broker for all three elements, and eventually settled on five projects that satisfied all the desiderata (one project was a later addition). As there was more interest than spaces available for team members, it was possible to screen for suitable background and matching interests. The six ongoing projects are as follows:

- Large-data statistical machine translation
- Construction of large latent-variable language models
- Resolution of name mentions in large email archives

- Network analysis for enhancing biomedical text retrieval
- Text-background separation in children's picture books
- High-throughput biological sequence alignment and processing

Of the six projects, four of them fall squarely in the area of human language technology: the first two are typical of problems in natural language processing, while the second two are problems in information retrieval. The final two projects represent attempts to push the boundaries of the MapReduce paradigm, into image processing and computational biology, respectively. Short project descriptions can be found on the course homepage.

5 Pedagogical Discussion

The design of any course is an exercise in tradeoffs, and this pilot project is no exception. In this section, I will attempt to justify course design decisions and discuss possible alternatives.

At the outset, I explicitly decided against a "traditional" course format that would involve carefully-paced delivery of content with structured exercises (e.g., problem sets or labs). Such a design would perhaps be capped off with a multi-week final project. The pioneering MapReduce course at the University of Washington represents an example of this design (Kimball et al., 2008), combining six weeks of standard classroom instruction with an optional four week final project. As an alternative, I organized my course around the research project. This choice meant that the time devoted to direct instruction on foundational concepts was very limited, i.e., the three-week boot camp.

One consequence of the boot-camp setup is some disconnect between the lecture material and implementation details. Students were expected to rapidly translate high-level concepts into low-level programming constructs and API calls without much guidance. There was only one "hands on" session in the boot camp, focusing on more mundane issues such as installation, configuration, connecting to the server, etc. Although that session also included overview of a simple Hadoop program, that by no means was sufficient to yield in-depth understanding of the framework.

The intensity of the boot camp was mitigated by the composition of the students. Since students were self-selected and further screened by me in terms of their computational background, they represent the highest caliber of students at the university. Furthermore, due to the novel nature of the material, students were highly motivated to rapidly acquire whatever knowledge was necessary outside the classroom. In reality, the course design forced students to spend the first few weeks of the project simultaneously learning about the research problem and the details of the Hadoop framework. However, this did not appear to be a problem.

Another interesting design choice is the mixing of students with different backgrounds in the same classroom environment. Obviously, the graduate students had stronger computer science backgrounds than the undergraduates overall, and the team leaders had far more experience on the particular research problem than everyone else by design. However, this was less an issue than one would have initially thought, partially due to the selection of the students. Since MapReduce requires a different approach to problem solving, significant learning was required from everyone, independent of prior experience. In fact, prior knowledge of existing solutions may in some cases be limiting, since it precludes a fresh approach to the problem.

6 Course Evaluation

Has the course succeeded? Before this question can be meaningfully answered, one needs to define measures for quantifying success. Note that the evaluation of the course is distinct from the evaluation of student performance (covered in Section 3.3). Given the explicit goal of integrating research and education, I propose the following evaluation criteria:

- Significance of research findings, as measured by the number of publications that arise directly or indirectly from this project.
- Placement of students, e.g., internships and permanent positions, or admission to graduate programs (for undergraduates).
- Number of projects with sustained research activities after the conclusion of the course.

- Amount of additional research support from other funding agencies (NSF, DARPA, etc.) for which the projects provided preliminary results.

Here I provide an interim assessment, as this paper goes to press in mid-April. Preliminary results from the projects have already yielded two separate publications: one on statistical machine translation (Dyer et al., 2008), the other on information retrieval (Elsayed et al., 2008). In terms of student placement, I believe that experience from this course has made several students highly attractive to companies such as Google, Yahoo, and Amazon—both for permanent positions and summer internships. It is far too early to have measurable results with respect to the final two criteria, but otherwise preliminary assessment appears to support the overall success of this course.

In addition to the above discussion, it is also worth mentioning that the course is emerging as a nexus of cloud computing on the Maryland campus (and beyond), serving to connect multiple organizations that share in having large-data problems. Already, the students are drawn from a variety of academic units on campus:

- The iSchool
- Department of Computer Science
- Department of Linguistics
- Department of Geography

And cross-cut multiple research labs:

- The Institute for Advanced Computer Studies
- The Laboratory for Computational Linguistics and Information Processing
- The Human-Computer Interaction Laboratory
- The Center for Bioinformatics and Computational Biology

Off campus, there are ongoing collaborations with the National Center for Biotechnology Information (NCBI) within the National Library of Medicine (NLM). Other information-based organizations around the Washington, D.C. area have also expressed interest in cloud computing technology.

7 Conclusion

This paper describes the design of an integrated research and educational initiative focused on tackling Web-scale problems in natural language processing and information retrieval using MapReduce. Preliminary assessment indicates that this project represents one viable approach to bridging classroom instruction and real-world research challenges. With the advent of clusters composed of commodity machines and "rent-a-cluster" services such as Amazon's EC2,[4] I believe that large-data issues can be practically incorporated into an HLT curriculum at a reasonable cost.

Acknowledgments

I would like to thank the generous hardware support of IBM and Google via the Academic Cloud Computing Initiative. Specifically, thanks go out to Dennis Quan and Eugene Hung from IBM for their tireless support of our efforts. This course would not have been possible without the participation of 13 enthusiastic, dedicated students, for which I feel blessed to have the opportunity to work with. In alphabetical order, they are: Christiam Camacho, George Caragea, Aaron Cordova, Chris Dyer, Tamer Elsayed, Denis Filimonov, Chang Hu, Greg Jablonski, Alan Jackoway, Punit Mehta, Alexander Mont, Michael Schatz, and Hua Wei. Finally, I would like to thank Esther and Kiri for their kind support.

References

Michele Banko and Eric Brill. 2001. Scaling to very very large corpora for natural language disambiguation. In *Proceedings of the 39th Annual Meeting of the Association for Computational Linguistics (ACL 2001)*, pages 26–33, Toulouse, France.

Thorsten Brants, Ashok C. Popat, Peng Xu, Franz J. Och, and Jeffrey Dean. 2007. Large language models in machine translation. In *Proceedings of the 2007 Joint Conference on Empirical Methods in Natural Language Processing and Computational Natural Language Learning*, pages 858–867, Prague, Czech Republic.

Eric Brill, Jimmy Lin, Michele Banko, Susan Dumais, and Andrew Ng. 2001. Data-intensive question answering. In *Proceedings of the Tenth Text REtrieval*

[4]http://aws.amazon.com/ec2

Conference (TREC 2001), pages 393–400, Gaithersburg, Maryland.

Jeffrey Dean and Sanjay Ghemawat. 2004. MapReduce: Simplified data processing on large clusters. In *Proceedings of the 6th Symposium on Operating System Design and Implementation (OSDI 2004)*, pages 137–150, San Francisco, California.

Chris Dyer, Aaron Cordova, Alex Mont, and Jimmy Lin. 2008. Fast, easy, and cheap: Construction of statistical machine translation models with MapReduce. In *Proceedings of the Third Workshop on Statistical Machine Translation at ACL 2008*, Columbus, Ohio.

Tamer Elsayed, Jimmy Lin, and Douglas Oard. 2008. Pairwise document similarity in large collections with MapReduce. In *Proceedings of the 46th Annual Meeting of the Association for Computational Linguistics (ACL 2008), Companion Volume*, Columbus, Ohio.

Sanjay Ghemawat, Howard Gobioff, and Shun-Tak Leung. 2003. The Google File System. In *Proceedings of the 19th ACM Symposium on Operating Systems Principles (SOSP-03)*, pages 29–43, Bolton Landing, New York.

Aaron Kimball, Sierra Michels-Slettvet, and Christophe Bisciglia. 2008. Cluster computing for Web-scale data processing. In *Proceedings of the 39th ACM Technical Symposium on Computer Science Education (SIGCSE 2008)*, pages 116–120, Portland, Oregon.

Multidisciplinary Instruction with the Natural Language Toolkit

Steven Bird
Department of Computer Science
University of Melbourne
sb@csse.unimelb.edu.au

Ewan Klein
School of Informatics
University of Edinburgh
ewan@inf.ed.ac.uk

Edward Loper
Computer and Information Science
University of Pennsylvania
edloper@gradient.cis.upenn.edu

Jason Baldridge
Department of Linguistics
University of Texas at Austin
jbaldrid@mail.utexas.edu

Abstract

The Natural Language Toolkit (NLTK) is widely used for teaching natural language processing to students majoring in linguistics or computer science. This paper describes the design of NLTK, and reports on how it has been used effectively in classes that involve different mixes of linguistics and computer science students. We focus on three key issues: getting started with a course, delivering interactive demonstrations in the classroom, and organizing assignments and projects. In each case, we report on practical experience and make recommendations on how to use NLTK to maximum effect.

1 Introduction

It is relatively easy to teach natural language processing (NLP) in a single-disciplinary mode to a uniform cohort of students. Linguists can be taught to program, leading to projects where students manipulate their own linguistic data. Computer scientists can be taught methods for automatic text processing, leading to projects on text mining and chatbots. Yet these approaches have almost nothing in common, and it is a stretch to call either of these NLP: more apt titles for such courses might be "linguistic data management" and "text technologies."

The Natural Language Toolkit, or NLTK, was developed to give a broad range of students access to the core knowledge and skills of NLP (Loper and Bird, 2002). In particular, NLTK makes it feasible to run a course that covers a substantial amount of theory and practice with an audience consisting of both linguists and computer scientists. NLTK is a suite of Python modules distributed under the GPL open source license via `nltk.org`. NLTK comes with a large collection of corpora, extensive documentation, and hundreds of exercises, making NLTK unique in providing a comprehensive framework for students to develop a computational understanding of language. NLTK's code base of 100,000 lines of Python code includes support for corpus access, tokenizing, stemming, tagging, chunking, parsing, clustering, classification, language modeling, semantic interpretation, unification, and much else besides. As a measure of its impact, NLTK has been used in over 60 university courses in 20 countries, listed on the NLTK website.

Since its inception in 2001, NLTK has undergone considerable evolution, based on the experience gained by teaching courses at several universities, and based on feedback from many teachers and students.[1] Over this period, a series of practical online tutorials about NLTK has grown up into a comprehensive online book (Bird et al., 2008). The book has been designed to stay in lock-step with the NLTK library, and is intended to facilitate "active learning" (Bonwell and Eison, 1991).

This paper describes the main features of NLTK, and reports on how it has been used effectively in classes that involve a combination of linguists and computer scientists. First we discuss aspects of the design of the toolkit that

[1](Bird and Loper, 2004; Loper, 2004; Bird, 2005; Hearst, 2005; Bird, 2006; Klein, 2006; Liddy and McCracken, 2005; Madnani, 2007; Madnani and Dorr, 2008; Baldridge and Erk, 2008)

Proceedings of the Third Workshop on Issues in Teaching Computational Linguistics (TeachCL-08), pages 62–70,
Columbus, Ohio, USA, June 2008.

arose from our need to teach computational linguistics to a multidisciplinary audience (§2). The following sections cover three distinct challenges: getting started with a course (§3); interactive demonstrations (§4); and organizing assignments and projects (§5).

2 Design Decisions Affecting Teaching

2.1 Python

We chose Python[2] as the implementation language for NLTK because it has a shallow learning curve, its syntax and semantics are transparent, and it has good string-handling functionality. As an interpreted language, Python facilitates interactive exploration. As an object-oriented language, Python permits data and methods to be encapsulated and re-used easily. Python comes with an extensive standard library, including tools for graphical programming and numerical processing, which means it can be used for a wide range of non-trivial applications. Python is ideal in a context serving newcomers and experienced programmers (Shannon, 2003).

We have taken the step of incorporating a detailed introduction to Python programming in the NLTK book, taking care to motivate programming constructs with linguistic examples. Extensive feedback from students has been humbling, and revealed that for students with no prior programming experience, it is almost impossible to over-explain. Despite the difficulty of providing a self-contained introduction to Python for linguists, we nevertheless have also had very positive feedback, and in combination with the teaching techniques described below, have managed to bring a large group of non-programmer students rapidly to a point where they could carry out interesting and useful exercises in text processing.

In addition to the NLTK book, the code in the NLTK core is richly documented, using Python docstrings and Epydoc[3] support for API documentation.[4] Access to the code documentation is available using the Python `help()` command at the interactive prompt, and this can be especially useful for checking the parameters and return type of functions.

[2] `http://www.python.org/`

[3] `http://epydoc.sourceforge.net/`

[4] `http://nltk.org/doc/api/`

Other Python libraries are useful in the NLP context: NumPy provides optimized support for linear algebra and sparse arrays (NumPy, 2008) and PyLab provides sophisticated facilities for scientific visualization (Matplotlib, 2008).

2.2 Coding Requirements

As discussed in Loper & Bird (2002), the priorities for NLTK code focus on its teaching role. When code is readable, a student who doesn't understand the maths of HMMs, smoothing, and so on may benefit from looking at how an algorithm is implemented. Thus consistency, simplicity, modularity are all vital features of NLTK code. A similar importance is placed on extensibility, since this helps to ensure that the code grows as a coherent whole, rather than by unpredictable and haphazard additions.

By contrast, although efficiency cannot be ignored, it has always taken second place to simplicity and clarity of coding. In a similar vein, we have tried to avoid clever programming tricks, since these typically hinder intelligibility of the code. Finally, comprehensiveness of coverage has never been an overriding concern of NLTK; this leaves open many possibilities for student projects and community involvement.

2.3 Naming

One issue which has absorbed a considerable amount of attention is the naming of user-oriented functions in NLTK. To a large extent, the system of naming *is* the user interface to the toolkit, and it is important that users should be able to guess what action might be performed by a given function. Consequently, naming conventions need to be consistent and semantically transparent. At the same time, there is a countervailing pressure for relatively succinct names, since excessive verbosity can also hinder comprehension and usability. An additional complication is that adopting an object-oriented style of programming may be well-motivated for a number of reasons but nevertheless baffling to the linguist student. For example, although it is perfectly respectable to invoke an instance method `WordPunctTokenizer().tokenize(text)` (for some input string `text`), a simpler version is also provided: `wordpunct_tokenize(text)`.

2.4 Corpus Access

The scope of exercises and projects that students can perform is greatly increased by the inclusion of a large collection of corpora, along with easy-to-use corpus readers. This collection, which currently stands at 45 corpora, includes parsed, POS-tagged, plain text, categorized text, and lexicons.[5]

In designing the corpus readers, we emphasized simplicity, consistency, and efficiency. *Corpus objects*, such as `nltk.corpus.brown` and `nltk.corpus.treebank`, define common methods for reading the corpus contents, abstracting away from idiosyncratic file formats to provide a uniform interface. See Figure 1 for an example of accessing POS-tagged data from different tagged and parsed corpora.

The corpus objects provide methods for loading corpus contents in various ways. Common methods include: `raw()`, for the raw contents of the corpus; `words()`, for a list of tokenized words; `sents()`, for the same list grouped into sentences; `tagged_words()`, for a list of (*word*, *tag*) pairs; `tagged_sents()`, for the same list grouped into sentences; and `parsed_sents()`, for a list of parse trees. Optional parameters can be used to restrict what portion of the corpus is returned, e.g., a particular section, or an individual corpus file.

Most corpus reader methods return a *corpus view* which acts as a list of text objects, but maintains responsiveness and memory efficiency by only loading items from the file on an as-needed basis. Thus, when we print a corpus view we only load the first block of the corpus into memory, but when we process this object we load the whole corpus:

```
>>> nltk.corpus.alpino.words()
['De', 'verzekeringsmaatschappijen',
'verhelen', ...]
>>> len(nltk.corpus.alpino.words())
139820
```

2.5 Accessing Shoebox Files

NLTK provides functionality for working with "Shoebox" (or "Toolbox") data (Robinson et al., 2007). Shoebox is a system used by many documentary linguists to produce lexicons and interlinear glossed text. The ability to work straightforwardly with Shoebox data has created a new incentive for linguists to learn how to program.

As an example, in the Linguistics Department at the University of Texas at Austin, a course has been offered on Python programming and working with corpora,[6] but so far uptake from the target audience of core linguistics students has been low. They usually have practical computational needs and many of them are intimidated by the very idea of programming. We believe that the appeal of this course can be enhanced by designing a significant component with the goal of helping documentary linguistics students take control of their *own* Shoebox data. This will give them skills that are useful for their research and also transferable to other activities. Although the NLTK Shoebox functionality was not originally designed with instruction in mind, its relevance to students of documentary linguistics is highly fortuitous and may prove appealing for similar linguistics departments.

3 Getting Started

NLP is usually only available as an elective course, and students will vote with their feet after attending one or two classes. This initial period is important for attracting and retaining students. In particular, students need to get a sense of the richness of language in general, and NLP in particular, while gaining a realistic impression of what will be accomplished during the course and what skills they will have by the end. During this time when rapport needs to be rapidly established, it is easy for instructors to alienate students through the use of linguistic or computational concepts and terminology that are foreign to students, or to bore students by getting bogged down in defining terms like "noun phrase" or "function" which are basic to one audience and new for the other. Thus, we believe it is crucial for instructors to understand and shape the student's expectations, and to get off to a good start. The best overall strategy that we have found is to use succinct nuggets of NLTK code to stimulate students' interest in both data and processing techniques.

[5] `http://nltk.org/corpora.html`

[6] `http://comp.ling.utexas.edu/courses/2007/corpora07/`

```
>>> nltk.corpus.treebank.tagged_words()
[('Pierre', 'NNP'), ('Vinken', 'NNP'), (',', ','), ...]
>>> nltk.corpus.brown.tagged_words()
[('The', 'AT'), ('Fulton', 'NP-TL'), ...]
>>> nltk.corpus.floresta.tagged_words()
[('Um', '>N+art'), ('revivalismo', 'H+n'), ...]
>>> nltk.corpus.cess_esp.tagged_words()
[('El', 'da0ms0'), ('grupo', 'ncms000'), ...]
>>> nltk.corpus.alpino.tagged_words()
[('De', 'det'), ('verzekeringsmaatschappijen', 'noun'), ...]
```

Figure 1: Accessing Different Corpora via a Uniform Interface

3.1 Student Expectations

Computer science students come to NLP expecting to learn about NLP algorithms and data structures. They typically have enough mathematical preparation to be confident in playing with abstract formal systems (including systems of linguistic rules). Moreover, they are already proficient in multiple programming languages, and have little difficulty in learning NLP algorithms by reading and manipulating the implementations provided with NLTK. At the same time, they tend to be unfamiliar with the terminology and concepts that linguists take for granted, and may struggle to come up with reasonable linguistic analyses of data.

Linguistics students, on the other hand, are interested in understanding NLP algorithms and data structures only insofar as it helps them to use computational tools to perform analytic tasks from "core linguistics," e.g. writing a set of CFG productions to parse some sentences, or plugging together NLP components in order to derive the subcategorization requirements of verbs in a corpus. They are usually not interested in reading significant chunks of code; it isn't what they care about and they probably lack the confidence to poke around in source files.

In a nutshell, the computer science students typically want to analyze the tools and synthesize new implementations, while the linguists typically want to use the tools to analyze language and synthesize new theories. There is a risk that the former group never really gets to grips with natural language, while the latter group never really gets to grips with processing. Instead, computer science students need to learn that NLP is not just an application of techniques from formal language theory and compiler construction, and linguistics students need to understand that NLP is not just computer-based housekeeping and a solution to the shortcomings of office productivity software for managing their data.

In many courses, linguistics students or computer science students will dominate the class numerically, simply because the course is only listed in one department. In such cases it is usually enough to provide additional support in the form of some extra readings, tutorials, and exercises in the opening stages of the course. In other cases, e.g. courses we have taught at the universities of Edinburgh, Melbourne, Pennsylvania, and Texas-Austin or in summer intensive programs in several countries, there is more of an even split, and the challenge of serving both cohorts of students becomes acute. It helps to address this issue head-on, with an early discussion of the goals of the course.

3.2 Articulating the Goals

Despite an instructor's efforts to add a cross-disciplinary angle, students easily "revert to type." The pressure of assessment encourages students to emphasize what they do well. Students' desire to understand what is expected of them encourages instructors to stick to familiar assessment instruments. As a consequence, the path of least resistance is for students to remain firmly monolingual in their own discipline, while acquiring a smattering of words from a foreign language, at a level we might call "survival linguistics" or "survival computer science." If they ever get to work in a multidisciplinary team they are likely only to play a type-cast role.

Asking computer science students to write their first essay in years, or asking linguistics students to write their first ever program, leads to stressed students who complain that they don't know what is expected of them. Nevertheless, students need to confront the challenge of becoming bilingual, of working hard to learn the basics of another discipline. In parallel, instructors need to confront the challenge of synthesizing material from linguistics and computer science into a coherent whole, and devising effective methods for teaching, learning, and assessment.

3.3 Entry Points

It is possible to identify several distinct pathways into the field of Computational Linguistics. Bird (2008) identifies four; each of these are supported by NLTK, as detailed below:

Text Processing First: NLTK supports variety of approaches to tokenization, tagging, evaluation, and language engineering more generally.

Programming First: NLTK is based on Python and the documentation teaches the language and provides many examples and exercises to test and reinforce student learning.

Linguistics First: Here, students come with a grounding in one or more areas of linguistics, and focus on computational approaches to that area by working with the relevant chapter of the NLTK book in conjunction with learning how to program.

Algorithms First: Here, students come with a grounding in one or more areas of computer science, and can use, test and extend NLTK'S reference implementations of standard NLP algorithms.

3.4 The First Lecture

It is important that the first lecture is effective at motivating and exemplifying NLP to an audience of computer science and linguistics students. They need to get an accurate sense of the interesting conceptual and technical challenges awaiting them. Fortunately, the task is made easier by the simple fact that language technologies, and language itself, are intrinsically interesting and appealing to a wide audience. Several opening topics appear to work particularly well:

The holy grail: A long term challenge, mythologized in science fiction movies, is to build machines that understand human language. Current technologies that exhibit some basic level of natural language understanding include spoken dialogue systems, question answering systems, summarization systems, and machine translation systems. These can be demonstrated in class without too much difficulty. The Turing test is a linguistic test, easily understood by all students, and which helps the computer science students to see NLP in relation to the field of Artificial Intelligence. The evolution of programming languages has brought them closer to natural language, helping students see the essentially linguistic purpose of this central development in computer science. The corresponding holy grail in linguistics is full understanding of the human language faculty; writing programs and building machines surely informs this quest too.

The riches of language: It is easy to find examples of the creative richness of language in its myriad uses. However, linguists will understand that language contains hidden riches that can only be uncovered by careful analysis of large quantities of linguistically annotated data, work that benefits from suitable computational tools. Moreover, the computational needs for exploratory linguistic research often go beyond the capabilities of the current tools. Computer scientists will appreciate the cognate problem of extracting information from the web, and the economic riches associated with state-of-the-art text mining technologies.

Formal approaches to language: Computer science and linguistics have a shared history in the area of philosophical logic and formal language theory. Whether the language is natural or artificial, computer scientists and linguists use similar logical formalisms for investigating the formal semantics of languages, similar grammar formalisms for modeling the syntax of languages, and similar finite-state methods for manipulating text. Both rely on the recursive, compositional nature of natural and artificial languages.

3.5 First Assignment

The first coursework assignment can be a significant step forwards in helping students get to grips with the material, and is best given out early, perhaps even in week 1. We have found it advisable for this assignment to include both programming and linguistics content. One example is to ask students to carry out NP chunking of some data (e.g. a section of the Brown Corpus). The `nltk.RegexpParser` class is initialized with a set of chunking rules expressed in a simple, regular expression-oriented syntax, and the resulting chunk parser can be run over POS-tagged input text. Given a Gold Standard test set like the CoNLL-2000 data,[7] precision and recall of the chunk grammar can be easily determined. Thus, if students are given an existing, incomplete set of rules as their starting point, they just have to modify and test their rules.

There are distinctive outcomes for each set of students: linguistics students learn to write grammar fragments that respect the literal-minded needs of the computer, and also come to appreciate the noisiness of typical NLP corpora (including automatically annotated corpora like CoNLL-2000). Computer science students become more familiar with parts of speech and with typical syntactic structures in English. Both groups learn the importance of formal evaluation using precision and recall.

4 Interactive Demonstrations

4.1 Python Demonstrations

Python fosters a highly interactive style of teaching. It is quite natural to build up moderately complex programs in front of a class, with the less confident students transcribing it into a Python session on their laptop to satisfy themselves it works (but not necessarily understanding everything they enter first time), while the stronger students quickly grasp the theoretical concepts and algorithms. While both groups can be served by the same presentation, they tend to ask quite different questions. However, this is addressed by dividing them into smaller clusters and having teaching assistants visit them separately to discuss issues arising from the content.

The NLTK book contains many examples, and the instructor can present an interactive lecture that includes running these examples and experimenting with them in response to student questions. In early classes, the focus will probably be on learning Python. In later classes, the driver for such interactive lessons can be an externally-motivated empirical or theoretical question.

As a practical matter, it is important to consider low-level issues that may get in the way of students' ability to capture the material covered in interactive Python sessions. These include choice of appropriate font size for screen display, avoiding the problem of output scrolling the command out of view, and distributing a log of the instructor's interactive session for students to study in their own time.

4.2 NLTK Demonstrations

A significant fraction of any NLP syllabus covers fundamental data structures and algorithms. These are usually taught with the help of formal notations and complex diagrams. Large trees and charts are copied onto the board and edited in tedious slow motion, or laboriously prepared for presentation slides. It is more effective to use live demonstrations in which those diagrams are generated and updated automatically. NLTK provides interactive graphical user interfaces, making it possible to view program state and to study program execution step-by-step. Most NLTK components have a demonstration mode, and will perform an interesting task without requiring any special input from the user. It is even possible to make minor modifications to programs in response to "what if" questions. In this way, students learn the mechanics of NLP quickly, gain deeper insights into the data structures and algorithms, and acquire new problem-solving skills.

An example of a particularly effective set of demonstrations are those for shift-reduce and recursive descent parsing. These make the difference between the algorithms glaringly obvious. More importantly, students get a concrete sense of many issues that affect the design of algorithms for tasks like parsing. The partial analysis constructed by the recursive descent parser bobs up and down as it steps forward and backtracks, and students often go wide-eyed as the parser retraces its steps and does "dumb" things like expanding N to *man* when it has already tried the rule unsuccessfully (but is now trying to match a bare NP rather than an NP with a PP modifier). Linguistics students who are extremely

[7] `http://www.cnts.ua.ac.be/conll2000/chunking/`

knowledgeable about context-free grammars and thus understand the representations gain a new appreciation for just how naive an algorithm can be. This helps students grasp the need for techniques like dynamic programming and motivates them to learn how they can be used to solve such problems much more efficiently.

Another highly useful aspect of NLTK is the ability to define a context-free grammar using a simple format and to display tree structures graphically. This can be used to teach context-free grammars interactively, where the instructor and the students develop a grammar from scratch and check its coverage against a testbed of grammatical and ungrammatical sentences. Because it is so easy to modify the grammar and check its behavior, students readily participate and suggest various solutions. When the grammar produces an analysis for an ungrammatical sentence in the testbed, the tree structure can be displayed graphically and inspected to see what went wrong. Conversely, the parse chart can be inspected to see where the grammar failed on grammatical sentences.

NLTK's easy access to many corpora greatly facilitates classroom instruction. It is straightforward to pull in different sections of corpora and build programs in class for many different tasks. This not only makes it easier to experiment with ideas on the fly, but also allows students to replicate the exercises outside of class. Graphical displays that show the dispersion of terms throughout a text also give students excellent examples of how a few simple statistics collected from a corpus can provide useful and interesting views on a text—including seeing the frequency with which various characters appear in a novel. This can in turn be related to other resources like Google Trends, which shows the frequency with which a term has been referenced in news reports or been used in search terms over several years.

5 Exercises, Assignments and Projects

5.1 Exercises

Copious exercises are provided with the NLTK book; these have been graded for difficulty relative to the concepts covered in the preceding sections of the book. Exercises have the tremendous advantage of building on the NLTK infrastructure, both code and documentation. The exercises are intended to be suitable both for self-paced learning and in formally assigned coursework.

A mixed class of linguistics and computer science students will have a diverse range of programming experience, and students with no programming experience will typically have different aptitudes for programming (Barker and Unger, 1983; Caspersen et al., 2007). A course which forces all students to progress at the same rate will be too difficult for some, and too dull for others, and will risk alienating many students. Thus, course materials need to accommodate self-paced learning. An effective way to do this is to provide students with contexts in which they can test and extend their knowledge at their own rate.

One such context is provided by lecture or laboratory sessions in which students have a machine in front of them (or one between two), and where there is time to work through a series of exercises to consolidate what has just been taught from the front, or read from a chapter of the book. When this can be done at regular intervals, it is easier for students to know which part of the materials to re-read. It also encourages them to get into the habit of checking their understanding of a concept by writing code.

When exercises are graded for difficulty, it is easier for students to understand how much effort is expected, and whether they even have time to attempt an exercise. Graded exercises are also good for supporting self-evaluation. If a student takes 20 minutes to write a solution, they also need to have some idea of whether this was an appropriate amount of time.

The exercises are also highly adaptable. It is common for instructors to take them as a starting point in building homework assignments that are tailored to their own students. Some instructors prefer to include exercises that do not allow students to take advantage of built-in NLTK functionality, e.g. using a Python dictionary to count word frequencies in the Brown corpus rather than NLTK's `FreqDist` (see Figure 2). This is an important part of building facility with general text processing in Python, since eventually students will have to work outside of the NLTK sandbox. Nonetheless, students often use NLTK functionality as part of their solutions, e.g., for managing frequencies and distributions. Again,

```
nltk.FreqDist(nltk.corpus.brown.words())

fd = nltk.FreqDist()
for filename in corpus_files:
    text = open(filename).read()
    for w in nltk.wordpunct_tokenize(text):
        fd.inc(w)

counts = {}
for w in nltk.corpus.brown.words():
    if w not in counts:
        counts[w] = 0
    counts[w] += 1
```

Figure 2: Three Ways to Build up a Frequency Distribution of Words in the Brown Corpus

this flexibility is a good thing: students learn to work with resources they know how to use, and can branch out to new exercises from that basis. When course content includes discussion of Unix command line utilities for text processing, students can furthermore gain a better appreciation of the pros and cons of writing their own scripts versus using an appropriate Unix pipeline.

5.2 Assignments

NLTK supports assignments of varying difficulty and scope: experimenting with existing components to see what happens for different inputs or parameter settings; modifying existing components and creating systems using existing components; leveraging NLTK's extensible architecture by developing entirely new components; or employing NLTK's interfaces to other toolkits such as Weka (Witten and Frank, 2005) and Prover9 (McCune, 2008).

5.3 Projects

Group projects involving a mixture of linguists and computer science students have an initial appeal, assuming that each kind of student can learn from the other. However, there's a complex social dynamic in such groups, one effect of which is that the linguistics students may opt out of the programming aspects of the task, perhaps with view that their contribution would only hurt the chances of achieving a good overall project mark. It is difficult to mandate significant collaboration across disciplinary boundaries, with the more likely outcome being, for example, that a parser is developed by a computer science team member, then thrown over the wall to a linguist who will develop an appropriate grammar.

Instead, we believe that it is generally more productive in the context of a single-semester introductory course to have students work individually on their own projects. Distinct projects can be devised for students depending on their background, or students can be given a list of project topics,[8] and offered option of self-proposing other projects.

6 Conclusion

We have argued that the distinctive features of NLTK make it an apt vehicle for teaching NLP to mixed audiences of linguistic and computer science students. On the one hand, complete novices can quickly gain confidence in their ability to do interesting and useful things with language processing, while the transparency and consistency of the implementation also makes it easy for experienced programmers to learn about natural language and to explore more challenging tasks. The success of this recipe is borne out by the wide uptake of the toolkit, not only within tertiary education but more broadly by users who just want try their hand at NLP. We also have encouraging results in presenting NLTK in classrooms at the secondary level, thereby trying to inspire the computational linguists of the future!

Finally, we believe that NLTK has gained much by participating in the Open Source software movement, specifically from the infrastructure provided by SourceForge.net and from the invaluable contributions of a wide range of people, including many students.

7 Acknowledgments

We are grateful to the members of the NLTK community for their helpful feedback on the toolkit and their many contributions. We thank the anonymous reviewers for their feedback on an earlier version of this paper.

[8] http://nltk.org/projects.html

References

Jason Baldridge and Katrin Erk. 2008. Teaching computational linguistics to a large, diverse student body: courses, tools, and interdepartmental interaction. In *Proceedings of the Third Workshop on Issues in Teaching Computational Linguistics*. Association for Computational Linguistics.

Ricky Barker and E. A. Unger. 1983. A predictor for success in an introductory programming class based upon abstract reasoning development. *ACM SIGCSE Bulletin*, 15:154–158.

Steven Bird and Edward Loper. 2004. NLTK: The Natural Language Toolkit. In *Companion Volume to the Proceedings of 42st Annual Meeting of the Association for Computational Linguistics*, pages 214–217. Association for Computational Linguistics.

Steven Bird, Ewan Klein, and Edward Loper. 2008. Natural Language Processing in Python. `http://nltk.org/book.html`.

Steven Bird. 2005. NLTK-Lite: Efficient scripting for natural language processing. In *4th International Conference on Natural Language Processing, Kanpur, India*, pages 1–8.

Steven Bird. 2006. NLTK: The Natural Language Toolkit. In *Proceedings of the COLING/ACL 2006 Interactive Presentation Sessions*, pages 69–72, Sydney, Australia, July. Association for Computational Linguistics.

Steven Bird. 2008. Defining a core body of knowledge for the introductory computational linguistics curriculum. In *Proceedings of the Third Workshop on Issues in Teaching Computational Linguistics*. Association for Computational Linguistics.

Charles C. Bonwell and James A. Eison. 1991. *Active Learning: Creating Excitement in the Classroom.* Washington, D.C.: Jossey-Bass.

Michael Caspersen, Kasper Larsen, and Jens Bennedsen. 2007. Mental models and programming aptitude. *SIGCSE Bulletin*, 39:206–210.

Marti Hearst. 2005. Teaching applied natural language processing: Triumphs and tribulations. In *Proceedings of the Second ACL Workshop on Effective Tools and Methodologies for Teaching NLP and CL*, pages 1–8, Ann Arbor, Michigan, June. Association for Computational Linguistics.

Ewan Klein. 2006. Computational semantics in the Natural Language Toolkit. In *Proceedings of the Australasian Language Technology Workshop*, pages 26–33.

Elizabeth Liddy and Nancy McCracken. 2005. Hands-on NLP for an interdisciplinary audience. In *Proceedings of the Second ACL Workshop on Effective Tools and Methodologies for Teaching NLP and CL*, pages 62–68, Ann Arbor, Michigan, June. Association for Computational Linguistics.

Edward Loper and Steven Bird. 2002. NLTK: The Natural Language Toolkit. In *Proceedings of the ACL Workshop on Effective Tools and Methodologies for Teaching Natural Language Processing and Computational Linguistics*, pages 62–69. Association for Computational Linguistics.

Edward Loper. 2004. NLTK: Building a pedagogical toolkit in Python. In *PyCon DC 2004*. Python Software Foundation.

Nitin Madnani and Bonnie Dorr. 2008. Combining open-source with research to re-engineer a hands-on introductory NLP course. In *Proceedings of the Third Workshop on Issues in Teaching Computational Linguistics*. Association for Computational Linguistics.

Nitin Madnani. 2007. Getting started on natural language processing with Python. *ACM Crossroads*, 13(4).

Matplotlib. 2008. Matplotlib: Python 2D plotting library. `http://matplotlib.sourceforge.net/`.

William McCune. 2008. Prover9: Automated theorem prover for first-order and equational logic. `http://www.cs.unm.edu/~mccune/mace4/manual-examples.html`.

NumPy. 2008. NumPy: Scientific computing with Python. `http://numpy.scipy.org/`.

Stuart Robinson, Greg Aumann, and Steven Bird. 2007. Managing fieldwork data with Toolbox and the Natural Language Toolkit. *Language Documentation and Conservation*, 1:44–57.

Christine Shannon. 2003. Another breadth-first approach to CS I using Python. In *Proceedings of the 34th SIGCSE Technical Symposium on Computer Science Education*, pages 248–251. ACM.

Ian H. Witten and Eibe Frank. 2005. *Data Mining: Practical machine learning tools and techniques.* Morgan Kaufmann.

Combining Open-Source with Research to Re-engineer a Hands-on Introductory NLP Course

Nitin Madnani **Bonnie J. Dorr**
Laboratory for Computational Linguistics and Information Processing
Institute for Advanced Computer Studies
Department of Computer Science
University of Maryland, College Park
{nmadnani,bonnie}@umiacs.umd.edu

Abstract

We describe our first attempts to re-engineer the curriculum of our introductory NLP course by using two important building blocks: (1) Access to an easy-to-learn programming language and framework to build hands-on programming assignments with real-world data and corpora and, (2) Incorporation of interesting ideas from recent NLP research publications into assignment and examination problems. We believe that these are extremely important components of a curriculum aimed at a diverse audience consisting primarily of first-year graduate students from both linguistics and computer science. Based on overwhelmingly positive student feedback, we find that our attempts were hugely successful.

1 Introduction

Designing an introductory level natural language processing course for a class of first year computer science and linguistics graduate students is a challenging task. It is important to strive for balance between breadth and depth—it is important not only to introduce the students to a variety of language processing techniques and applications but also to provide sufficient detail about each. However, we claim that there is another important requirement for a successful implementation of such a course. Like any other graduate-level course offered to first year students, it should encourage them to approach solutions to problems as researchers. In order to meet such a requirement, the course should have two important dimensions:

1. Access to a programming framework that provides the tools and data used in the real world so as to allow the students to explore each topic hands-on and easily attempt creative solutions to problems. The framework should be simple enough to use so that students are not bogged down in its intricacies and can focus on the course concepts.

2. Exposure to novel and innovative research in each topic. One of the most valuable contributions of a large community, such as the NLP and CL community, is the publicly accessible repository of research publications for a range of topics. While the commonly used textbooks describe established and mainstream research methods for each topic in detail, more recent research papers are usually omitted. By using such papers as the bases for programming assignments—instantiated in the framework described earlier—and exam questions, students can gain important insights into how new solutions to existing problems are formulated; insights that can only come from a hands-on approach to problem solving.

In this paper, we describe our attempts to engineer such a course. In section 2, we describe the specific goals we had in mind for such a course and how it differs from the previous version of the introductory course we taught at our institution. Section 3 discusses how we fully integrated an open-source programming framework into our curriculum and used it for programming assignments as well as in-class

Proceedings of the Third Workshop on Issues in Teaching Computational Linguistics (TeachCL-08), pages 71–79,
Columbus, Ohio, USA, June 2008.

sessions. In a similar vein, section 4 describes our preliminary efforts to combine interesting research ideas for various topics with the framework above. We also have definite plans to expand the course curriculum to take more novel ideas from recent NLP literature for each topic and adapt them to instructive hands-on assignments. Furthermore, we are developing extensions and add-ons for the programming framework that we plan to contribute to the project. We outline these plans in section 6 and conclude in section 7.

2 Goals

We wanted our course curriculum to fulfill some specific goals that we discuss below, provide motivation wherever appropriate.

- **A Uniform Programming Framework**. The previous version of our introductory course took a more fragmented approach and used different programming languages and tools for different assignments. For example, we used an in-house HMM library written in C for any HMM-based assignments and Perl for some other assignments. As expected, such an approach requires students to familiarize themselves with a different programming interface for each assignment and discourages students to explore on their own. To address this concern, we chose the Python (Python, 2007) programming language and the Natural Language Toolkit (Loper and Bird, 2002), written entirely in Python, for all our assignments and programming tasks. We discuss our use of NLTK in more detail in the next section.

- **Real-world Data & Corpora**. In our previous course, students did not have access to any of the corpora that are used in actual NLP research. We found this to be a serious shortcoming and wanted to ensure that our new curriculum allowed students to use real corpora for evaluating their programming assignments.

- **Exposure to Research**. While we had certainly made it a point to introduce recent research work in our lectures for all topics in the previous course, we believed that a much richer integration was required in order to allow a more realistic peek into NLP research.

- **Satisfying a Diverse Audience**. We wanted the curriculum to appeal to both computer science and linguistics students since they the course was cross-listed in both departments.

- **Continuing Interest**. A large number of the students enrolled in the course were undecided about what research area to pursue. We wanted to present a fair picture of what NLP research actually entails and encourage any interested students to take the more advanced part of the course being offered later in the year.

3 Incorporating Open Source

We use the Python programming language and NLTK as our programming framework for the curriculum. Python is currently one of the most popular programming languages—it is fully object oriented and multi-platform, natively supports high-level dynamic data types such as lists and hashes (termed *dictionaries* in Python), has very readable syntax and, most importantly, ships with an extensive standard library for almost every conceivable task. Although Python already has most of the functionality needed to perform very simple NLP tasks, its still not powerful enough for most standard ones. This is where the Natural Language Toolkit (NLTK) comes in. NLTK[1], written entirely in Python, is a collection of modules and corpora, released under an open-source license, that allows students to learn and conduct research in NLP (Bird et al., 2008). The most important advantage of using NLTK is that it is entirely self-contained. Not only does it provide convenient functions and wrappers that can be used as building blocks for common NLP tasks, it also provides raw and pre-processed versions of standard corpora used frequently in NLP literature. Together, Python and NLTK constitute one of the most potent tools for instruction of NLP (Madnani, 2007) and allow us to develop hands-on assignments that can appeal to a broad audience including both linguistics and computer science students.

[1] `http://nltk.org`

```
Query: economy

Clinton 76 ############################################################################
 Carter 21 #####################
 GWBush 61 #############################################################
 Reagan 48 ################################################
   Bush 15 ###############
  Nixon 12 ############

Query: aid

Clinton  2 ##
 Carter  1 #
 GWBush  5 #####
 Reagan  9 #########
   Bush  2 ##
  Nixon  7 #######
```

Figure 1: An Excerpt from the output of a Python script used for an in-class exercise demonstrating the simplicity of the Python-NLTK combination.

In order to illustrate the simplicity and utility of this tool to the students, we went through an in-class exercise at the beginning of the class. The exercise asked the students to solve the following simple language processing problem:

Find the frequency of occurrences of the following words in the state-of-the-union addresses of the last 6 American Presidents: war, peace, economy & aid. Also draw histograms for each word.

We then went through a step-by-step process of how one would go about solving such a problem. The solution hinged on two important points:

(a) NLTK ships with a corpus of the last 50 years of state-of-the-union addresses and provides a native conditional frequency distribution object to easily keep track of conditional counts.

(b) Drawing a histogram in Python is as simple as the statement `print '#'*n` where n is the count for each query word.

Given these two properties, the Python solution for the problem was only 20 lines long. Figure 1 shows an excerpt from the output of this script. This exercise allowed us to impress upon the students that the programming framework for the course is simple and fun so that they may start exploring it on their own. We describe more concrete instances of NLTK usage in our curriculum below.

3.1 HMMs & Part-of-speech Tagging

Hidden Markov Models (Rabiner, 1989) have proven to be a very useful formalism in NLP and have been used in a wide range of problems, e.g., parsing, machine translation and part-of-speech (POS) tagging. In our previous curriculum, we had employed an in-house C++ implementation of HMMs for our assignments. As part of our new curriculum, we introduced Markov models (and HMMs) in the context of POS tagging and in a much more hands-on fashion. To do this, we created an assignment where students were required to implement Viterbi decoding for an HMM and output the best POS tag sequence for any given sentence. There were several ways in which NLTK made this extremely simple:

- Since we had the entire source code of the HMM module from NLTK available, we factored out the part of the code that handled the HMM training, parameterized it and provided that to students as a separate module they they could use to train the HMMs. Such refactoring not only allows for cleaner code boundaries but it also allows the students to use a variety of training parameters (such as different forms of smoothed distributions for the transition and emission probabilities) and measure their effects with little effort. Listing 1 shows how the refactoring was accomplished: the training code was put into a separate module called `hmmtrainer` and automatically called in the

Listing 1: A skeleton of the refactored NLTK HMM code used to build a hands-on HMM assignment

```
import hmmtrainer
import nltk.LidStoneProbDist as lidstone
class hmm:
  def __init__(self):
    params = hmmtrainer.train(smooth=lidstone)
    self.params = params

  def decode(self, word_sequence)

  def tag(self, word_sequence)
```

main hmm class when instantiating it. The students had to write the code for the decode and tag methods of this class. The HMM training was setup to be able to use a variety of smoothed distributions, e.g. Lidstone, Laplace etc., all available from NLTK.

- NLTK ships with the tokenized and POS tagged version of the Brown corpus—one of the most common corpora employed for corpus linguistics and, in particular, for evaluating POS taggers. We used Section A of the corpus for training the HMMs and asked the students to evaluate their taggers on Section B.

Another advantage of this assignment was that the if students were interested in how the supervised training process actually worked, they could simply examine the hmmtrainer module that was also written entirely in Python. An assignment with such characteristics in our previous course would have required knowledge of C++, willingness to wade through much more complicated code and would certainly not have been as instructive.

3.2 Finite State Automata

Another topic where we were able to leverage the strengths of both NLTK and Python was when introducing the students to finite state automata. Previously, we only discussed the fundamentals of finite state automata in class and then asked the students to apply this knowledge to morphological parsing by using PC-Kimmo (Koskenniemi, 1983). However, working with PC-Kimmo required the students to directly fill entries in transition tables using a very rigid syntax.

Listing 2: An illustration of the simple finite state transducer interface in NLTK

```
from nltk_contrib.fst import fst
f = fst.FST('test') #instantiate
f.add_state('1') # add states
f.add_state('2')
f.add_state('3')
f.initial_state = 1 # set initial
f.set_final('2') # set finals
f.set_final('3')
f.add_arc('1','2','a','A') # a -> A
f.add_arc('1','3','b','B') # b -> B
print f.transduce(['a','a','b','b'])
```

In the new curriculum, we could easily rely on the finite state module that ships with NLTK to use such automata in a very natural way as shown in Listing 2. With such an easy to use interface, we could concentrate instead on the more important concepts underlying the building and cascading of transducers to accomplish a language processing task.

As our example task, we asked the students to implement the Soundex Algorithm, a phonetic algorithm commonly used by libraries and the Census Bureau to represent people's names as they are pronounced in English. We found that not only did the students easily implement such a complex transducer, they also took the time to perform some analysis on their own and determine the shortcomings of the Soundex algorithm. This was only possible because of the simple interface and short development cycle provided by the Python-NLTK combination. In addition, NLTK also provides a single method[2] that can render the transducer as a postscript or image file that can prove extremely useful for debugging.

In our new version of the course, we consciously chose to use primarily open-source technologies in the curriculum. We feel that it is important to say a few words about this choice: an open-source project

[2]This method interfaces with an existing installation of *Graphviz*, a popular open-source graph drawing software (Ellson et al., 2004).

not only allows instructors to examine the source code and re-purpose it for their own use (as we did in section 3.1) but it also encourages students to delve deep into the programming framework if they are curious about how something works. In fact, a few of our students actually discovered subtle idiosyncrasies and bugs in the NLTK source while exploring on their own, filed bug reports where necessary and shared the findings with the entire class. This experience allowed all students to understand the challenges of language processing.

More importantly, we believe an open-source project fosters collaboration in the community that it serves. For example, a lot of the functionality of NLTK hinges on important technical contributions, such as our SRILM interface described in section 6, from the large academic NLP community that can be used by any member of the community for research and for teaching.

4 Incorporating Research

Besides employing a uniform programming framework that the students could pick up easily and learn to explore on their own, the other important goal of the new curriculum was to incorporate ideas and techniques from interesting NLP research publications into assignments and exams. The motivation, of course, was to get our students to think about and possibly even implement these ideas. Since we cannot discuss all instances in the curriculum where we leveraged research publications (due to space considerations), we only discuss two such instances in detail below.

The first topic for which we constructed a more open-ended research-oriented assignment was lexical semantics. We focused, in particular, on the WordNet (Fellbaum, 1998) database. WordNet is a very popular lexical database and has been used extensively in NLP literature over the years. In the previous course, our assignment on lexical semantics asked the students to use the online interface to WordNet to learn the basic concept of a *synset* and the various relations that are defined over synsets such as hyponymy, hypernymy etc. A very simple change would have been to ask the students to use the WordNet interface included with NLTK to perform the same analysis. However, we thought that a more interesting assignment would be to explore the structure of the four WordNet taxonomies (Noun, Verb, Adjective and Adverb). This taxonomy can be simplified and thought of as a directed acyclic graph $G = (V, E)$ where each synset $u \in V$ is a node and each edge $(u, v) \in E$ represents that v is a hypernym of u. Given such a graph, some very interesting statistics can be computed about the topology of WordNet itself (Devitt and Vogel, 2004). In our assignment, we asked the students to use the NLTK WordNet interface to compute some of these statistics automatically and answer some interesting questions:

(a) What percentage of the nodes in the Noun taxonomy are leaf nodes?

(b) Which are the nine most general root nodes in the Noun taxonomy and what is the node distribution across these roots?

(c) Compute the *branching factor* (number of descendants) for each node in the Noun taxonomy both including and excluding leaf nodes. What percentage of nodes have a branching factor less than 5? Less than 20? Does this tell something you about the shallowness/depth of the taxonomy?

(d) If we plot a graph with the number of senses of each verb in the Verb taxonomy against its polysemy rank, what kind of graph do we get? What conclusion can be drawn from this graph?

(e) Compare the four taxonomies on average polysemy, both including and excluding monosemous words. What conclusions can you draw from this?

Of course, the assignment also contained the usual questions pertaining to the content of the WordNet database rather than just its structure. We believe that this assignment was much more instructive because not only did it afford the students a close examination into the usage as well as structure of a valuable NLP resource, but also required them to apply their knowledge of graph theory.

The second instance where we used a research paper was when writing the HMM question for the final exam. We thought it would be illuminating to ask the students to apply what they had learned in class about HMMs to an instance of HMM used in an actual NLP scenario. For this purpose, we chose the HMM described in (Miller et al., 1999) and as shown in Figure 2. As part of the question, we explained the information retrieval task: generate a ranked list of documents relevant to a user query $U = \langle u_i \rangle$, where the rank of the document D is based on the probability $P(D \text{ is relevant}|U)$. We further explained that by applying Bayes' theorem to this quantity and assuming a uniform prior over document selection, the only important quantity was the probability of the query U being generated by a relevant document D, or $P(U|D \text{ is relevant})$. The rest of the question demonstrated how this generative process could be modeled by the HMM in Figure 2:

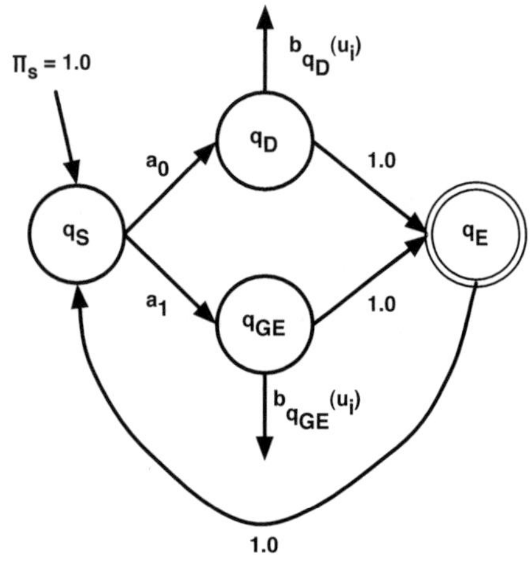

Figure 2: An HMM used and described in a popular research publication formed the basis of a question in the final exam.

- Start at the initial state q_S.
- Transition with the probability a_0 to state q_D which represents choosing a word directly from document D OR transition with probability a_1 to state q_{GE} which represents choosing a word from "General English", i.e., a word unrelated to the document but that occurs commonly in other queries.
- If in state q_D, emit the current, say i^{th}, query word either directly from document D with emission probability $b_{q_D}(u_i)$. Otherwise, if in state q_{GE}, emit the current query word from "General English" with emission probability $b_{q_{GE}}(u_i)$.
- Transition to the end state q_E.
- If we have generated all the words in the query, then stop here. If not, transition to q_S and repeat.

Given this generative process, we then asked the students to answer the following questions:

(a) Derive a simplified closed-form expression for the posterior probability $P(U|D \text{ is relevant})$ in terms of the transition probabilities $\{a_0, a_1\}$ and the emissions probabilities $\{b_{q_D}(u_i), b_{q_{GE}}(u_i)\}$. You may assume that $U = \langle u_i \rangle_{i=1}^{n}$.

(b) What HMM algorithm will you use to compute $P(U|D \text{ is relevant})$ when implementing this model?

(c) How will you compute the maximum likelihood estimate for the emission probability $b_{q_D}(u_i)$?

(d) What about $b_{q_{GE}}(u_i)$? Is it practical to compute the actual value of this estimate? What reasonable approximation might be used in place of the actual value?

This question not only required the students to apply the concepts of probability theory and HMMs that they learned in class but also to contemplate more open-ended research questions where there may be no one right answer.

For both these and other instances where we used ideas from research publications to build assignments and exam questions, we encouraged the students to read the corresponding publications after they had submitted their solutions. In addition, we discussed possible answers with them in an online forum set up especially for the course.

5 Indicators of Success

Since this was our first major revision of the curriculum for an introductory NLP course, we were interested in getting student feedback on the changes that we made. To elicit such feedback, we designed a survey that asked all the students in the class (a total of 30) to rate the new curriculum on a scale of one to five on various criteria, particularly for the experience of using NLTK for all programming assignments and on the quality of the assignments themselves.

Figure 3: Histogram of student feedback on the experience of using the Python-NLTK combination.

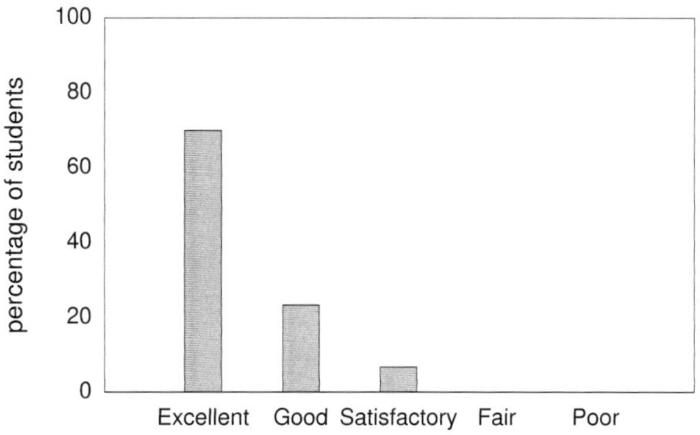

Figure 4: Histogram of student feedback on the quality of course assignments.

Figures 3 and 4 show the histograms of the students' survey responses for these two criteria. The overwhelmingly positive ratings clearly indicate that we were extremely successful in achieving the desired goals for our revised curriculum. As part of the survey, we had also asked the students to provide any comments they had about the curriculum. We received a large number of positive comments some of which we quote below:

"Using Python and NLTK for assignments removed any programming barriers and enabled me to focus on the course concepts."

"The assignments were absolutely fantastic and supplemented the material presented in class."

"A great experience for the students."

The first comment—echoed by several linguistics as well as computer science students—validates our particular choice of programming language and framework. In the past, we had observed that linguistics students with little programming background spent most of their time figuring out how to wield the programming language or tool to accomplish simple tasks. However, the combination of Python and NLTK provided a way for them to work on computational solutions without taking too much time away from learning the core NLP concepts.

While it is clearly apparent to us that the students really liked the new version of the curriculum, it would also have been worthwhile to carry out a comparison of students' reviews of the old and new curricula. The most frequent comments that we saw in older versions of the course were similar to the following:

"Although I feel you did a decent job repeating and pointing out the interesting facts of the book, I don't think you really found many compelling examples of using these techniques in practice."

The feedback we received for the revamped curriculum, such as the second comment above, clearly indicated that we had addressed this shortcoming of the older curriculum. However, due to significant format changes in the review forms between various offerings of this course, it is not possible to conduct a direct, retroactive comparison. It is our intent to offer such comparisons in the future.

6 Future Plans

Given the success that we had in our first attempt to re-engineer the introductory NLP course, we plan to continue: (1) our hands-on approach to programming assignments in the NLTK framework and, (2) our practice of adapting ideas from research publications as the bases for assignment and examination problems. Below we describe two concrete ideas for the next iteration of the course.

1. **Hands-on Statistical Language Modeling**. For this topic, we have so far restricted ourselves to the textbook (Jurafsky and Martin, 2000); the in-class discussion and programming assignments have been missing a hands-on component. We have written a Python interface to the SRI Language Modeling toolkit (Stolcke, 2002) for use in our research work. This interface uses the Simplified Wrapper & Interface Generator (SWIG) to generate a Python wrapper around our C code that does all the heavy lifting via the SRILM libraries. We are currently working on integrating this module into NLTK which would allow all NLTK users, including our students in the next version of the course, to build and query statistical language models directly inside their Python code. This module, combined with the large real-world corpora, would provide a great opportunity to perform hands-on experiments with language models and to understand the various smoothing methods. In addition, this would also allow a language model to be used in an assignment for any other topic should we need it.

2. **Teaching Distributional Similarity**. The idea that a language possesses *distributional structure*—first discussed at length by Harris (1954)—says that one can describe a language in terms of relationships between the occurrences of its *elements* (words, morphemes, phonemes). The name for the phenomenon is derived from an element's *distribution*—sets of other elements in particular positions that occur with the element in utterances or sentences. This work led to the concept of *distributional similarity*—words or phrases that share the same distribution, i.e., the same set of words or in the same context in a corpus, tend to have similar meanings. This is an extremely popular concept in corpus linguistics and forms the basis of a large body of work. We believe that this is an important topic that should be included in the curriculum. We plan to do so in the context of lexical paraphrase acquisition or synonyms automatically from corpora, a task that relies heavily on this notion of distributional similarity. There has been a lot of work in this area in the past years (Pereira et al., 1993; Gasperin et al., 2001; Glickman and Dagan, 2003; Shimohata and Sumita, 2005), much of which can be easily replicated using the Python-NLTK combination. This would allow for a very hands-on treatment and would allow the students to gain insight into this important, but often omitted, idea from computational linguistics.

7 Conclusion

Our primacy goal was to design an introductory level natural language processing course for a class of first year computer science and linguistics graduate students. We wanted the curriculum to encourage the students to approach solutions to problems with the mind-set of a researcher. To accomplish this, we relied on two basic ideas. First, we used a programming framework which provides the tools and data used in the real world so as to allow hands-on exploration of each topic. Second, we adapted ideas from recent research papers into programming assignments and exam questions to provide students with insight into the process of formulating a solution to common NLP problems. At the end of the course, we asked all students to provide feedback and the verdict from both linguistics and computer science students was overwhelmingly in favor of the new more hands-on curriculum.

References

Steven Bird, Ewan Klein, Edward Loper, and Jason Baldridge. 2008. Multidisciplinary Instruction with the Natural Language Toolkit. In *Proceedings of the Third ACL Workshop on Issues in Teaching Computational Linguistics*.

Ann Devitt and Carl Vogel. 2004. The Topology of

WordNet: Some metrics. In *Proceedings of the Second International WordNet Conference (GWC2004)*.

J. Ellson, E.R. Gansner, E. Koutsofios, S.C. North, and G. Woodhull. 2004. Graphviz and Dynagraph – Static and Dynamic Graph Drawing Tools. In *Graph Drawing Software*, pages 127–148. Springer-Verlag.

Christiane Fellbaum. 1998. *WordNet: An Electronic Lexical Database*. Bradford Books.

Caroline Gasperin, P. Gamallo, A. Agustini, G. Lopes, and Vera de Lima. 2001. Using syntactic contexts for measuring word similarity. In *Workshop on Knowledge Acquisition Categorization, ESSLLI*.

Oren Glickman and Ido Dagan. 2003. Identifying lexical paraphrases from a single corpus: A case study for verbs. In *Recent Advantages in Natural Language Processing (RANLP'03)*.

Zellig Harris. 1954. Distributional Structure. *Word*, 10(2):3.146–162.

Daniel Jurafsky and James H. Martin. 2000. *Speech and Language Processing: An Introduction to Natural Language Processing, Computational Linguistics, and Speech Recognition*. Prentice Hall.

Kimmo Koskenniemi. 1983. Two-level morphology: a general computational model for word-form recognition and production. Publication No. 11, University of Helsinki: Department of General Linguistics.

Edward Loper and Steven Bird. 2002. NLTK: The Natural Language Toolkit. In *Proceedings of ACL Workshop on Effective Tools and Methodologies for Teaching NLP and CL*, pages 62–69.

Nitin Madnani. 2007. Getting Started on Natural Language Processing with Python. *ACM Crossroads*, 13(4).

D. R. Miller, T. Leek, and R. M. Schwartz. 1999. A hidden Markov model information retrieval system. In *Proceedings of SIGIR*, pages 214–221.

Fernando Pereira, Naftali Tishby, and Lillian Lee. 1993. Distributional clustering of english words. In *Proceedings of ACL*, pages 183–190.

Python. 2007. The Python Programming Language. `http://www.python.org`.

Lawrence R. Rabiner. 1989. A tutorial on hidden markov models and selected applications in speech recognition. *Proceedings of the IEEE*, 77(2):257–286.

Mitsuo Shimohata and Eiichiro Sumita. 2005. Acquiring synonyms from monolingual comparable texts. In *Proceedings of IJCNLP*, pages 233–244.

Andreas Stolcke. 2002. SRILM – an extensible language modeling toolkit. In *Proceedings of International Conference on Spoken Language Processing (ICSLP)*.

Zero to Spoken Dialogue System in One Quarter: Teaching Computational Linguistics to Linguists Using Regulus

Beth Ann Hockey
Department of Linguistics,
UARC
UC Santa Cruz
Mail-Stop 19-26, NASA Ames
Moffett Field, CA 94035-1000
bahockey@ucsc.edu

Gwen Christian
Department of Linguistics
UCSC
Santa Cruz, CA 95064, USA
jchristi@ucsc.edu

Abstract

This paper describes a Computational Linguistics course designed for Linguistics students. The course is structured around the architecture of a Spoken Dialogue System and makes extensive use of the dialogue system tools and examples available in the Regulus Open Source Project. Although only a quarter long course, students learn Computational Linguistics and programming sufficient to build their own Spoken Dialogue System as a course project.

1 Introduction

Spoken Dialogue Systems model end-to-end execution of conversation and consequently require knowledge of many areas of computational linguistics, speech technology and linguistics. The structure of Spoken Dialogue Systems offers a ready-made structure for teaching a computational linguistics course. One can work through the components and cover a broad range of material in a grounded and motivating way. The course described in this paper was designed for linguistics students, upper-division undergraduate and graduate, many having limited experience with programming or computer science. By the end of a quarter long course, students were able to build a working spoken dialogue systems and had a good introductory level understanding of the related computational linguistics topics.

When this course was first being contemplated, it became apparent that there were a number of somewhat unusual properties that it should have, and a number of useful goals for it to accomplish. The Linguistics Department in which this course is given had only sporadic offerings of computational courses, due in part to having no faculty with a primary focus in Computational Linguistics. linguistics students are very interested in having courses in this area, but even in the University as a whole availability is limited. A course on information extraction is offered in the Engineering School and while some linguistics students are equipped to take that course, many do not have sufficient computer science background or programming experience to make that a viable option.

This course, in the Linguistics department, needed to be for linguistics students, who might not have well-developed computer skills. It needed to fit into a single quarter, be self-contained, depend only on linguistics courses as prerequisites, and give students at least an overview of a number of areas of CL. These students are also interested in connections with industry; now that there are industry jobs available for linguists, students are eager for internships and jobs where they can apply the skills learned in their linguistics courses. Given this, it was also important that the students learn to program during the course, both to make engineering courses more accessible, and to attract potential employers.

In addition, since the department was interested in finding ways to expand computational linguistics offerings, it clearly would be good if the course appealed to the students, the department's faculty and to higher levels of the University administration.

Proceedings of the Third Workshop on Issues in Teaching Computational Linguistics (TeachCL-08), pages 80–86,
Columbus, Ohio, USA, June 2008.

2 Class Demographics

Students in the course are a mix of graduates and upper-division undergraduates with a solid background in syntax and semantics but are not expected to have much in the way of programming experience. Familiarity with Windows, Unix and some minimal experience with shell scripting are recommended but not required. Students have been very successful in the course starting with no programming experience at all. Because the Linguistics department is especially strong in formal linguistics, and the courses typically require extensive problem sets, linguistics students have good aptitude for and experience working with formal systems and this aptitude and skill set seems to transfer quite readily to programming.

3 Regulus Open Source Platform

The Regulus Open Source Platform is a major resource for the course. Regulus is designed for corpus-based derivation of efficient domain-specific speech recognisers from general linguistically-motivated unification grammars. The process of creating an application-specific Regulus recogniser starts with a general unification grammar (UG), together with a supplementary lexicon containing extra domain-specific vocabulary. An application-specific UG is then automatically derived using Explanation Based Learning (EBL) specialisation techniques (van Harmelen and Bundy, 1988). This corpus-based EBL method is parameterised by 1) a small domain-specific training corpus, from which the system learns the vocabulary and types of phrases that should be kept in the specialised grammar, and 2) a set of "operationality criteria", which control the specialised grammar's generality. The application-specific UG is then compiled into a Nuance-compatible CFG. Processing up to this point is all carried out using Open Source Regulus tools. Two Nuance utilities then transform the output CFG into a recogniser. One of these uses the training corpus a second time to convert the CFG into a PCFG; the second performs the PCFG-to-recogniser compilation step. This platform has been used the base for an number of applications including The Clarissa Procedure Browser (Clarissa, 2006) and MedSLT (Bouillon et al., 2005)

The Regulus website (Regulus, 2008) makes available a number of resources, including compilers, an integrated development environment, a Regulus resource grammar for English, online documentation and a set of example dialogue and translation systems. These examples range from completely basic to quite complex. This material is all described in detail in the Regulus book (Rayner et al., 2006), which documents the system and provides a tutorial. As noted in reviews of the book, (Roark, 2007) (Bos, 2008) it is very detailed. To quote Roark, "the tutorial format is terrifically explicit which will make this volume appropriate for undergraduate courses looking to provide students with hands-on exercises in building spoken dialog systems." Not only does the Regulus-based dialogue architecture supply an organizing principle for the course but a large proportion of the homework comes from the exercises in the book. The examples serve as starting points for the students projects, give good illustrations of the various dialogue components and are nice clean programming examples. The more research-oriented material in the Regulus book also provides opportunities for discussion of topics such as unification, feature grammars, ellipsis processing, dialogue-state update, Chomsky hierarchy and compilers. Reviewers of the book have noted a potential problem: although Regulus itself is open source it is currently dependent on two commercial pieces of software, SICStus Prolog and Nuance speech recognition platform (8.5). Nuance 8.5 is a speech recognition developer platform that is widely used for build telephone call centers. This developer kit supplies the acoustic models which model the sounds of the language, the user supplies a language model which defines the range of language that will be recognized for a particular application. This dependance on these commercial products has turned out not to be a serious problem for us since we were able to get a research license from Nuance and purchase a site license for SICStus Prolog. However, beyond the fact that we were able to get licenses, we are not convinced that eliminating the commercial software would be an educational win. While, for example, SWI Prolog might work as well in the course the commercial SISCtus Prolog given a suitable port of Regulus, we think that having the students work with a widely used commercial speech recognition product such as Nuance, is beneficial training for students looking for jobs or internships. Using Nuance also avoids frustration because its performance is dramatically better than the free alternatives.

4 Other Materials

The course uses a variety of materials in addition to the Regulus platform and book. For historical and current views of research in dialogue and speech, course sessions typically begin with an example project or system, usually with a video or a runnable version. Examples of system web materials that we use include: (Resurrected)SHRDLU (`http://www.semaphorecorp.com/misc/shrdlu.html`), TRIPS and TRAINS (`http://www.cs.rochester.edu/research/cisd/projects/trips/movies/TRIPS\_Overview/`), Galaxy (`http://groups.csail.mit.edu/sls//applications/jupiter.shtml`), VocalJoyStick (`http://ssli.ee.washington.edu/vj/`), and ProjectListen (`http://www.cs.cmu.edu/~listen/mm.html`)and NASA's Clarissa Procedure Browser (`http://ti.arc.nasa.gov/projects/clarissa/gallery.php?ta\=\&gid\=\&pid\=`).

Jurasfsky and Martin (Jurafsky and Martin, 2000) is used as an additional text and various research papers are given as reading in addition to the Regulus material. Jurafsky and Martin is also good source for exercises. The Jurafsky and Martin material and the Regulus material are fairly complementary and fit together well in the context of this type of course. Various other exercises are used, including two student favorites: a classic 'construct your own ELIZA' task, and a exercise in reverse engineering a telephone call center, which is an original created for this course.

5 Programming languages

Prolog is used as the primary language in the course for several reasons. First, Prolog was built for processing language and consequently has a natural fit to language processing tasks. Second, as a high-level language, Prolog allows students to stay on a fairly conceptual level and does not require them to spend time learning how to handle low-level tasks. Prolog is good for rapid prototyping; a small amount of Prolog code can do a lot of work and in a one quarter class this is an important advantage. Also, Prolog is very close to predicate logic, which the linguistics students already know from their semantics classes. When the students look at Prolog and see something familiar, it builds confidence and helps make the task of learning to program seem less daunting. The declarative nature of Prolog, which often frustrates computer science students who were well trained in procedural programming, feels natural for the linguists. And finally, the Regulus Open Source System is written mainly in Prolog, so using Prolog for the course makes the Regulus examples maximally accessible.

Note that Regulus does support development of Java dialogue processing components, and provides Java examples. However, the Java based examples are two to three times longer, more complicated and less transparent than their Prolog counterparts, for the same functionality. We believe that the Java based materials would be very good for a more advanced course on multimodal applications, where the advantages of Java would be evident, but in a beginning course for linguists, we find Prolog pedagogically superior.

A potential downside to using Prolog is that it is not a particularly mainstream programming language. If the course was solely about technical training for immediate employment, Java or C++ would probably be better. However, because most students enter the course with limited programming experience, the most important programming outcomes for the course are that they end up with evidence that they can complete a non-trivial programming project, that they gain the experience of debugging and structuring code and that they end up better able to learn additional computer science subsequent to the course. The alternative these students have for learning programming is to take traditional programming courses, starting with an extremely basic introduction to computers course and taking 1-2 additional quarter long courses to reach the level of programming sophistication that they reach in one quarter in this course. In addition, taking the alternative route, they would learn no Computational Linguistics, and would likely find those courses much less engaging.

6 Course Content

Figure 6, depicts relationships between the dialogue system components and related topics both in Linguistics and in Computational Linguistics and/or Computer Science. The course follows the flow of the Dialogue System processing through the various components, discussing topics related to each component. The first two weeks of the course are used as an overview. Spoken Dialogue Systems are put in the context of Computational Linguistics, Speech Technology, NLP and current commercial and research state of the art. General CL tools and techniques are introduced and a quick tour is made of the various dialogue system components. In addition to giving the students background about the field, we want them to be functioning at a basic level with the software at the end of two weeks so that they can begin work on their projects. Following the two week introduction, about two weeks are devoted to each component.

The speech recognition discussion is focused mainly on language modeling. This is an area of particular strength for Regulus and the grammar-based modeling is an easy place for linguists to start. Covering the details of speech recognition algorithms in addition to the other material being covered would be too much for a ten week course. In addition, the department has recently added a course on speech recognition and text-to-speech, so this is an obvious thing to omit from this course. With the Nuance speech recognition platform, there is plenty for the students to learn as users rather than as speech recognition implementers. In practice, it is not unusual for a Spoken Dialogue System implementer to use a speech recognition platform rather than building their own, so the students are getting a realistic experience.

For the Input Management, Regulus has implemented several types of semantic representations, from a simple linear list representation that can be used with the Alterf robust semantics tool, to one that handles complex embedding. So the Input Manager related component can explore the trade offs in processing and representation, using Regulus examples.

The Dialogue Managment section looks at simple finite state dialogue management as well as the dialogue state update approach that has typically been used in Regulus based applications. Many other topics are possible depending on the available time.

The Output Management unit looks at various aspects of generation, timing of actions and could also discuss paraphrase generation or prosodic mark up.

Other topics of a system wide nature such as N-best processing or help systems can be discussed at the end of the course if time allows.

7 Improvements for '08

The course is currently being taught for Spring quarter and a number of changes have been implemented to address what we felt were the weak points of the course as previously taught. It was generally agreed that the first version of the course was quite successful and had many of the desired properties. Students learned Computational Linguistics and they learned how to program. The demo session of the students' projects held at the end of the course was attended by much of the linguistics department, plus a few outside visitors. Attendees were impressed with how much the students had accomplished. In building on that success, we wanted to improve the following areas: enrollment, limiting distractions from the spoken dialogue material, building software engineering skills, making connections with industry and/or research, and visibility.

The first time the course was given, enrollment was six students. This level of enrollment was no doubt in part related to the fact that the course was announced relatively late and students did not have enough lead time to work it into their schedules. The small size was intimate, but it seemed as though it would be better for more students to be able to benefit from the course. For the current course, students knew a year and a half in advance that it would be offered. We also had an information session about the course as part of an internship workshop, and apparently word of mouth was good. With addition of a course assistant the maximum we felt we could handle without compromising the hands-on experience was twenty. Demand greatly exceeded supply and we ended up with twenty two students initially enrolled. As of the deadline for dropping without

Di lo Pro essi
Dialogu Manager

have been successful in running the software with BootCamp. The twice weekly lab sessions also give students a chance do installation and practical lab exercises in an environment in which the course assistant is able see what they are doing, and give them assistance. Observing and getting help from more computationally savy classmates is also common in the labs. Athough the measures taken to reduce the software installation burden still leave some room for improvement, students were able to use Regulus and Nuance successfully, on average, in less than half the time required the first time the course was taught.

The other distracting activity was building the backend for the course projects. Spoken Dialogue Systems are usually an interface technology, but the students in the first offering of the course had to build their projects end to end. While this was not a complete loss, since they did get useful programming experience, it seemed as though it would be an improvement if students could focus more on the spoken dialogue aspects. The approach for doing this in the current course is to recruit Project Partners from industry, government, academic research projects and other university courses. Our students build the spoken dialogue system components and then work with their Project Partner to connect to the Project Partner's system. The students will then demonstrate the project as a whole, that is, their dialogue system working with the Project Partner's material/system, at the course end demo sessions. We have project partners working in areas such as: robotics, telephone based services, automotive industry, and virtual environments. There are a number of potential benefits to this approach. Students are able to spend most of their time on the spoken dialogue system and yet have something interesting to connect to. In fact, they have access to systems that are real research projects, and real commercial products that are beyond what our students would be capable of producing on their own. Students gain the experience of doing a fairly realistic software collaboration, in which they are the spoken dialogue experts. Project partners are enthusiastic because they get to try projects they might not have time or resources to do. Industry partners get to check out potential interns and research partners may find potential collaborators. In the previous version of the course, half of the students who finished the course subsequently worked on Spoken Dialogue oriented research projects connected with the department. One of the students had a successful summer internship with Ford Motors as a result of having taken the course. The research and industry connection was already there, but the Project Partner program strengthens it and expands the opportunities beyond projects connected with the department.

One enhancement to students' software engineering skills in the current version of the course is that students are using version control from day one. Each student in the course is being provided with a Subversion repository with a Track ticket system hosted by Freepository.com. Part of the incentive for doing this was to protect Project Partners' IP, so that materials provided by (particularly commercial) Project Partners would not be housed at the University, and would only be accessible to relevant student(s), the Project Partner, the instructor and the course assistant. The repositories also support remote collaboration making a wider range of organizations workable as project partners. With the repositories the students gain experience with version control and bug-tracking. Having the version control and ticket system should also make the development of their projects easier. Another way we are hoping to enhance the students software skills is through simply having more assistance available for students in this area. We have added the previously mentioned lab sections in the instructional labs, we have arranged for the course assistant to have substantial time available for tutoring, and we are posting tutorials as needed on the course website.

The final area of improvement that we wanted to address is visibility. This is a matter of some practical importance for the course, the addition of CL to the department's offerings, and the students. Visibility among students has improved with word of mouth and with the strategically timed information session held the quarter prior to holding the course. The course end demo session in the first offering of the course did a good job of bringing it to the attention of the students and faculty in the Linguistics Department. For the current course, the Project Partner program provides considerable visibility for students, the department, and the University, among industry, government and other Universities. We are also expanding the demo session at the end of the course. This time the demo session will be held as a University wide event, and will be held at the main UC Santa Cruz campus and a second time at the University's satellite Silicon Valley Center, in order to tap into different potential audiences. The session at the Silicon Valley Center has potential for giving students good exposure to potential employers, and both sessions have good potential for highlighting the Linguistics department.

8 Summary and Conclusion

The course presented in this paper has three key features. First it is designed for linguistics students. This means having linguistics and not computer science as prerequisites and necessitates teaching students programming and computer science when they may start with little or no background. Second, the course takes the architecture of a Spoken Dialogue System as the structure of the course, working through the components and discussing CL topics as they relate to the components. The third feature is the extensive use of the Regulus Open Source platform as key resource for the course. Regulus material is used for exercises, as a base for construction of students' course projects, and for introducing topics such as unification, feature grammars, Chomsky hierarchy, and dialogue management. We have found this combination excellent for teaching CL to linguistics students. The grammar-based language modeling in Regulus, the use of Prolog and relating linguistic topics as well as computational ones to the various dialogue system components, gives linguistics students familiar material to build on. The medium vocabulary type of Spoken Dialogue system supported by the Regulus platform, makes a very motivating course project and students are able to program by the end of the course.

We discuss a number of innovations we have introduced in the latest version of the course, such as the Project Partner program, use of instructional labs and subversion repositories, and expanded course demo session. Since we are teaching the course for the second time during Spring Quarter, we will be able to report on the outcome of these innovations at the workshop.

Acknowledgments

We would like to thank Nuance, for giving us the research licenses for Nuance 8.5 and Vocalizer that helped make this course and this paper possible.

References

Johan Bos. 2008. A review of putting linguistics into speech recognition. the regulus grammar compiler. *Natural Language Engineering*, 14(1).

P. Bouillon, M. Rayner, N. Chatzichrisafis, B.A. Hockey, M. Santaholma, M. Starlander, Y. Nakao, K. Kanzaki, and H. Isahara. 2005. A generic multi-lingual open source platform for limited-domain medical speech translation. In *In Proceedings of the 10th Conference of the European Association for Machine Translation (EAMT)*, Budapest, Hungary.

Clarissa, 2006. http://www.ic.arc.nasa.gov/projects/clarissa/. As of 1 Jan 2006.

D. Jurafsky and J. H. Martin. 2000. *Speech and Language Processing: An Introduction to Natural Language Processing, Computational Linguistics and Speech Recognition*. Prentice Hall Inc, New Jersey.

M. Rayner, B.A. Hockey, and P. Bouillon. 2006. *Putting Linguistics into Speech Recognition: The Regulus Grammar Compiler*. CSLI Press, Chicago.

Regulus, 2008. http://www.issco.unige.ch/projects/regulus/, http://sourceforge.net/projects/regulus/. As of 1 Jan 2008.

Brian Roark. 2007. A review of putting linguistics into speech recognition: The regulus grammar compiler. *Computational Linguistics*, 33(2).

T. van Harmelen and A. Bundy. 1988. Explanation-based generalization = partial evaluation (research note). *Artificial Intelligence*, 36:401–412.

The North American Computational Linguistics Olympiad (NACLO)

Dragomir R. Radev
SI, EECS, and Linguistics
University of Michigan
radev@umich.edu

Lori S. Levin
Language Technologies Institute
Carnegie-Mellon University
lsl@cs.cmu.edu

Thomas E. Payne
Department of Linguistics
University of Oregon
tpayne@uoregon.edu

Abstract

1 Introduction

NACLO (North American Computational Linguistics Olympiad) is an annual Olympiad-style contest for high school students, focusing on linguistics, computational linguistics, and language technologies.

The goal of NACLO is to increase participation in these fields by introducing them before students reach college. Since these subjects are not normally taught in high school, we do not expect students to have any background of these areas before the contest. The contest consists of self-contained problems that can be solved with analytical thinking, but in the course of solving each problem, the students learn something about a language, culture, linguistic phenomenon, or computational tool.

The winners of NACLO are eligible to participate in the International Linguistics Olympiad as part of the US team.

1.1 History of the LO and ILO

The International Olympiad in Linguistics is one of twelve international Science Olympiads (the others include Mathematics, Physics, Chemistry, Biology, Informatics, Philosophy, Astronomy, Geography, and Earth Science). It has existed since 2003 and has, so far, been held exclusively in Europe (Russia, Estonia, Bulgaria, and the Netherlands). ILO 2007 took place in Zelenogorsk near St. Petersburg, Russia whereas ILO 2008 will be in Slantchev Bryag near Burgas, Bulgaria. ILO 2009 will be held in Poland.

Individual national linguistics Olympiads have been held in Russia since 1965 (based on an initiative by Andrey Zaliznyak) and in other countries more recently[1]. Recently, a collection of problems from different decades appeared in Russian (Belikov et al., 2007).

1.2 Linguistics Contests in the US

Thomas Payne pioneered LO-style competitions in the USA by organizing three consecutive contests for middle and high school students in the Eugene, Oregon area in 1998-2000. In the course of publicizing NACLO, we have discovered that other local linguistics contests have taken place in Tennessee, San Jose, and New York City.

1.3 Origin of NACLO

NACLO began with a planning workshop funded by NSF in September 2006. The attendees included faculty and graduate students from about ten universities as well as representatives from NSF and ACL. Two high school teachers were present. The workshop opened with presentations from organizers of other Olympiads and contests in linguistics and computer programming. In particular we received excellent advice from Ivan Derzhanski, representing the International Linguistics Olympiad, and Boris Iomdin, representing the Moscow Olympiad. The remainder of the workshop dealt with scheduling the first contest, elect-

[1] The first author of this paper participated in the Bulgarian national LO in the early 1980s.

Proceedings of the Third Workshop on Issues in Teaching Computational Linguistics (TeachCL-08), pages 87–96,
Columbus, Ohio, USA, June 2008.

ing committee chairs, and making organizational decisions.

1.4 Pedagogical goals

We have two goals in organizing NACLO. We want to increase broad participation and diversity in all language-related careers. We want every student to have a fun and educational experience and have a positive attitude toward taking linguistics and language technologies courses in college. However, we also want to conduct a talent search for the most promising future researchers in our field. NACLO uses two mechanisms to be sure that we reach all levels of participation. The first mechanism is to separate an open round with easier problems from an invitation-only round with harder problems. The second mechanism is related to grading the problems. Forty percent of the score is for a correct answer and sixty percent is for explaining the answer. The students who write the most insightful explanations are the focus of our talent search.

When publicizing NACLO in high schools we have been focusing on certain aspects of linguistics and computer science. With respect to linguistics, we emphasize that languages have rules and patterns that native speakers are not aware of; that there are procedures by which these rules and patterns can be discovered in your own language; and that the same procedures can be used to discover rules and patterns in languages other than your own. With respect to computer science the term *computational thinking* has been coined (Wing 2006) to refer to those parts of the field that are not about computers or programming: thinking algorithmically, using abstraction to model a problem, structuring and reducing a search space, etc.

1.5 Organization at the national level

NACLO has two co-chairs, currently Lori Levin, Carnegie Mellon University, and Thomas Payne, University of Oregon. Dragomir Radev is the program chair and team coach. Amy Troyani, a high school teacher with board certification, is the high school liaison and advisor on making the contest appropriate and beneficial to high school students.

NACLO has several committees. James Pustejovsky currently chairs the sponsorship committee. The other committees are currently unchaired, although we would like to thank William Lewis (outreach and publicity) and Barbara Di Eugenio (followup) for chairing them in the first year. NACLO is not yet registered as a non-profit organization and does not yet have a constitution. We would welcome assistance in these areas.

The national level organization provides materials that are used at many local sites. The materials include a comprehensive web site (http://www.naclo.cs.cmu.edu), practice problems, examples of flyers and press releases, PowerPoint presentations for use in high schools, as well as contest booklets from previous competitions.

The contest is held on the same day in all locations (universities and "online" sites as described below). In 2007 there was a single round with 195 participants. In 2008 there was an open round with 763 participants and an invitation-only round with 115 participants. Grading is done centrally. Each problem is graded at one location to ensure consistency.

Three national prizes are awarded for first, second, and third place. National prizes are also given for the best solution to each problem. Local hosts can also award prizes for first, second, and third place at their sites based on the national scores.

1.6 Funding

The main national expenses are prizes, planning meetings, and the trip to the International Linguistics Olympiad (ILO). The trip to the ILO is the largest expense, including airfare for eight team members (two teams of four), a coach, and two chaperones. The national level sponsors are the National Science Foundation (2007, 2008), Google (2007, 2008), Cambridge University Press (2007, 2008), and the North American Chapter of the Association for Computational Linguistics (2007). The organizers constantly seek additional sponsors.

1.7 Publicity before the contest

At the national level, NACLO is publicized through its own web site as well as on LinguistList and Language Log. From there, word spreads through personal email and news groups. No press releases have been picked up by national papers that we know of. Local level publicity depends on the organization of local schools and the hosting university's high school outreach programs. In Pittsburgh, publicity is facilitated by a central mailing list for gifted program coordinators in the city and county. Some of the other local organizers (including James Pustejosvky at Brandeis, Alina Johnson at the University of Michigan and Barry Schiffman at Columbia University as well as several others) sent mail to literally hundreds of high schools in their areas. Word of mouth from the 2007 contest also helped reach out to more places.

1.8 Registration

NSF REU-funded Justin Brown at CMU created an online registration site for the 2008 contest which proved very helpful. Without such a site, the overhead of dealing with close to 1,000 students, teachers, and other organizers would have been impossible.

1.9 Participation of graduate and undergraduate students

Graduate and undergraduate students participate in many activities including: web site design, visiting high schools, formulating problems, testing problems, advising on policy decisions, and facilitating local competitions.

2 Problem selection

We made a difficult decision early on not to require knowledge of linguistics, programming or mathematics. Requiring these subjects would have reduced diversity in our pool of contestants as well as its overall size. Enrollment in high school programming classes has dropped, perhaps because of a perception that programming jobs are not interesting. NACLO does not require students to know programming, but by introducing a career option, it gives them a reason to take programming classes later.

2.1 Problem types

The NACLO problem sets include two main categories of problems: "traditional" and "computational/formal". The ILO includes mostly traditional problems which include translations from unknown languages, glyph decoding, calendar systems, kinship systems, mathematical expressions and counting systems, among others. The other category deals with linguistic phenomena (often in English) as well as algorithms and formal analyses of text.

2.2 Problem committee

A problem committee was formed each year to work on the creation, pre-testing, and grading of problems. The members in 2007 included Emily Bender, John Blatz, Ivan Derzhanski, Jason Eisner, Eugene Fink, Boris Iomdin, Mahesh Joshi, Anagha Kulkarni, Will Lewis, Patrick Littell, Ruslan Mitkov, Thomas Payne, James Pustejovsky, Roy Tromble, and Dragomir Radev (chair). In 2008, the following people were members: Emily Bender, Eric Breck, Lauren Collister, Eugene Fink, Adam Hesterberg, Joshua Katz, Stacy Kurnikova, Lori Levin, Will Lewis, Patrick Littell, David Mortensen, Barbara Partee, Thomas Payne, James Pustejovsky, Richard Sproat, Todor Tchervenkov, and Dragomir Radev (chair).

2.3 Problem pool

At all times, the problem committee maintains a pool of problems which are constantly being evaluated and improved. Professional linguists and language technologists contribute problems or problem ideas that reflect cutting-edges issues in their disciplines. These are edited and tested for age appropriateness, and the data are thoroughly checked with independent experts.

2.4 Booklets

The three booklets (one for 2007 and two for 2008) were prepared using MS Publisher. Additionally, booklets with solutions were prepared in MS Word. All of these are available from the NACLO web site.

2.5 List of problems

This is the list of problems for NACLO 2007 (8 problems) and 2008 (12 problems). They can be divided into two categories: traditional (2007: C, D, G and 2008: A, C, D, E, G, J, K) and formal/computational (2007: A, B, E, F, H and 2008: B, F, H, I, L). The traditional problems addressed topics such as phonology, writing systems, calendar systems, and cognates, among others. The other category included problems on stemming, finite state automata, clustering, sentence similarity identification, and spectrograms.

2007

A. English (Molistic)
B. English (Encyclopedia)
C. Ancient Greek
D. Hmong
E. English (Verb forms)
F. English (Spelling correction)
G. Huishu (Phonology)
H. English (Sentence processing)

2008 (A-E Open; F-L Invitational)

A. Apinaye (Brazil)
B. Hindi
C. Ilocano (Philippines)
D. Swedish and Norwegian
E. Aymara (South America)
F. Japanese
G. Manam Pile (Papua New Guinea)
H. English (Stemming)
I. Rotokas (Automata; Bougainville Island)
J. Irish
K. Mayan (Calendar)
L. English (Spectrograms)

Figure 1: List of languages used in NACLO 2007 and 2008.

3 Contest administration

NACLO is run in a highly distributed fashion and involves a large number of sites across the USA in Canada.

3.1 Local administration

NACLO is held at hosting universities and also "online". The online category includes students who cannot get to one of the hosting universities, but instead are monitored by a teacher at a convenient location, usually the student's high school. There were three hosting universities (Carnegie-Mellon, Brandeis, and Cornell) in 2007 and thirteen hosting universities (the three above + U. Michigan, U. Illinois, U. Oregon, Columbia, Middle Tennessee State, San Jose State, U. Wisconsin, U. Pennsylvania, U. Ottawa, and U. Toronto) in 2008. Any university in the US or Canada may host NACLO. Local organizers are responsible for providing a room for the contest, contacting high local high schools, and facilitating the contest on the specified contest date. Local organizers may decide on the number of participants. The number of participants at the 2008 sites ranged from a handful to almost 200 (CMU-Pitt).

Local organizers may choose their level of investment of time and money. They may spend only a few hours recruiting participants from one or two local high schools and may spend a small amount of money on school visits and copying. But they may also run large scale operations including extensive fundraising and publicity. The site with the largest local participation, Carnegie Mellon/University of Pittsburgh, donated administrative staff time, invested hundreds of volunteer hours, and raised money for snacks and souvenirs from local sponsors[2]. The CMU-Pitt site also hosts a problem club for faculty and students where problems are proposed, fleshed out, and tested. At the University of Oregon, a seminar course was taught on Language Task Creation (formulation of problems) for which university students received academic credit.

3.2 Remote ("online") sites

We had about 65 such sites in 2008. All local teachers and other facilitators did an amazing job following the instructions for administering the competition and for promptly returning the submissions by email or regular mail.

3.3 Clarifications

During each of the three competitions, the jury was online (in some cases for 8 hours in a row) to provide live clarifications. Each local facilitator was asked to be online during the contest and relay to the jury any questions from the students. The jury then, typically within 10 minutes, either replied "no clarification needed" (the most frequent reply) or provided an answer which was than posted online for all facilitators to see. We received dozens of clarifications requests at each of the rounds.

3.4 Grading

Grading was done by the PC with assistance from local colleagues. To ensure grade consistency, each problem was assigned to a single

[2] We are grateful to the Pittsburgh sponsors: M*Modal, Vivísimo, JustSystems Evans Research, and Carnegie Mellon's Leonard Gelfand Center for Service Learning and Outreach.

grader or team of graders. Graders were asked to provide grading rubrics which assigned individual points for both "practice" (that is, getting the right answers) and "theory" (justifying the answers).

3.5 Results from 2007

195 students participated in 2007. The winners are shown here. One of the students was a high school sophomore (15 years old) while three were seniors at the time of the 2007 NACLO.

1. Rachel Zax, Ithaca, NY
2. Ryan Musa, Ithaca, NY
3. Adam Hesterberg, Seattle, WA
4. Jeffrey Lim, Arlington, MA
5. (tie) Rebecca Jacobs, Encino, CA
5. (tie) Michael Gottlieb, Tarrytown, NY
7. (tie) Mitha Nandagopalan, San Jose, CA
7. (tie) Josh Falk, Pittsburgh, PA

Alternate. Anna Tchetchetkine, San Jose, CA

Figure 2: List of team members from 2007. Mitha was unable to travel and was replaced by Anna Tchetchetkine.

3.6 2008 Winners

The 2008 contest included 763 participants in the Open Round and 115 participants in the Invitational Round. The winners of the Invitational Round are listed below. These are the eight students who are eligible to represent the USA at the 2008 ILO. As of the writing of this paper, all eight were available for the trip. One of the eight is a high school freshman (9th grade).

1. Guy Tabachnick, New York, NY
2. Jeffrey Lim, Arlington, MA
3. Josh Falk, Pittsburgh, PA
4. Anand Natarajan, San Jose, CA
5. Jae-Kyu Lee, Andover, MA
6. Rebecca Jacobs, Encino, CA
7. Hanzhi Zhu, Shrewsbury, MA
8. Morris Alper, San Jose, CA

Figure 3: List of team members from 2008.

3.7 Canadian Participation

Canada participated for the first time in 2008 (about 20 students from Toronto, a handful from Ottawa and one from Vancouver). Two students did really well at the 2008 Open (one ranked second and two tied for 13th) but were not in the top 20 at the Invitational.

3.8 Diversity

About half of the participants in NACLO were girls in 2007 and 2008. In 2007, 25 out of the top 50 students were female.

The two US teams that went to the ILO in 2007 included three girls, out of eight total team members (two teams of four). The 2008 teams include only one girl.

3.9 Other statistics

Some random statistics: (a) of the top 20 students in 2008, 14 are from public schools, (b) 26 states, 3 Canadian provinces, and the District of Columbia were represented in 2008.

4 Preparation for the ILO

Preparation for the ILO was a long and painful process. We had to obtain visas for Russia, fund and arrange for the trip, and do a lot of practices.

4.1 Teams

One of the students who was eligible to be on the second USA team was unable to travel. We went down the list of alternates and picked a different student to replace her.

4.2 Funding

The ILO covered room and board for the first team and the team coach. The second team was largely self-funded (including airfare and room and board). Everyone else was funded as part of the overall NACLO budget. The University of Michigan covered the coach's airfare.

4.3 Training

We ran multiple training sessions. The activities included individual problem solving, team problem solving (using Skype's chat facility), readings, as well as live lectures (both at the summer school in Estonia and on the day before the main ILO in Russia).

4.4 Travel logistics

Four students, two chaperones, and one parent left early to attend a summer school organized by the Russian team in Narva, Estonia. The third chaperone and three students traveled directly to the ILO. The eighth student traveled with her parents and did some sightseeing in Russia prior to the ILO.

5 Participation in the ILO

The ILO was organized by a local committee from St. Petersburg chaired by Stanislav Gurevych. The organization was extraordinary. Everything (problem selection, grading, hotel, activities, food) was excellent.

5.1 Organization of the ILO

The ILO was held at a decent hotel in Zelenogorsk, a suburb of St. Petersburg on the Baltic Sea. The first day included an orientation, the second day was the individual contest and team building activities, the third day – an excursion to St. Petersburg, the fourth day – the team contest and awards ceremony.

5.2 Problems

The problems given at the ILO were quite diverse and difficult. The hardest problems were the one in the Ndom language which involved a nonstandard number system and the Hawaiian problem given at the team contests which involved a very sophisticated kinship system.

Turkish/Tatar
Braille
Ndom (Papua New Guinea)
Movima (Bolivia)
Georgian (Caucasus)
Hawaiian

Figure 4: List of languages used in ILO 2007.

5.3 Results

Adam Hesterberg scored the highest score in the individual contest. One of the two US teams (Rebecca Jacobs, Joshua Falk, Michael Gottlieb, and Anna Tchetchetkine) tied for first place in the team event.

6 Future directions

The unexpected interest in the NACLO poses a number of challenges for the organizers. Further challenges arise from our desire to cover more computational problems.

6.1 Grading and decentralization?

Grading close to 5,000 submissions from 763 students in 2008 took a toll on our problem committee. The process took more than two weeks. We are considering different options for future years, e.g., reducing the number of problems in the first round or involving some sort of self-selection (e.g., asking each potential participant to do a practice test and obtain a minimal score on it). These options are suboptimal as they detract from some of the stated goals of the NACLO and we will not consider them seriously unless all other options (e.g., recruiting more graders). have been exhausted.

6.2 Problem diversity

We would like to include more problem types, especially on the computational end of the contest. This is somewhat of a conflict with the ILO which includes mostly "traditional" LO problems. One possibility is to have the first round be more computational whereas the invitational round would be more aimed at picking the team members for the ILO by focusing more on traditional problems.

6.3 Practice problems

We will be looking to recruit a larger pool of problem writers who can contribute problems of various levels of difficulty (including very easy problems and problems based on the state of the art in research in NLP). We are also looking for volunteers to translate problems from Russian, including the recently published collection "Zadachi Lingvisticheskyh Olimpiad".

6.4 Other challenges

The biggest challenges for the NACLO in both years were funding and time management.

In 2007, four of the students had to pay for their own airfare and room and board. At the time of writing, the budget for 2008 is still not fully covered. The current approach with regard to sponsorship is not sustainable since NSF cannot fund recurring events and the companies that we approached either gave nothing or gave a relatively small amount compared to the overall annual budget.

The main organizers of the NACLO each spent several hundred hours (one of them claims "the equivalent to 20 ACL program committee chairmanships"), mostly above and beyond their regular appointments. For NACLO to scale up and be successful in the future, a much wider pool of organizers will be needed.

6.5 Other countries

Dominique Estival told us recently that an LO will take place in Australia in Winter 2008 (that is, Summer 2008 in the Northern Hemisphere). OzLO (as it is called) will be collaborating with NACLO on problem sets. Other countries such as the United Kingdom and the Republic of Ireland are considering contests as well. One advantage that these countries all have is that they can share (English-language) problem sets with NACLO.

6.6 Participant self-selection

Some Olympiads provide self-selection problems. Students who score poorly on these problem sets are effectively discouraged from participation in the official contest. If the number of participants keeps growing, we may need to consider this option for NACLO.

6.7 More volunteers

NACLO exerted a tremendous toll on the organizers. Thousands of hours of volunteer work went into the event each year. NACLO desperately needs more volunteers to help at all levels (problem writing, local organization, web site maintenance, outreach, grading, etc).

7 Overall assessment

While it will take a long time to properly assess the impact of NACLO 2007 and 2008, we have some preliminary observations to share.

7.1 Openness

We made a very clear effort to reach out to all high school students in the USA and Canada. Holding the contest online helped make it truly within everyone's reach. Students and teachers overwhelmingly appreciated the opportunity to participate at no cost (other than postage to send the submissions back to the jury) and at their own schools. Students who participated at the university sites similarly expressed great satisfaction at the opportunity to meet with peers who share their interests.

7.2 Diversity and outreach

We were pleased to see that the number of male and female participants was nearly equal. A number of high schools indicated that clubs in Linguistics were being created or were in the works.

7.3 Success at the ILO

Even though the US participated for the first time at the ILO, the performance shown there (including first place individually and a tie for first place in the team contest) was outstanding.

Acknowledgments

We want to thank everyone who helped turn NACLO into a successful event. Specifically, Amy Troyani from Taylor Allderdice High School in Pittsburgh, Mary Jo Bensasi of CMU, all problem writers and graders (which include the PC listed above as well as Rahel Ringger and Julia Workman) and all local contest organizers (James Pustejovsky, Lillian Lee, Claire Cardie, Mitch Marcus, Kathy McKeown, Barry Schiffman, Lori Levin, Catherine Arnott Smith, Richard Sproat, Roxana Girju, Steve Abney, Sally Thomason, Aleka Blackwell, Roula Svorou, Thomas Payne, Stan Szpakowicz, Diana Inkpen, Elaine Gold). James Pustejovsky was also the sponsorship chair, with help from Paula Chesley. Ankit Srivastava, Ronnie Sim and Willie Costello co-wrote some of the problems with members of the PC. Eugene Fink helped with the solutions booklets, Justin Brown worked on the web site, and Adam Hesterberg was an invaluable member of the team throughout. Other people who deserve our gratitude include Cheryl Hickey, Alina Johnson, Patti Kardia, Josh Cannon, Christina Hunt, Jennifer Wofford, and Cindy Robinson. Finally, NACLO couldn't have happened without the leadership and funding provided by NSF and Tanya Korelsky in particular as well as the generous sponsorship from Google, Cambridge University Press, and the North American Chapter of the ACL (NAACL).

The authors of this paper are also thankful to Martha Palmer for giving us feedback on an earlier draft.

NACLO was partially funded by the National Science Foundation under grant IIS 0633871 Planning Workshop for a Computational Linguistics Olympiad.

References

Vasileios Hatzivassiloglou and Kathleen McKeown. 1997. Predicting the Semantic Orientation of Adjectives, ACL 1997.

Jeannette Wing, Computational Thinking, CACM vol. 49, no. 3, March 2006, pp. 33-35.

V. I. Belikov, E. V. Muravenko and M. E. Alexeev, editors. Zadachi Lingvisticheskikh Olimpiad. MTsNMO. Moscow, 2007.

Appendix A. Summary of freeform comments

"I think it's a great outreach tool to high schools. I was especially impressed by the teachers who came and talked to [the linguistics professors] about starting a linguistics club"

"The problems are great. One of our undergraduates expressed interest in a linguistics puzzle contest (on the model of Google's and MS's puzzle contests) at the undergrad level."

"We got a small but very high-quality group of students. To get a larger group, we'd need to start earlier."

"Things could be more streamlined. I think actually *less* communication, but at key points in the process, would be more effective."

"It also would have been nice if there were a camp, like with the other US olympiads, so that more students would get the chance to learn about linguistics"

"Just get the word out to as many schools as possible. You could also advertise on forums like AOPS, Cogito, and even CollegeConfidential ... where students are looking for intellectual challenges".

"The problems helped develop the basic code breaking."

"Having a camp would be a huge benefit, but otherwise I think the contest was done very well. Thank you for bringing it to the US."

"Maybe send a press release to school newspapers and ask them to print something about it."

"My 9 students enjoyed participating even though none of them made it to the second round. Several have indicated that they want to do it again next year now that they know what it is like."

"I used every opportunity to utter the phrase "computational linguistics" to other administrators, at meetings, with parents, students, other teachers. People inevitably want to know more!"

"As I mentioned previously, we are all set to start up a new math/WL club next year. YAY!"

"Advertise with world language professional organizations (i.e., ACTFL) and on our ListServs (i.e., FLTeach)"

"It was wonderful. KUDOS!"

"There were several practice sessions, about half run by a math teacher (who organizes many of the competitions of this nature) and half by the Spanish teacher. Also, several of the English teachers got really excited about it (especially the teacher who teaches AP English Language, who teaches often about logical reasoning) and offered extra credit to the students who took it."

"The preparation for the naclo was done entirely by the math club."

"It was a very useful competition. First, it raised awareness about linguistics among our students. They knew nothing about this area before, and now they are looking for opportunities to study linguistics and some started visiting linguistic research seminars at the University of Washington."

"The Olympiad was interesting to most students because it was very different from all the other math Olympiads we participate in. Students saw possibilities for other application of their general math skills. In addition, the students who won (reasonably succeeded in) this Olympiad were not the same students that usually win math contests at our school. This was very useful for their confidence, and showed everybody that broadening skills is important."

"I was the only one to take the contest from my school, so it didn't really increase awareness that much. I, however, learned a lot about linguistics, and the people who I told about the contest seemed to find it interesting also."

"As a result of this competition, an Independent-Study Linguistics Course was offered this spring for a few interested students."

"Three students who participated in NACLO are now doing an Independent Study course with my colleague from th

e World Languages dept (who had a linguistics course in college)"

"I'd like to see more linguistic indoctrination, so that math nerds are converted over to the good side."

"next year I will teach a Computational Linguistics seminar"

Appendix B. Related URLs

```
http://www.naclo.cs.cmu.edu/
http://www.cogito.org/ContentRedirect.aspx?
    ContentID=16832
http://www.cogito.org/Interviews/
    InterviewsDetail.aspx?ContentID=16901
http://www.ilolympiad.spb.ru/
http://cty.jhu.edu/imagine/PDFs/Linguistics.pdf
http://www.nsf.gov/news/news_summ.jsp?
    cntn_id=109891
http://photofile.name/users/anna_stargazer/2949079/
```

Figure 5: List of additional references URLs.

Appendix C. Sample problems

We include here some sample problems as well as one solution. The rest of the solutions are available on the NACLO Web site.

C.1. Molistic

This is a problem from 2007 written by Dragomir Radev and based on [Hatzivassiloglou and McKeown 1997].

> Imagine that you heard these sentences:
>
> Jane is molistic and slatty.
> Jennifer is cluvious and brastic.
> Molly and Kyle are slatty but danty.
> The teacher is danty and cloovy.
> Mary is blitty but cloovy.
> Jeremiah is not only sloshful but also weasy.
> Even though frumsy, Jim is sloshful.
> Strungy and struffy, Diane was a pleasure to watch.
> Even though weasy, John is strungy.
> Carla is blitty but struffy.
> The salespeople were cluvious and not slatty.
>
> 1. Then which of the following would you be likely to hear?
>
> a. Meredith is blitty and brastic.
> b. The singer was not only molistic but also cluvious.
> c. May found a dog that was danty but sloshful.
>
> 2. What quality or qualities would you be looking for in a person?
>
> a. blitty
> b. weasy
> c. sloshful
> d. frumsy
>
> 3. Explain all your answers. (Hint: The sounds of the words are not relevant to their meanings.)

Figure 6: "Molistic" problem from 2007.

C.2. Garden Path

This is another problem from 2007.

> True story: a major wireless company recently started an advertising campaign focusing on its claim that callers who use its phones experience fewer dropped calls.
>
> The billboards for this company feature sentences that are split into two parts. The first one is what the recipient of the call hears, and the second one - what the caller actually said before realizing that the call got dropped. The punch line is that dropped calls can lead to serious misunderstandings. We will use the symbol // to separate the two parts of such sentences.
>
> (1) Don't bother coming // early.
> (2) Take the turkey out at five // to four.
> (3) I got canned // peaches.
>
> These sentences are representative of a common phenomenon in language, called "garden path sentences". Psychologically, people interpret sentences incrementally, before waiting to hear the full text. When they hear the ambiguous start of a garden path sentence, they assume the most likely interpretation that is consistent with what they have heard so far. They then later backtrack in search of a new parse, should the first one fail.
>
> In the specific examples above, on hearing the first part, one incorrectly assumes that the sentence is over. However, when more words arrive, the original interpretation will need to be abandoned.
>
> (4) All Americans need to buy a house // is a large amount of money.
> (5) Melanie is pretty // busy.
> (6) Fat people eat // accumulates in their bodies.
>
> 1. Come up with two examples of garden path sentences that are not just modifications of the ones above and of each other. Split each of these two sentences into two parts and indicate how hearing the second part causes the hearer to revise his or her current parse.
>
> For full credit, your sentences need to be such that the interpretation of the first part should change as much as possible on hearing the second part. For example, in sentence (6) above, the interpretation of the word "fat" changes from an adjective ("fat people") to a noun ("fat [that] people eat..."). Note: sentences like "You did a great job..., // NOT!" don't count.
>
> 2. Rank sentences (4), (5), (6) as well as the two sentences from your solution to H1 above, based on how surprised the hearer is after hearing the second part. What, in your opinion, makes a garden path sentence harder to process by the hearer?

Figure 7: "Garden Path" problem from 2007.

C.3. Ilocano

This 2008 problem was written by Patrick Littell of the University of Pittsburgh.

The Ilocano language is one of the major languages of the Philippines, spoken by more than 8 million people. Today is it written in the Roman alphabet, which was introduced by the Spanish, but before that Ilocano was written in the *Baybayin* script. *Baybayin* (which literally means "spelling") was used to write many Philippine languages and was in use from the 14th to the 19th centuries.

1. Below are twelve Ilocano words written in Baybayin. Match them to their English translations, listed in scrambled order below.

___________ (×12)

{ to look, is skipping for joy, is becoming a skeleton, to buy, various skeletons, various appearances, to reach the top, is looking, appearance, summit, happiness, skeleton }

2. Fill in the missing forms.

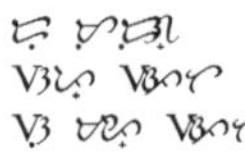

___________ (×3)

___________ (the/a) purchase

___________ is buying

3. Explain your answers to 1 and 2.

Figure 8: Ilocano problem from 2008.

Practical: 11 points

1. Translations (1/2 point each)

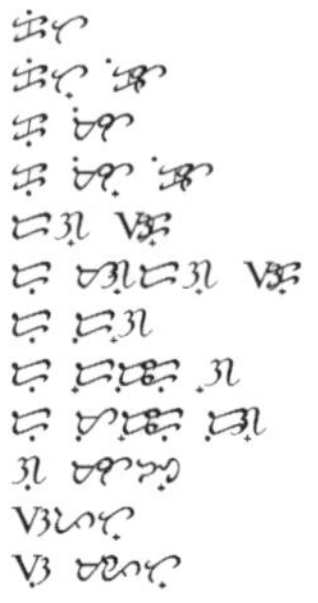

appearance
various appearances
to look
is looking
happiness
is skipping for joy
skeleton
various skeletons
is becoming a skeleton
to buy
summit
to reach the top

2. Missing forms (1 point each)

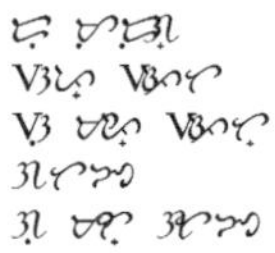

to become a skeleton
various summits
is reaching the top
(the/a) purchase
is buying

Assign ½ point each if the basic symbols (the consonants) are correct, and the other ½ point if the diacritics (the vowels) are correct.

Theoretical: 9 points

* The first step in this problem must be to divide the English items into semantically similar groups (**1 pt**) and divide the Baybayin items into groups based on shared symbols (**1 pt**).

* From this they can deduce that the group including 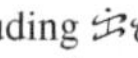 must correspond to the "look/appearances" group (4 members each), that including 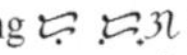 to the "skeleton" group (3 members each), and  must be "to buy" (1 each). For getting this far they should get another **2 points**.

* Figuring out the nature of the Baybayin alternations is the tricky part. A maximally good explanation will discover that there are two basic processes:

- From the basic form, copy the initial two symbols and add them to the beginning. The first should retain whatever diacritic it might have, but the second should have its diacritic (if any) replaced by a cross below.
- Insert  as the second symbol, and move the initial symbol's diacritic (if any) to this one. Add an underdot to the first symbol.

* Discovering these two processes, and determining that the third process is the result of doing both, is worth **3 points**. Discovering these two processes, and describing the third as an unrelated process – that is, not figuring out that it's just a combination of the first two – is worth **2 points**. Figuring out these processes without reference to the diacritics is worth **1 point**, whether or not they correctly determine the nature of the third process.

* All that remains is to match up which processes indicate which categories, which shouldn't be hard if they've gotten this far. Their description of how to determine this is worth another **1 point**.

* The remaining **1 point** is reserved to distinguish particularly elegant solutions described with unusual clarity.

Competitive Grammar Writing*

Jason Eisner
Department of Computer Science
Johns Hopkins University
Baltimore, MD 21218, USA
jason@cs.jhu.edu

Noah A. Smith
Language Technologies Institute
Carnegie Mellon University
Pittsburgh, PA 15213, USA
nasmith@cs.cmu.edu

Abstract

Just as programming is the traditional introduction to computer science, writing grammars by hand is an excellent introduction to many topics in computational linguistics. We present and justify a well-tested introductory activity in which teams of mixed background compete to write probabilistic context-free grammars of English. The exercise brings together symbolic, probabilistic, algorithmic, and experimental issues in a way that is accessible to novices and enjoyable.

1 Introduction

We describe a hands-on group activity for novices that introduces several central topics in computational linguistics (CL). While the task is intellectually challenging, it requires no background other than linguistic intuitions, no programming,[1] and only a very basic understanding of probability.

The activity is especially appropriate for mixed groups of linguists, computer scientists, and others, letting them collaborate effectively on small teams and learn from one another. A friendly competition among the teams makes the activity intense and enjoyable and introduces quantitative evaluation.

1.1 Task Overview

Each 3-person team is asked to write a generative context-free grammar that generates as much of English as possible (over a small fixed vocabulary). Obviously, writing a *full* English grammar would take years even for experienced linguists. Thus each team will only manage to cover a few phenomena, and imperfectly.

To encourage precision but also recall and linguistic creativity, teams are rewarded for generating sentences that are (prescriptively) grammatical but are not anticipated by other teams' grammars. This somewhat resembles scoring in the Boggle word game, where players are rewarded for finding valid words in a grid that are not found by other players.

A final twist is that the exercise uses *probabilistic* context-free grammars (PCFGs); the actual scoring methods are based on sampling and cross-entropy. Each team must therefore decide how to allocate probability mass among sentences. To avoid assigning probability of zero when attempting to parse another team's sentences, a team is allowed to "back off" (when parsing) to a simpler probability model, such as a part-of-speech bigram model, also expressed as a PCFG.

1.2 Setting

We have run this activity for six consecutive years, as a laboratory exercise on the *very first* afternoon of an intensive 2-week summer school on various topics in human language technology.[2] We allot 3.5 hours in this setting, including about 15 minutes for setup, 30 minutes for instructions, 15 minutes for evaluation, and 30 minutes for final discussion.

The remaining 2 hours is barely enough time for team members to get acquainted, understand the requirements, plan a strategy, and make a small dent in

* This work was supported by NSF award 0121285, "ITR/IM+PE+SY: Summer Workshops on Human Language Technology: Integrating Research and Education," and by a Fannie and John Hertz Foundation Fellowship to the second author. We thank David A. Smith and Markus Dreyer for co-leading the lab in 2004–2007 and for implementing various improvements in 2004–2007 and for providing us with data from those years. The lab has benefited over the years from feedback from the participants, many of whom attended the JHU summer school thanks to the generous support of NAACL. We also thank the anonymous reviewers for helpful comments.

[1] In our setup, students do need the ability to invoke scripts and edit files in a shared directory, e.g., on a Unix system.

[2] This 2-week course is offered as a prelude to the Johns Hopkins University summer research workshops, sponsored by the National Science Foundation and the Department of Defense. In recent years the course has been co-sponsored by the North American ACL.

Proceedings of the Third Workshop on Issues in Teaching Computational Linguistics (TeachCL-08), pages 97–105,
Columbus, Ohio, USA, June 2008. ©2008 Association for Computational Linguistics

the problem. Nonetheless, participants consistently tell us that the exercise is enjoyable and pedagogically effective, almost always voting to stay an extra hour to make further progress.

Our 3-person teams have consisted of approximately one undergraduate, one junior graduate student, and one more senior graduate student. If possible, each team should include at least one member who has basic familiarity with some syntactic phenomena and phrasal categories. Teams that wholly lack this experience have been at a disadvantage in the time-limited setting.

1.3 Resources for Instructors

We will maintain teaching materials at `http://www.clsp.jhu.edu/grammar-writing`, for both the laboratory exercise version and for homework versions: scripts, data, instructions for participants, and tips for instructors. While our materials are designed for participants who are fluent in English, we would gladly host translations or adaptations into other languages, as well as other variants and similar assignments.

2 Why Grammar Writing?

A computer science curriculum traditionally starts with *programming*, because programming is accessible, hands-on, and necessary to motivate or understand most other topics in computer science. We believe that *grammar writing* should play the same role in computational linguistics—as it often did before the statistical revolution[3]—and for similar reasons.

Grammar writing remains central because many theoretical and applied CL topics center around grammar formalisms. Much of the field tries to design expressive formalisms (akin to programming languages); solve linguistic problems within them (akin to programming); enrich them with probabilities; process them with efficient algorithms; learn them from data; and connect them to other modules in the linguistic processing pipeline.

Of course, there are interesting grammar formalisms at all levels of language processing. One might ask why *syntax* is a good level at which to begin education in computational linguistics.

First, starting with syntax establishes at the start that there are formal and computational methods specific to natural language. Computational linguistics is not merely a set of applied tasks to be solved with methods already standardly taught in courses on machine learning, theory of computation,[4] or knowledge representation.

Second, we have found that syntax captures students' interest rapidly. They quickly appreciate the linguistic phenomena, see that they are non-trivial, and have little trouble with the CFG formalism.

Third, beginning specifically with PCFGs pays technical dividends in a CL course. Once one understands PCFG models, it is easy to understand the simpler finite-state models (including n-gram models, HMMs, etc.) and their associated algorithms, either by analogy or by explicit reduction to special cases of PCFGs. CFGs are also a good starting point for more complex syntactic formalisms (BNF, categorial grammars, TAG, LFG, HPSG, etc.) and for compositional semantics. Indeed, our exercise motivates these more complex formalisms by forcing students to work with the more impoverished PCFG formalism and experience its limitations.

3 Educational Goals of the Exercise

Our grammar-writing exercise is intended to serve as a touchstone for discussion of many subsequent topics in NLP and CL (which are *italicized* below). As an instructor, one can often refer back later to the exercise to remind students of their concrete experience with a given concept.

Generative probabilistic models. The first set of concepts concerns *language models*. These are easiest to understand as processes for generating text. Thus, we give our teams a script for *generating random sentences* from their grammar and their backoff

[3]The first author was specifically inspired by his experience writing a grammar in Bill Woods's NLP course at Harvard in 1987. An anonymous reviewer remarks that such assignments were common at the time. Our contributions are to introduce statistical and finite-state elements, to make the exercise into a game, and to provide reusable instructional materials.

[4]Courses on theory of computation do teach pushdown automata and CFGs, of course, but they rarely touch on parsing or probabilistic grammars, as this exercise does. Courses on compilers may cover parsing algorithms, but only for restricted grammar families such as unambiguous LR(1) grammars.

model—a helpful way to observe the generative capacity and qualitative behavior of any model.

Of course, in practice a generative grammar is most often run "backwards" to *parse an observed sentence* or score its *inside probability*, and we also give the teams a script to do that. Most teams do actually run these scripts repeatedly to test their grammars, since both scripts will be central in the evaluation (where sentences are randomly generated from one grammar and scored with another grammar).

It is common for instructors of NLP to show examples of randomly-generated text from an n-gram model (e.g., Jurafsky and Martin, 2000, pp. 202–203), yet this amusing demonstration may be misinterpreted as merely illustrating the inadequacy of n-gram models. Our use of a hand-crafted PCFG *combined with* a bigram-based (HMM) backoff grammar demonstrates that although the HMM is much worse at *generating* valid English sentences (precision), it is much better at robustly assigning nonzero probability when *analyzing* English sentences (recall).

Finally, generative models do more than assign probability. They often involve linguistically meaningful *latent variables*, which can be recovered given the observed data. Parsing with an appropriate PCFG thus yields a intuitive and useful analysis (a *syntactic parse tree*), although only for the sentences that the PCFG covers. Even parsing with the simple backoff grammar that we initially provide yields some coarser analysis, in the form of a part-of-speech tagging, since this backoff grammar is a right-branching PCFG that captures part-of-speech bigrams (for details see §1.1, §4.1, and Table 2). In fact, parsing with the backoff PCFG is isomorphic to Viterbi decoding in an *HMM part-of-speech tagger*, a topic that is commonly covered in NLP courses.

Modeling grammaticality. The next set of concepts concerns linguistic grammaticality. During the evaluation phase of our exercise (see below), students must make *grammaticality judgments* on other teams' randomly generated sentences—which are usually nonsensical, frequently hard for humans to parse, and sometimes ungrammatical. This concrete task usually prompts questions from students about how grammaticality ought to be defined, both for purposes of the task and in principle. It could also be used to discuss why some of the sentences are so hard for humans to understand (e.g., garden-path and frequency effects) and what *parsing strategies* humans or machines might use.

The exercise of modeling grammaticality with the CFG formalism, a formalism that appears elsewhere in the computer science curriculum, highlights some important differences between natural languages and formal languages. A natural language's true grammar is unknown (and may not even exist: perhaps the CFG formalism is inadequate). Rather, a grammar must be *induced or constructed* as an approximate model of corpus data and/or certain native-speaker intuitions. A natural language also differs from a programming language in including *ambiguous sentences*. Students observe that the parser *uses probabilities to resolve ambiguity*.

Linguistic analysis. Grammar writing is an excellent way to get students thinking about *linguistic phenomena* (e.g., adjuncts, embedded sentences, *wh*-questions, clefts, point absorption of punctuation marks). It also forces students to think about appropriate *linguistic formalisms*. Many phenomena are tedious to describe within CFGs (e.g., agreement, movement, subcategorization, selectional restrictions, morphological inflection, and phonologically-conditioned allomorphy such as a vs. an). They can be treated in CFGs only with a large number of repetitive rules. Students appreciate these problems by grappling with them, and become very receptive to designing expressive improvements such as feature structures and slashed categories.

Parameter tuning. Students observe the *effects of changing the rule probabilities* by running the scripts. For example, teams often find themselves generating unreasonably long (or even infinite) sentences, and must damp down the probabilities of their recursive rules. Adjusting the rule probabilities can also change the score and optimal tree that are returned by the parser, and can make a big difference in the final evaluation (see §5). This appreciation for the role of numerical parameters helps motivate future study of *machine learning* in NLP.

Quantitative evaluation. As an engineering pursuit, NLP research requires objective evaluation measures to know how well systems work.

Our first measure is the *precision* of each team's

probabilistic grammar: how much of its probability mass is devoted to sentences that are truly grammatical? Estimating this requires human grammaticality judgments on a *random sample* C of sentences generated from all teams' grammars. These binary judgments are provided by the participants themselves, introducing the notion of linguistic *annotation* (albeit of a very simple kind). Details are in §4.3.3.

Our second measure is an upper-bound approximation to *cross-entropy* (or log-perplexity—in effect, the *recall* of a probability model): how well does each team's probabilistic model (this time including the backoff model of §1.1) anticipate unseen data that are truly grammatical? (Details in §4.3.3.)

Note that in contrast to parsing competitions, we do not evaluate the quality of the parse trees (e.g., PARSEVAL). Our cross-entropy measure evaluates only the grammars' ability to predict word strings (language modeling). That is because we impose no annotation standard for parse trees: each team is free to develop its own theory of syntax. Furthermore, many sentences will only be parsable by the backoff grammar (e.g., a bigram model), which is not expected to produce a full syntactic analysis.

The lesson about cross-entropy evaluation is slightly distorted by our peculiar choice of test data. In principle, the instructors might prepare a batch of grammatical sentences ahead of time and split them into a *test set* (used to evaluate cross-entropy at the end) and a *development set* (provided to the students at the start, so that they know which grammatical phenomena are important to handle). The activity could certainly be run in this way to demonstrate *proper experimental design* for evaluating a language model (discussed further in §5 and §6). We have opted for the more entertaining "Boggle-style" evaluation described in §1.1, where teams try to stump one another by generating difficult test data, using the fixed vocabulary. Thus, we evaluate each team's cross-entropy on all grammatical sentences in the collection C, which was generated *ex post facto* from all teams' grammars.

4 Important Details

4.1 Data

A few elements are provided to participants to get them started on their grammars.

Vocabulary. The terminal vocabulary Σ consists of words from early scenes of the film *Monty Python and the Holy Grail* along with some inflected forms and function words, for a total vocabulary of 220 words. For simplicity, only 3rd-person pronouns, nouns, and verbs are included. All words are case-sensitive for readability (as are the grammar nonterminals), but we do not require or expect sentence-initial capitalization.

All teams are restricted to this vocabulary, so that the sentences that they generate will not frustrate other teams' parsers with out-of-vocabulary words. However, they are free to use words in unexpected ways (e.g., using castle in its verbal sense from chess, or building up unusual constructions with the available function words).

Initial lexicon. The initial *lexical rules* take the form $T \rightarrow w$, where $w \in \Sigma^+$ and $T \in \mathcal{T}$, with $\mathcal{T}$ being a set of six coarse part-of-speech tags:

Noun: 21 singular nouns starting with consonants

Det: 9 singular determiners

Prep: 14 prepositions

Proper: 8 singular proper nouns denoting people (including multiwords such as Sir Lancelot)

VerbT: 6 3rd-person singular present transitive verbs

Misc: 183 other words, divided into several commented sections in the grammar file

Students are free to change this tagset. They are especially encouraged to refine the Misc tag, which includes 3rd-person plural nouns (including some proper nouns), 3rd-person pronouns (nominative, accusative, and genitive), additional 3rd-person verb forms (plural present, past, stem, and participles), verbs that cannot be used transitively, modals, adverbs, numbers, adjectives (including some comparative and superlative forms), punctuation, coordinating and subordinating conjunctions, *wh*-words, and a few miscellaneous function words (to, not, 's).

The initial lexicon is ambiguous: some words are associated with more than one tag. Each rule has weight 1, meaning that a tag T is equally likely to rewrite as any of its allowed nonterminals.

Initial grammar. We provide the "S1" rules in Table 1, so that students can try generating and parsing

1	S1	→	NP VP .
1	VP	→	VerbT NP
20	NP	→	Det Nbar
1	NP	→	Proper
20	Nbar	→	Noun
1	Nbar	→	Nbar PP
1	PP	→	Prep NP

Table 1: The S1 rules: a starting point for building an English grammar. The start symbol is S1. The weights in the first column will be normalized into generative probabilities; for example, the probability of expanding a given NP with NP → Det Nbar is actually $20/(20+1)$.

1	S2	→	
1	S2	→	_Noun
1	S2	→	_Misc
1	_Noun	→	Noun
1	_Noun	→	Noun _Noun
1	_Noun	→	Noun _Misc
1	_Misc	→	Misc
1	_Misc	→	Misc _Noun
1	_Misc	→	Misc _Misc

Table 2: The S2 rules (simplified here where $\mathcal{T} = \{\text{Noun}, \text{Misc}\}$): a starting point for a backoff grammar. The start symbol is S2. The _Noun nonterminal generates those phrases that start with Nouns. Its 3 rules mean that following a Noun, there is 1/3 probability each of stopping, continuing with another Noun (via _Noun), or continuing with a Misc word (via _Misc).

sentences right away. The S1 and lexical rules together implement a very small CFG. Note that no Misc words can yet be generated. Indeed, this initial grammar will only generate some simple grammatical SVO sentences in singular present tense, although they may be unboundedly long and ambiguous because of recursion through Nbar and PP.

Initial backoff grammar. The provided "S2" grammar is designed to assign positive probability to any string in Σ^* (see §1.1). At least initially, this PCFG generates only right-branching structures. Its nonterminals correspond to the states of a weighted finite-state machine, with start state S2 and one state per element of $\mathcal{T}$ (the coarse parts of speech listed above). Table 2 shows a simplified version.

From each state, transition into any state except the start state S2 is permitted, and so is stopping. These rules can be seen as specifying the *transitions* in a bigram hidden Markov model (HMM) on part-of-speech tags, whose *emissions* are specified by the lexical rules. Since each rule initially has weight 1, all part-of-speech sequences of a given length are equally likely, but these weights could be changed to arbitrary transition probabilities.

Arthur is the king .
Arthur rides the horse near the castle .
riding to Camelot is hard .
do coconuts speak ?
what does Arthur ride ?
who does Arthur suggest she carry ?
are they suggesting Arthur ride to Camelot ?
Guinevere might have known .
it is Sir Lancelot who knows Zoot !
neither Sir Lancelot nor Guinevere will speak of it .
the Holy Grail was covered by a yellow fruit .
do not speak !
Arthur will have been riding for eight nights .
Arthur , sixty inches , is a tiny king .
Arthur and Guinevere migrate frequently .
he knows what they are covering with that story .
the king drank to the castle that was his home .
when the king drinks , Patsy drinks .

Table 3: Example sentences. Only the first two can be parsed by the initial S1 and lexical rules.

Start rules. The initial grammar S1 and the initial backoff grammar S2 are tied together by a single symbol START, which has two production rules:

99	START	→	S1
1	START	→	S2

These two rules are obligatory, but their weights may be changed. The resulting model, rooted at START, is a *mixture* of the S1 and S2 grammars, where the weights of these two rules implement the mixture coefficients. This is a simple form of backoff smoothing by linear interpolation (Jelinek and Mercer, 1980). The teams are warned to pay special attention to these rules. If the weight of START → S1 is decreased relative to START → S2, then the model relies more heavily on the backoff model—perhaps a wise choice for keeping cross-entropy small, if the team has little faith in S1's ability to parse the forthcoming data.

Sample sentences. A set of 27 example sentences in Σ^+ (subset shown in Table 3) is provided for linguistic inspiration and as practice data on which to run the parser. Since only 2 of these sentences can be parsed with the initial S1 and lexical rules, there is plenty of room for improvement. A further development set is provided midway through the exercise (§4.3.2).

4.2 Computing Environment

We now describe how the above data are made available to students along with some software.

4.2.1 Scripts

We provide scripts that implement two important capabilities for PCFG development. Both scripts are invoked with a set of grammar files specified on the command line (typically all of them, "`*.gr`"). A PCFG is obtained by concatenating these files and stripping their comments, then normalizing their rule weights into probabilities (see Table 1), and finally checking that all terminal symbols of this PCFG are legal words of the vocabulary Σ.

The **random generation** script prints a sample of n sentences from this PCFG. The generator can optionally print trees or flat word sequences. A start symbol other than the default S1 may be specified (e.g., NP, S2, START, etc.), to allow participants to test subgrammars or the backoff grammar.[5]

The **parsing** script prints the most probable parse tree for each sentence read from a file (or from the standard input). A start symbol may again be specified; this time the default is START. The parser also prints each sentence's probability, total *number of parses*, and the fraction of the probability that goes to the best parse.

Tree outputs can be pretty-printed for readability.

4.2.2 Collaborative Setup

Teams of three or four sit at adjacent workstations with a shared filesystem. The scripts above are publicly installed; a handout gives brief usage instructions. The instructor and teaching assistant roam the room and offer assistance as needed.

Each team works in its own shared directory. The Emacs editor will warn users who are simultaneously editing the same file. Individual participants tend to work on different sub-grammar files; all of a team's files can be concatenated (as `*.gr`) when the scripts are run. (The directory initially includes separate files for the S1 rules, S2 rules, and lexical rules.) To avoid unexpected interactions among these grammar fragments, students are advised to divide work based on nonterminals; e.g., one member of a team may claim jurisdiction over all rules of the form VP_plural $\rightarrow \cdots$.

4.3 Activities

4.3.1 Introductory Lecture

Once students have formed themselves into teams and managed to log in at adjacent computers, we begin with an 30-minute introductory lecture. No background is assumed. We explain PCFGs simply by showing the S1 grammar and hand-simulating the action of the random sentence generator.

We explain the goal of extending the S1 grammar to cover more of English. We explain how each team's precision will be evaluated by human judgments on a sample, but point out that this measure gives no incentive to increase coverage (recall). This motivates the "Boggle" aspect of the game, where teams must also be able to parse one another's grammatical sentences, and indeed assign them as high a probability as possible. We demonstrate how the parser assigns a probability by running it on the sentence that we earlier generated by hand.[6]

We describe how the parser's probabilities are turned into a cross-entropy measure, and discuss strategy. Finally, we show that parsing a sentence that is not covered by the S1 grammar will lead to infinite cross-entropy, and we motivate the S2 backoff grammar as an escape hatch.

4.3.2 Midpoint: Development data

Once or more during the course of the exercise, we take a snapshot of all teams' S1 grammars and sample 50 sentences from each. The resulting collection of sentences, in random order, is made available to all teams as a kind of development data. While we do not filter for grammaticality as in the final evaluation, this gives all participants an idea of what they will be up against when it comes time

[5] For some PCFGs, the stochastic process implemented by the script has a nonzero probability of failing to terminate. This has not caused problems to date.

[6] The probability will be tiny, as a product of many rule probabilities. But it may be higher than expected, and students are challenged to guess why: there are additional parses beyond the one we hand-generated, and the parser sums over all of them.

to parse other teams' sentences. Teams are on their honor not to disguise the true state of their grammar at the time of the snapshot.

4.3.3 Evaluation procedure

Grammar development ends at an announced deadline. The grammars are now evaluated on the two measures discussed in §3. The instructors run a few scripts that handle most of this work.

First, we generate a collection C by sampling 20 sentences from each team's probabilistic grammar, using S1 as the start symbol. (Thus, the backoff S2 grammar is not used for generation.)

We now determine, for each team, what fraction of its 20-sentence sample was grammatical. The participants play the role of grammaticality judges. In our randomized double-blind procedure, each individual judge receives (in his or her team directory) a file of about 20 sentences from C, with instructions to delete the ungrammatical ones and save the file, implying coarse Boolean grammaticality judgments.[7] The files are constructed so that each sentence in C is judged by 3 different participants; a sentence is considered grammatical if ≥ 2 judges thinks that it is.

We define the test corpus $\hat{C}$ to consist of all sentences in C that were judged grammatical. Each team's full grammar (using START as the start symbol to allow backoff) is used to parse $\hat{C}$. This gives us the $\log_2$-probability of each sentence in $\hat{C}$; the cross-entropy score is the sum of these $\log_2$-probabilities divided by the length of $\hat{C}$.

4.3.4 Group discussion

While the teaching assistant is running the evaluation scripts and compiling the results, the instructor leads a general discussion. Many topics are possible, according to the interests of the instructor and participants. For example: What linguistic phenomena did the teams handle, and how? Was the CFG formalism adequately expressive? How well would it work for languages other than English?

What strategies did the teams adopt, based on the evaluation criteria? How were the weights chosen?

[7]Judges are on their honor to make fair judgments rather than attempt to judge other teams' sentences ungrammatical. Moreover, such an attempt might be self-defeating, as they might unknowingly be judging some of their own team's sentences ungrammatical.

		cross-entropy	new rules	
team	precision	(bits/sent.)	lex.	other
A	0.30	**35.57**	202	111
B	0.00	54.01	304	80
C	**0.80**	38.48	179	48
D	0.25	49.37	254	186
E	0.55	39.59	198	114
F	0.00	39.56	193	37
G	0.65	40.97	71	15
H	0.30	36.53	176	9
I	0.70	36.17	181	54
J	0.00	∞	193	29

Table 4: Teams' evaluation scores in one year, and the number of new rules (not including weight changes) that they wrote. Only teams A and H modified the relative weights of the START rules (they used 80/20 and 75/25, respectively), giving them competitive perplexity scores. (Cross-entropy in this year was approximated by an upper bound that uses only the probability of each sentence's single best parse.)

How would you build a better backoff grammar?[8]

How would you organize a real long-term effort to build a full English grammar? What would such a grammar be good for? Would you use any additional tools, data, or evaluation criteria?

5 Outcomes

Table 4 shows scores achieved in one year (2002).

A valuable lesson for the students was the importance of backoff. None but the first two of the example sentences (Table 3) are parseable with the small S1 grammar. Thus, the best way to reduce perplexity was to upweight the S2 grammar and perhaps spend a little time improving its rules or weights. Teams that spent all of their time on the S1 grammar may have learned a lot about linguistics, but tended to score poorly on perplexity.

Indeed, the winning team in a later year spent nearly all of their effort on the S2 grammar. They placed almost all their weight on the S2 grammar, whose rules they edited and whose parameters they estimated from the example sentences and development data. As for their S1 grammar, it generated only a small set of grammatical sentences with ob-

[8]E.g., training the model weights, extending it to trigrams, or introducing syntax into the S2 model by allowing it to invoke nonterminals of the S1 grammar.

scure constructions that other teams were unlikely to model well in *their* S1 grammars. This gave them a 100% precision score on grammaticality while presenting a difficult parsing challenge to other teams. This team gamed our scoring system, exploiting the idiosyncrasy that S2 would be used to parse but not to generate. (See §3 for an alternative system.)

We conducted a *post hoc* qualitative survey of the grammars from teams in 2002. Teams were not asked to provide comments, and nonterminal naming conventions often tend to be inscrutable, but the intentions are mostly understandable. All 10 teams developed more fine-grained parts of speech, including coordinating conjunctions, modal verbs, number words, adverbs. 9 teams implemented singular and plural features on nouns and/or verbs, and 9 implemented the distinction between base, past, present, and gerund forms of verbs (or a subset of those). 7 teams brought in other features like comparative and superlative adjectives and personal vs. possessive pronouns. 4 teams modeled pronoun case. Team C created a "location" category.

7 teams explicitly tried to model questions, often including rules for *do*-support; 3 of those teams also modeled negation with *do*-insertion. 2 teams used gapped categories (team D used them extensively), and 7 teams used explicit $\bar{X}$ nonterminals, most commonly within noun phrases (following the initial grammar). Three teams used a rudimentary subcategorization frame model, distinguishing between sentence-taking, transitive, and intransitive verbs, with an exploded set of production rules as a result. Team D modeled appositives.

The amount of effort teams put into weights varied, as well. Team A used 11 distinct weight values from 1 to 80, giving 79 rules weights > 1 (next closest was team 10, with 7 weight values in $[1, 99]$ and only 43 up-weighted rules). Most teams set fewer than 25 rules' weights to something other than 1.

6 Use as a Homework Assignment

Two hours is not enough time to complete a *good* grammar. Our participants are ambitious but never come close to finishing what they undertake; Table 4 reflects incomplete work. Nonetheless, we believe that the experience still successfully fulfills many of the goals of §2–3 in a short time, and the participants enjoy the energy in a roomful of peers racing toward a deadline. The fact that the task is open-ended and clearly impossible keeps the competition friendly.

An alternative would be to allot 2 weeks or more as a homework assignment, allowing teams to go more deeply into linguistic issues and/or backoff modeling techniques. A team's grade could be linked to its performance. In this setting, we recommend limiting the team size to 1 or 2 people each, since larger teams may not be able to find time or facilities to work side-by-side for long.

This homework version of our exercise might helpfully be split into two assignments:

Part 1 (non-competitive, smaller vocabulary). "Extend the initial S1 grammar to cover a certain small set of linguistic phenomena, as illustrated by a development set [e.g., Table 3]. You will be evaluated on the cross-entropy of your grammar on a test set that closely resembles the development set [see §3], and perhaps also on the acceptability of sentences sampled from your grammar (as judged by you, your classmates, or the instructor). You will also receive qualitative feedback on how correctly and elegantly your grammar solves the linguistic problems posed by the development set."

Part 2 (competitive, full 220-word vocabulary). "Extend your S1 grammar from Part 1 to generate phenomena that stump other teams, and add an S2 grammar to avoid being stumped by them. You will be evaluated as follows ... [see §4.3.3]."

We have already experimented with simpler non-competitive grammar-writing exercises (similar to Part 1) in our undergraduate NLP courses. Given two weeks, even without teammates, many students do a fine job of covering several non-trivial syntactic phenomena. These assignments are available for use by others (see §1.3). In some versions, students were asked to write their own random generator, judge their own sentences, explain how to evaluate perplexity, or guess why the S2 grammar was used.

7 Conclusion

We hope that other instructors can make use of these materials or ideas. Our competitive PCFG-writing game touches upon many core CL concepts, is challenging and enjoyable, allows collaboration, and is suitable for cross-disciplinary and intro courses.

References

F. Jelinek and R. L. Mercer. 1980. Interpolated estimation of Markov source parameters from sparse data. In *Proc. of Workshop on Pattern Recognition in Practice*.

D. Jurafsky and J.H. Martin. 2000. *Speech and Language Processing*. Prentice Hall.

Studying Discourse and Dialogue with SIDGrid*

Gina-Anne Levow
Department of Computer Science
University of Chicago
Chicago, IL 60611, USA
levow@cs.uchicago.edu

Abstract

Teaching Computational Linguistics is inherently multi-disciplinary and frequently poses challenges and provides opportunities in teaching to a student body with diverse educational backgrounds and goals. This paper describes the use of a computational environment (SIDGrid) that facilitates interdisciplinary instruction by providing support for students with little computational background as well as extending the scale of projects accessible to students with more advanced computational skills. The environment facilitates the use of hands-on exercises and is being applied to interdisciplinary instruction in Discourse and Dialogue.

1 Introduction

Teaching Computational Linguistics poses many challenges but also provides many opportunities. Students in Computational Linguistics courses come from diverse academic backgrounds, including computer science, linguistics, and psychology. The students enter with differing experience and exposure to programming, computational and mathematical models, and linguistic, psycholinguistic and sociolinguistic theories that inform the practice and study of computational linguistics. However, studying in a common class provides students with the opportunity to gain exposure to diverse perspectives on their research problems and to apply computational tools and techniques to expand the range and scope of problems they can investigate.

While there are many facets of these instructional challenges that must be addressed to support a successful course with a multi-disciplinary class and perspective, this paper focuses on the use and development of a computational environment to support laboratory exercises for students from diverse backgrounds. The framework aims to facilitate collaborative projects, reduce barriers of entry for students with little prior computational experience, and to provide access to large-scale distributed processing resources for students with greater computational expertise to expand the scope and scale of their projects and exercises.

Specifically, we exploit the Social Informatics Data Grid (SIDGrid) framework developed as part of the NSF-funded Cyberinfrastructure project, "Cyberinfrastructure for Collaborative Research in the Social and Behavioral Sciences (PI: Stevens)", to support hands-on annotation and analysis exercises in a computational linguistics course focused on discourse and dialogue. We begin by describing the SIDGrid framework for annotation, archiving, and analysis of multi-modal, multi-measure data. We then describe the course setting and the application of SIDGrid functionality to expand exercise and project possibilities. Finally, we discuss the impact of this framework for multi-disciplinary instruction in computational linguistics as well as the limitations of the current implementation of the framework.

*The work is supported by a University of Chicago Academic Technology Innovation Grant.

Proceedings of the Third Workshop on Issues in Teaching Computational Linguistics (TeachCL-08), pages 106–113,
Columbus, Ohio, USA, June 2008.

2 SIDGrid Framework

2.1 Motivation

Recent research programs in multi-modal environments, including understanding and analysis of multi-party meeting data and oral history recording projects, have created an explosion of multi-modal data sets, including video and audio recordings, transcripts and other annotations, and increased interest in annotation and analysis of such data. A number of systems have been developed to manage and support annotation of multi-modal data, including Annotation Graphs (Bird and Liberman, 2001), Exmeralda (Schmidt, 2004), NITE XML Toolkit (Carletta et al., 2003), Multitool (Allwood et al., 2001), Anvil (Kipp, 2001), and Elan (Wittenburg et al., 2006). The Social Informatics Data Grid (SIDGrid), developed under the NSF Cyberinfrastructure Program, aims to extend the capabilities of such systems by focusing on support for large-scale, extensible distributed data annotation, sharing, and analysis. The system is open-source and multi-platform and based on existing open-source software and standards. The system greatly eases the integration of annotation with analysis though user-defined functions both on the client-side for data exploration and on the TeraGrid for large-scale distributed data processing. A web-accessible repository supports data search, sharing, and distributed annotation. While the framework is general, analysis of spoken and multi-modal discourse and dialogue data is a primary application.

The details of the system are presented below. Sections 2.2, 2.3, and 2.4 describe the annotation client, the web-accessible data repository, and the portal to the TeraGrid, respectively, as shown in Figure 1 below.

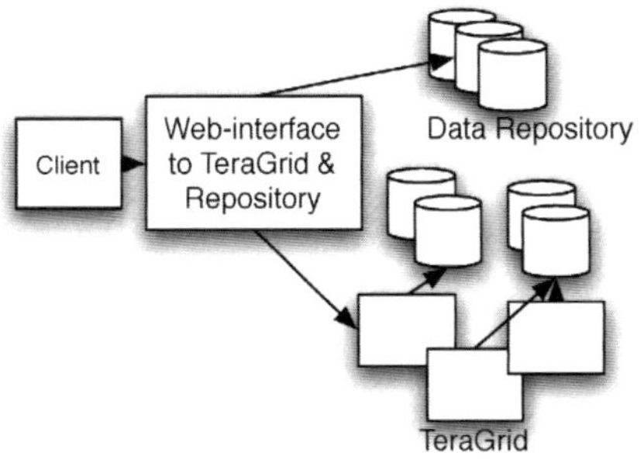

Figure 1: System Architecture

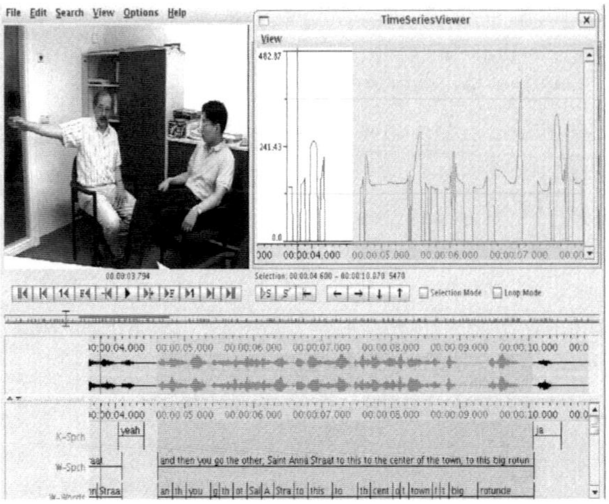

Figure 2: Screenshot of the annotation client interface, with video, time-aligned textual annotations, and time series displays.

2.2 The SIDGrid Client

The SIDGrid client provides an interactive multi-modal annotation interface, building on the open-source ELAN annotation tool from the Max Planck Institute[1]. A screenshot appears in Figure 2. ELAN supports display and synchronized playback of multiple video files, audio files, and arbitrarily many annotation "tiers" in its "music-score"-style graphical interface. The annotations are assumed to be time-aligned intervals with, typically, text content; the system leverages Unicode to provide multilingual support. Time series such as pitch tracks or motion capture data can be displayed synchronously. The user may interactively add, edit, and do simple search in annotations. For example, in multi-modal multi-party spoken data, annotation tiers corresponding to aligned text transcriptions, head nods, pause, gesture, and reference can be created.

The client expands on this functionality by allowing the application of user-defined analysis programs to media, time series, and annotations associated with the current project, such as a conversation, to yield time series files or annotation tiers displayed in the client interface. Any program with a command-line or scriptable interface installed on the user's system may be added to a pull-down list for invocation. For example, to support a prosodic

[1] http://www.mpi.nl/tools/elan.html

analysis of multi-party meeting data, the user can select a Praat (Boersma, 2001) script to perform pitch or intensity tracking. Also, the client provides integrated import and export capabilities for the central repository. New and updated experiments and annotations may be uploaded directly to the archive from within the client interface. Existing experiments may be loaded from local disk or downloaded from the repository for additional annotation.

2.3 The SIDGrid Repository

The SIDGrid repository provides a web-accessible, central archive of multi-modal data, annotations, and analyses. This archive facilitates distributed annotation efforts by multiple researchers working on a common data set by allowing shared storage and access to annotations, while keeping a history of updates to the shared data, annotations, and analysis.

The browser-based interface to the archive allows the user to browse or search the on-line data collection by media type, tags, project identifier, and group or owner. Once selected, all or part of any experiment may be downloaded. In addition to lists of experiment names or thumbnail images, the web interface also provides a streaming preview of the selected media and annotations, allowing verification prior to download. (Figure 3)

All data is stored in a MySQL database. Annotation tiers are converted to an internal time-span based representation, while media and time series files are linked in unanalyzed. This format allows generation of ELAN format files for download to the client tool without regard to the original source form of the annotation file. The database structure further enables the potential for flexible search of the stored annotations both within and across multiple annotation types.

2.4 The TeraGrid Portal

The large-scale multimedia data collected for multimodal research poses significant computational challenges. Signal processing of gigabytes of media files requires processing horsepower that may strain many local sites, as do approaches such as multi-dimensional scaling for semantic analysis and topic segmentation. To enable users to more effectively exploit this data, the SIDGrid provides a portal to the TeraGrid (Pennington, 2002), the largest distributed cyberinfrastructure for open scientific research, which uses high-speed network connections to link high performance computers and large scale data stores distributed across the United States. While the TeraGrid has been exploited within the astronomy and physics communities, it has been little used by the computational linguistics community.

The SIDGrid portal to the TeraGrid allows large-scale experimentation by providing access to large-scale distributed processing clusters to enable parallel processing on very high capacity servers. The SIDGrid portal to the TeraGrid allows the user to specify a set of files in the repository and a program or programs to run on them on the Grid-based resources. Once a program is installed on the Grid, the processing can be distributed automatically to different TeraGrid nodes. Software supports arbitrarily complex workflow specifications, but the current SIDGrid interface provides simple support for high degrees of data-parallel processing, as well as a graphical display indicating the progress of the distributed program execution, as shown in Figure 4. The results are then reintegrated with the original experiments in the on-line repository. Currently installed programs support distributed acoustic analysis using Praat, statistical analysis using R, and matrix computations using Matlab and Octave.

2.5 Software Availability

The client software is freely available. Access to the public portion of the repository is possible through the project website at `https://sidgrid.ci.uchicago.edu`; full access to the repository to create new experiments may also be requested there.

3 Course Setting and Activities

We explore the use of this framework in a course which focuses on a subarea of Computational Linguistics, specifically discourse and dialogue, targeted at graduate students interested in research in this area. This topic is the subject of research not only in computational speech and language processing, but also in linguistics, psychology, sociology, anthropology, and philosophy. Research in this area draws on a growing, large-scale collection of text and multi-modal interaction data that often relies on

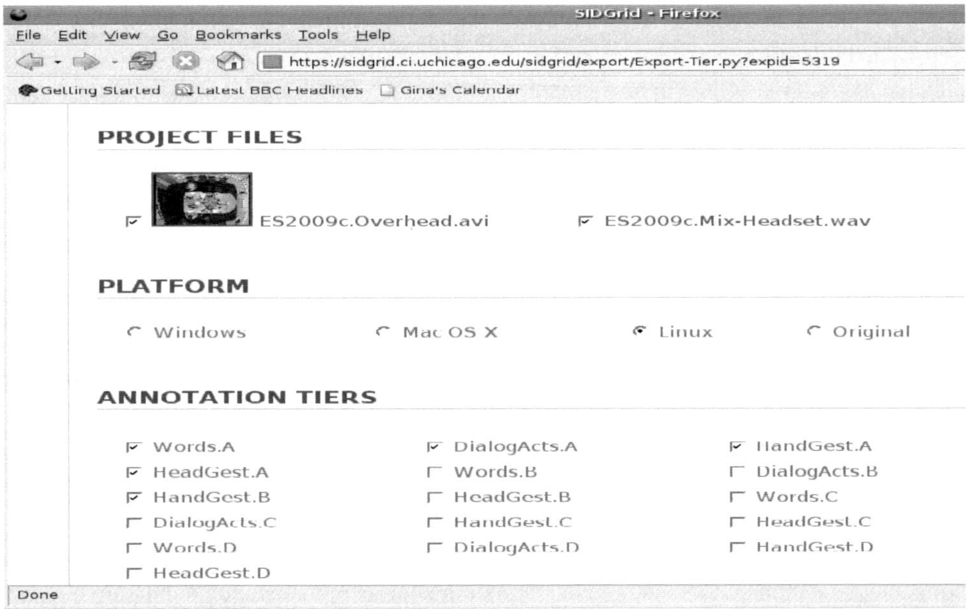

Figure 3: Screenshot of the archive download interface, with thumbnails of available video and download and analysis controls.

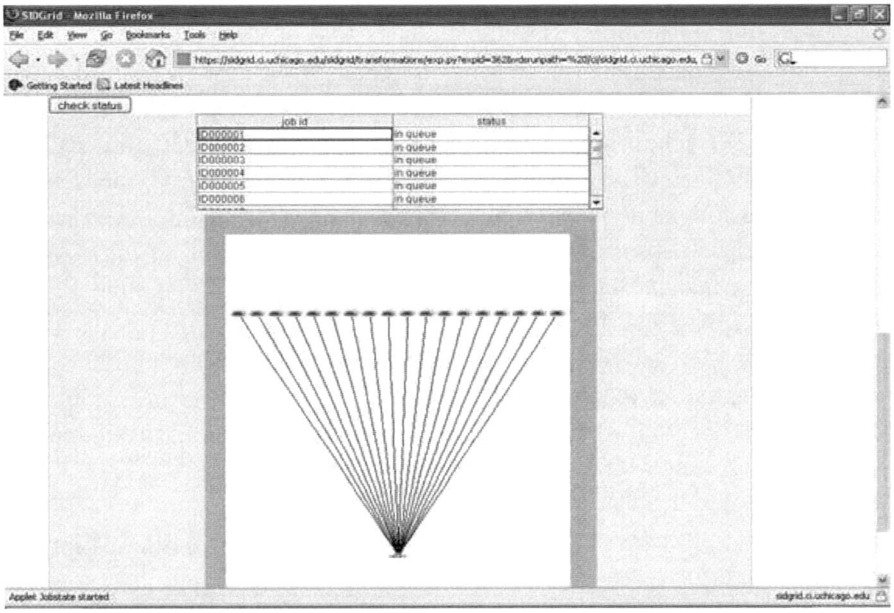

Figure 4: Progress of execution of programs on TeraGrid. Table lists file identifiers and status. Graph shows progress.

computational tools to support annotation, archiving, and analysis. However, prior offerings of this course through the Computer Science Department had attracted primarily Computer Science graduate students, even though readings for the course spanned the range of related fields. In collaboration with researchers in co-verbal gesture in the Psychology department, we hoped to increase the attraction and accessibility of the course material and exercises to a more diverse student population. After advertising the course to a broader population through the Linguistics Department mailing list, emphasizing the use of computational tools but lack of requirements for previous programming experience, the resulting class included members of the Linguistics, Slavic Studies, Psychology, and Computer Science Departments, about half of whom had some prior programming experience, but few were expert.

3.1 Hands-on Exercises

Currently, we have only included a small number of software tools as proof-of-concept and to enable particular course exercises in discourse and dialogue. This first set of exercises explores three main problems in this area: topic segmentation, dialogue act tagging, and turn-taking.

The topic segmentation exercise investigates the impact of segment granularity and automatic speech recognition errors on topic segmentation of conversational speech. The data is drawn from the Cross-Language Speech Retrieval Track of the Cross-language Evaluation Forum (CLEF CL-SR) (Pecina et al., 2007) collection. This collection includes automatic transcriptions of interviews from an oral history project, accompanied by manual segmentation created as part of the MALACH project (Franz et al., 2003). The exercise employs the web-based portal to the TeraGrid to perform segmentation of multiple interviews in parallel on the Grid, followed by evaluation in parallel. We perform segmentation using LCSeg (Galley et al., 2003) and evaluate using the p_k and WindowDiff metrics. Students identify the best segmentation parameters for these interviews and perform error analysis to assess the effect of ASR errors.

The dialogue act tagging exercise involves both annotation and analysis components. The students are asked to download and annotate a small portion of a conversation from the AMI corpus (Carletta et al., 2005) with dialogue act tags. The AMI corpus of multiparty meetings includes recorded video, recorded audio, aligned manual transcriptions, and manually annotated head and hand gesture. Students annotate from text alone, with audio, with video, and with all modalities. Local "transformations", programs or scripts associated with the annotation client, can also provide prosodic analysis of features such as pitch and intensity. Students are asked to assess the influence of different features on their annotation process and to compare to a gold standard annotation which is later provided. The automatic analysis phase is performed on the web-based portal to assess the impact of different feature sets on automatic tagging. The tagging is done in the Feature Latent Semantic Analysis framework (Serafin and Di Eugenio, 2004), augmented with additional prosodic and multi-modal features drawn from the annotation. Since this analysis requires Singular Value Decomposition of the potentially large Feature-by-Dialogue-Act matrices, it is often impractical to execute on single personal or even departmental servers. Furthermore, feature extraction, such as pitch tracking, of the full conversation can itself strain the computational resources available to students. Grid-based processing overcomes both of these problems.

Exercises on turn-taking follow similar patterns. An initial phase requires annotation and assessment exercises by the students in the ELAN-based client tool and downloaded from the web-based repository. Subsequent phases of the exercises include application and investigation of automatic techniques using the web-based environment and computational resources of the TeraGrid. Clearly, many other exercises could be framed within this general paradigm, and we plan to extend the options available to students as our interests and available software and data sets permit.

4 Impact on Interdisciplinary Instruction

We designed these hands-on exercises to allow students to investigate important problems in discourse and dialogue through exploration of the data and application of automatic techniques to recognize these phenomena. We aimed in addition to exploit the cyberinfrastructure framework to achieve three main goals: lower barriers of entry to use of computational tools by students with little prior programming experience, enable students with greater computational skills to expand the scale and scope of their experiments, and to support collaborative projects and a broader, interdisciplinary perspective on research in discourse and dialogue.

4.1 Enabling All Users

A key goal in employing this architecture was to enable students with little or no programming experience to exploit advanced computational tools and techniques. The integration of so-called "transformations", actually arbitrary program applications, in both the annotation client and the web-based portal to the TeraGrid, supports this goal. In both cases, drop-down menus to select programs and text- and check-boxes to specify parameters provide graphical user interfaces to what can otherwise be complex command-line specifications. In particular, the web-based portal removes requirements for local installation of software, shielding the user from problems due to complex installations, variations in platforms and operating systems, and abstruse command-line syntax. In addition, the web-based archive provides simple mechanisms to browse and download a range of data sources. The students all found the archive, download, and transformation mechanisms easy to use, regardless of prior programming experience. It is important to remember that the goal of this environment is not to replace existing software systems for Natural Language Processing, such the Natural Language Toolkit (NLTK) (Bird and Loper, 2004), but rather to provide a simpler interface to such software tools and to support their application to potentially large data sets, irrespective of the processing power of the individual user' system.

4.2 Enabling Large-Scale Experimentation

A second goal is to enable larger-scale experimentation by both expert and non-expert users. The use of the web-based portal to the TeraGrid provides such opportunities. The portal provides access to highly distributed parallel processing capabilities. For example, in the case of the segmentation of the oral history interviews above, the user can select several interviews, say 60, to segment by checking the associated check-boxes in the interface. The portal software will automatically identify available processing nodes and distribute the segmentation jobs for the corresponding interviews to each of the available nodes to be executed in parallel. Not only are there many processing nodes, but these nodes are of very high capacity in terms of CPU speed, number of CPUs, and available memory.

The multigigabyte data files associated with the growing number of multi-modal discourse and dialogue corpora, such as the AMI and ICSI Meeting Recorder collections, make such processing power highly desirable. For example, pitch tracking for such corpora is beyond the memory limitations of any single machine in the department, while such tasks are quickly processed on the powerful TeraGrid machines.

Expert users are also granted privileges to upload their own user-defined programs to be executed on the Grid. Finally, web services also enable execution of arbitrary read-only queries on the underlying database of annotations, media files, and time-series data through standard Structure Query Language (SQL) calls. All these capabilities enhance the scope of problems that more skilled programmers can employ in the study of discourse and dialogue phenomena.

4.3 Interdisciplinary Collaboration and Perspectives

The web-based archive in the SIDGrid framework also provides support for group distributed collaborative projects. The archive provides a Unix-style permission structure that allows data sharing within groups. The process of project creation, annotation, and experimentation maintains a version history. Uploads of new annotations create new versions; older versions are not deleted or overwritten. Experimental runs are also archived, providing an experiment history and shared access to intermediate and final results. Script and software versions are also maintained. While the version control is not nearly as sophisticated as that provided by GForge or Subversion, this simple model requires no special training and facilitates flexible, web-based distributed access and collaboration.

Finally, the interleaving of annotation and automated experimented permitted by this integrated architecture provides the students with additional insight into different aspects of research on discourse and dialogue. Students from linguistics and psychology gain greater experience in automatic analysis and recognition of discourse phenomena, while more computationally oriented students develop a greater appreciation of the challenges of annotation and theoretical issues in analysis of dialogue data.

5 Challenges and Costs

The capabilities and opportunities for study of computational approaches to discourse and dialogue afforded within the SIDGrid framework do require some significant investment of time and effort. Incorporating new data sets and software packages requires programming expertise. The framework can, in principle, incorporate arbitrary data types: media, physiological measures, manual and automatic annotations, and even motion tracking. The data must be converted into the ELAN .eaf format to be deployed effectively by the annotation client and interpreted correctly by the archive's underlying database. Converters have been created for several established formats[2], such as Annotation Graphs (Bird and Liberman, 2001), ANVIL (Kipp, 2001), and EXMARaLDA(Schmidt, 2004), and projects are underway to improve interoperability between formats. However, new formats such as the CLEF Cross-language Speech Retrieval SGML format and NITE XML(Carletta et al., 2003) format for the AMI data used here, required the implementation of software to convert the source format to one suitable for use by SIDGrid.

Incorporating new Grid-based "transformation" programs can also range in required effort. For self-contained programs in supported frameworks - currently, Perl, Python, Praat, and Octave - adding a new program requires only a simple browser-based upload. Compiled programs, such as LCSeg here, must be compatible with the operating systems and 64-bit architecture on the Grid servers, often requiring recompilation and occasionally addition of libraries to existing Grid installations. Finally, software with licensing restrictions can only run on a local cluster rather than on the full TeraGrid. Thus, public domain programs and systems that rely on such are preferred; for example, Octave-based programs are preferred to Matlab-based ones.

Finally, one must remember that the SIDGrid framework is itself an ongoing research project. It provides many opportunities to enhance interdisciplinary instruction in Computational Linguistics, especially in areas involving multi-modal data. However, the functionality is still under active development, and current system users are beta-testers. The use of the system, both in coursework and in research, has driven improvements and expansions in service.

6 Conclusions and Future Directions

We have explored the use of the SIDGrid framework for annotation, archiving, and analysis of multimodal data to enhance hands-on activities in the study of discourse and dialogue in a highly interdisciplinary course setting. Our preliminary efforts have demonstrated the potential for the framework to lower barriers of entry for students with less programming experience to apply computational techniques while enabling large-scale investigation of discourse and dialogue phenomena by more expert users. Annotation, analysis, and automatic recognition exercises relating to topic segmentation, dialogue act tagging, and turn-taking give students a broader perspective on research and issues in discourse and dialogue. These exercises also allow students to contribute to class discussion and collaborative projects drawing on their diverse disciplinary backgrounds. We plan to extend our current suite of hands-on exercises to cover other aspects of discourse and dialogue, both in terms of data sets and software, including well-known toolkits such as NLTK. We hope that this expanded framework will encourage additional interdisciplinary collaborative projects among students.

Acknowledgments

We would like to thank Susan Duncan and David McNeill for their participation in this project as well as the University of Chicago Academic Technology Innovation program. We would also like to thank Sonjia Waxmonsky for her assistance in implementing the course exercises, and the entire SIDGRID team for providing the necessary system infrastruc-

[2]www.multimodal-annotation.org

ture. We are particularly appreciative of the response to our bug reports and functionality requests by Tom Uram and Sarah Kenny.

References

Jens Allwood, Leif Groenqvist, Elisabeth Ahlsen, and Magnus Gunnarsson. 2001. Annotations and tools for an activity based spoken language corpus. In *Proceedings of the Second SIGdial Workshop on Discourse and Dialogue*, pages 1–10.

S. Bird and M. Liberman. 2001. A formal framework for linguistic annotation. *Speech Communication*, 33(1,2):23–60.

Steven Bird and Edward Loper. 2004. Nltk: The natural language toolkit. In *Proceedings of the ACL demonstration session*, pages 214–217.

P. Boersma. 2001. Praat, a system for doing phonetics by computer. *Glot International*, 5(9–10):341–345.

J. Carletta, S. Evert, U. Heid, J. Kilgour, J. Robertson, and H. Voormann. 2003. The NITE XML Toolkit: flexible annotation for multi-modal language data. *Behavior Research Methods, Instruments, and Computers, special issue on Measuring Behavior*, 35(3):353–363.

Jean Carletta, Simone Ashby, Sebastien Bourban, Mike Flynn, Mael Guillemot, Thomas Hain, Jaroslav Kadlec, Vasilis Karaiskos, Wessel Kraaij, Melissa Kronenthal, Guillaume Lathoud, Mike Lincoln, Agnes Lisowska, Iain A. McCowan, Wilfried Post, Dennis Reidsma, and Pierre Wellner. 2005. The AMI meetings corpus. In *Proceedings of the Measuring Behavior 2005 symposium on Annotating and measuring Meeting Behavior*.

M. Franz, B. Ramabhadran, T. Ward, and M. Picheny. 2003. Automated transcription and topic segmentation of large spoken archives. In *Proceedings of EUROSPEECH*.

Michel Galley, Kathleen McKeown, Eric Fosler-Lussier, and Hongyan Jing. 2003. Discourse segmentation of multi-party conversation. In *Proceedings of ACL'03*.

M. Kipp. 2001. Anvil- a generic annotation tool for multimodal dialogue. In *Proceedings of the 7th European Conference on Speech Communication and Technology (Eurospeech)*, pages 1367–1370.

Pavel Pecina, Petra Hoffmannova, Gareth J. F. Jones, Ying Zhang, and Douglas W. Oard. 2007. Overview of the clef-2007 cross language speech retrieval track. In *Working Notes for CLEF 2007*.

Rob Pennington. 2002. Terascale clusters and the TeraGrid. In *Proceedings for HPC Asia*, pages 407–413. Invited talk.

T. Schmidt. 2004. Transcribing and annotating spoken language with EXMARaLDA. In *Proceedings of the LREC-Workshop on XML-based richly annotated corpora*.

Riccardo Serafin and Barbara Di Eugenio. 2004. Flsa: Extending latent semantic analysis with features for dialogue act classification. In *Proceedings of the 42nd Meeting of the Association for Computational Linguistics (ACL'04), Main Volume*, pages 692–699, Barcelona, Spain, July.

P. Wittenburg, H. Brugman, A. Russel, A. Klassmann, and H. Sloetjes. 2006. Elan: a professional framework for multimodality research. In *Proceedings of Language Resources and Evaluation Conference (LREC) 2006*.

Teaching NLP to Computer Science Majors via Applications and Experiments

Reva Freedman
Department of Computer Science
Northern Illinois University
DeKalb, IL 60115
rfreedman@niu.edu

Abstract

Most computer science majors at Northern Illinois University, whether at the B.S. or M.S. level, are professionally oriented. However, some of the best students are willing to try something completely different. NLP is a challenge for them because most have no background in linguistics or artificial intelligence, have little experience in reading traditional academic prose, and are unused to open-ended assignments with gray areas. In this paper I describe a syllabus for Introduction to NLP that concentrates on applications and motivates concepts through student experiments. Core materials include an introductory linguistics textbook, the Jurafsky and Martin textbook, the NLTK book, and a Python textbook.

1 Introduction

Northern Illinois University is a large public university (25,000 students) located about 60 miles west of Chicago. Most computer science majors come from the suburbs and exurbs of Chicago or small towns near the university. Their preferred career path is generally to obtain a programming job in local industry, preferably in a hi-tech area. Most students take the Introduction to NLP course out of a desire to do something different from their required courses.

In this paper I describe the issues I have found in teaching NLP to this population, and the syllabus I have developed as a result. Since the students enjoy programming and see system development as the core issue of computer science, I concentrate on applications and their structure. I motivate many of the issues involved using data and systems from the web and in-class experiments. I explicitly teach the linguistics background that they need.

2 Student background

I started from the following assumptions derived from several years of teaching Introduction to Artificial Intelligence and Introduction to NLP at NIU.

Linguistic background:

1. Students have never studied linguistics.
2. Students are not familiar with the common syntactic constructions of English taught in traditional English grammar, and are often unsure about parts of speech.
3. Students have little experience with languages other than English.

Programming:

4. Students are not familiar with programming languages other than conventional imperative languages such as C++, Java, and .NET.
5. Students like to program and to build working systems.
6. Students expect to have programming languages explicitly taught in class.

Academic approach:

7. Students live on the web and are uncomfortable having to use offline reference materials.
8. Students are not comfortable with or interested in traditional academic prose or research papers.
9. Students are taking the course for fun and to do something different. They are unlikely to need specific NLP content in their future careers.

Proceedings of the Third Workshop on Issues in Teaching Computational Linguistics (TeachCL-08), pages 114–119,
Columbus, Ohio, USA, June 2008.

10. Students taking NLP are unlikely to have time in their program to take another artificial intelligence course (although there are exceptions).

3 Course goals

From these presuppositions I have developed the following general principles to provide a positive experience for both students and teacher:

1. Teach the linguistic content explicitly, at a level suitable for beginners.
2. Concentrate on applications, using them to motivate algorithms.
3. Concentrate on student involvement at all levels: in-class experiments, take-home experiments to be discussed in class, and practical programming projects.
4. Concentrate on a few basic principles that are repeated in many contexts, such as rule-based vs. Bayesian approaches and the role of world knowledge in working systems.

From these presuppositions I have developed a syllabus that maintains student interest, provides students a basic background in NLP, and also provides them with useful skills and knowledge that they may not otherwise encounter in their program of study.

The course has three goals:

1. Give students a general background in the issues involved in handling both speech and written text, some of the most common applications, and some of the most widely used algorithms.
2. Provide students with a productive experience in a modern programming language.
3. Teach students a number of useful concepts that they might not otherwise come across in their course of study. These topics include:

- Bayes' Law
- Dynamic programming
- Hidden Markov models
- Regular expressions and finite-state machines
- Context-free grammars

The following sections of the paper describe the most important units of the course, showing how they use the principles stated above to contribute to these goals.

4 Introducing NLP

The first goal of the course is to define the NLP task and explain why it is harder and less determinate than many of the problems they have studied in their other courses.

I start by encouraging students to list all the meanings they can for "I made her duck", based on the five meanings given by Jurafsky and Martin (2000, section 1.2). For a view of a system that can deal with such issues, I then introduce Figure 1.1 of Bird, Klein, and Loper (2008, henceforce referred to as the NLTK textbook), which shows a pipeline architecture for a spoken dialogue system. I use this opportunity to discuss each component and possible data representations.

5 Providing linguistic background

I introduce three kinds of background knowledge, related to speech, words and sentences, and human factors issues.

5.1 Background for speech processing

To provide essential background for discussing speech processing, I introduce the concepts of *phone* and *phoneme*. I also teach give a brief introduction to the IPA so that I can use it in examples. I use the following sections from Stewart and Vaillette (2001), a textbook for introductory linguistics classes:

File 3.1: International Phonetic Alphabet (IPA)
File 3.2: English consonants
File 3.3: English vowels
File 3.5: English transcription exercises
File 4.1: Phones vs. phonemes

These sections were chosen to provide the background students need while providing maximum opportunities for interaction. Students have found this approach more accessible than the rather terse treatment in Jurafsky and Martin (2000, ch. 4). I do the following activities, familiar to teachers of introductory linguistics classes, in class:

- Putting one's fingers on the glottis to experience the difference between voiced and unvoiced

consonants
- Putting one's hand in front of one's mouth to experience the difference between aspirated and unaspirated consonants
- Reading IPA transcription in pairs

I also introduce students to the idea that both pronunciation and other areas of human language generation are affected by context. For example, using Figure 5.7 of Jurafsky and Martin (2000) as a guide, I try to generate as many as possible of the sixteen most common pronunciations of *because* shown in that figure.

5.2 Background for text processing

As background for the text processing section, I lecture on a few core aspects of syntax and related topics that will be needed during the semester. These topics include the following:

- What is a word?
- How many parts of speech are there?
- Lexical ambiguity
- Syntactic ambiguity, including PP attachment, attachment of gerunds, and coordination ambiguity
- Difference between syntactic structure and intention

5.3 Background in human factors issues

This section includes several topics that experience has shown will be needed during the semester.

The first is the difference between descriptive and prescriptive linguistics. I take class polls on various sociolinguistic issues, including pronunciation, word choice and sentence structure, using File 10.10: Language variation from Stewart and Vaillette (2001) as a basis.

I take a poll on the pronunciation of the word *office*, choosing that word since the distribution of its first vowel is sensitive both to geography and speaker age. The poll gives me an opportunity to introduce some of the human factors issues related to corpus collection and the issue of statistical significance. We also examine some data collection tasks found on the Internet, using them to discuss experimental design and how it relates to the data collected.

Finally, I begin a discussion on the difference between rule-based and statistical systems that will recur frequently during the semester. This is a good place to discuss the importance of separating training data and test data.

6 Python

6.1 Basic Python

The next step is to teach basic Python so that there will be time for some practice programs before the first major programming project. As computer science majors, the students tend to find that the treatment in the NLTK textbook does not answer enough of their technical questions, such as issues on argument handling and copying of objects vs. references to them.

I give several lectures on Python, including the following topics:

- Basic data structures
- Basic control structures
- Functions and modules
- Objects
- File handling

I have found Lutz (2008) to be the most readable introductory textbook. I use Chun (2007) as a reference for topics not covered by Lutz, such as regular expressions and some of the I/O options.

6.2 Using Python for basic language handling

This unit basically covers the material in chapters 2, 3, and 6 of the NLTK textbook. The goal is to show students how easily some of these problems can be handled with an appropriate programming language. Many of them are quite uncomfortable with the idea of a list not implemented with pointers, but in the end they cope well with a language that does not have all the baggage of C++.

I give a simple assignment that involves finding the most common words in a corpus. A secondary purpose of this assignment is to reinforce the earlier lecture on the difficulty of defining a word. I lard the input text for the assignment with problematic cases such as hyphenated multiword expressions, e.g., "the orange-juice based confection."

7 Rule-based dialogue systems using regular expressions

Since later in the course we will be comparing rule-based systems to statistics-based systems, this is an appropriate time to introduce rule based systems. We experiment in class with Eliza, trying both to make it work and make it fail. I give out a list of versions available on the web, and students can easily find more. In class I often use the emacs built-in version.

I then give out copies of the original Eliza paper (Weizenbaum, 1966), which contains the original script in an appendix. If time permits, I also discuss PARRY (Parkison, Colby and Faught, 1977), which has a much more linguistically sophisticated design but there is no simulator available for it.

I introduce regular expressions at this point for two reasons. In addition to being required for continued use of the NLTK textbook, regular expressions are an important idea that is not otherwise included in our curriculum. We experiment with Rocky Ross' interactive web site (Pascoe, 2005) and occasionally with other simulators. I also assign a simple homework using regular expressions in Python.

The first major project in the course is to write an shallow interactive written dialogue system, i.e., an Eliza-type program. Students have the choice of choosing a more realistic, limited domain, such as a database front-end, or of picking a specific case (e.g., a linguistic issue) that they would like Eliza to handle. This project is implemented in Python as a rule-based system with heavy use of regular expressions. Before they write their code, students do a five-minute presentation of their domain, including a sample conversation. After the projects are due, they present their results to the class.

8 Spelling correction and Bayes' Law

Bayes' Law is another core topic that students are generally unfamiliar with, even though statistics is required in our program. To provide a contrast to rule-based systems, and to introduce this core topic, I present Kernighan, Church and Gale's (1990) Bayesian approach to spelling correction, as explained by Jurafsky and Martin (2000, section 5.5).

Kernighan et al. choose as the preferred correction the one that maximizes $P(t|c)P(c)$, where t is the typo and c is a candidate correction. In a previous paper (Freedman, 2005), I discuss in detail an assignment where students choose a corpus and replicate Kernighan's calculations. They then compare their results to results from their favorite word processor.

Students are generally surprised at how similar the results are from what they originally see as an unmotivated calculation. They are always surprised to learn that spelling correction is generally not done by a lookup process. They are also surprised to learn that learn that results were largely independent of the corpus chosen.

I also demonstrate approximating word frequencies by page counts in Google, along with a discussion of the advantages and disadvantages of doing so. In general, students prefer to use one of the NLTK corpora or a corpus obtained from the web.

9 Machine translation: rule-based and statistical models

This unit has several purposes. In addition to showing students how the same problem can be attacked in remarkably different ways, including multiple levels of rule-based and statistically-based systems, machine translation gives students a look at a fielded application that is good enough to be viable but sill obviously needs improvement.

To the extent that information is publicly available, I discuss the architecture of one of the oldest machine translation systems, Systran (Babelfish), and one of the newest, Microsoft Live Translator. The latter uses components from MindNet, Microsoft's knowledge representation project, which provides another opportunity to reinforce the importance of world knowledge in artificial intelligence and NLP in particular. It also provides an initial opportunity to discuss the concept of machine learning as opposed to hand-crafting rules or databases.

As the assignment for this unit, students choose a short text in a foreign language. They use multiple web-based translation systems to translate it into English, and analyze the results. In addition to the systems mentioned above, the Reverso system has done well in these experiments.

Popular inputs include administrative text (e.g., citizenship rules) from a bilingual country and chapter 1 of Genesis. One student started with a French version of the Tolkien poem "... one ring to rule them all..." Although translation of poetry obviously poses different issues than technical text, a fruitful discussion emerged from the fact that two of the systems misparsed one or more of the lines of the poem.

10 POS identification, parsing and author identification

This unit of the course covers key sections of chapters 4, 7, 8 and 9 of the NLTK textbook. Although one student originally stated that "I really don't care about parts of speech," students find this material more interesting after seeing how many of the machine translation errors are caused by parsing errors. Still, I only cover POS assignment enough to use it for chunking and parsing.

The application chosen for this unit involves author identification. I introduce students to the basics of the Federalist Papers controversy. Then I discuss the approach of Mosteller and Wallace (1984), which depends largely on words used much more frequently by one author than the other, such as *while* and *whilst*.

I suggest to students that more interesting results could perhaps be obtained if data about items such as part of speech use and use of specific constructions of English were added to the input. As an alternative assignment, I give students transcripts of tutoring by two different professors and invite them to identify the authors of additional transcripts from a test set. A secondary goal of this assignment is for students to see the level of cleanup that live data can require.

This assignment also shows students the relative difficulty level of chunking vs. parsing better than any lecture could. This is useful because students otherwise tend to find chunking too ad hoc for their taste.

I do teach several approaches to parsing since many students will not otherwise see context-free grammars in their studies. Having had the experiences with machine translation systems helps prevent the reaction of a previous class to Earley's algorithm: "we understand it; it's just not interesting." I also frame Earley's algorithm as another example of dynamic programming.

11 Speech understanding

Students generally find speech a much more compelling application than written text. In this unit I discuss how basic speech processing works. This unit provides a nice review of the basics of phonology taught at the beginning of the semester. It also provides a nice review of Bayes' Law because the approach used, based on Jurafsky and Martin (2000, ch. 5.7–5.9) uses Bayes' Law in a fashion similar to spelling correction.

The assignment for this unit involves experimenting with publicly available speech understanding systems to see how well they work. The assignment involves comparing two automated 411 systems, Google's new system (1-800-GOOG411), which was built specifically for data collection, and Jingle (1-800-FREE411), which is advertising-supported. I also encourage students to report on their own experiments with bank, airline, and other systems.

I give at least one anonymous questionnaire every semester. Students generally report that the level of detail is appropriate. They generally vote for more topics as opposed to more depth, and they always vote for more programming assignments and real systems rather than theory.

12 Future work

I am considering replacing author identification by question answering, both because it is an important and practical topic and because I think it would provide better motivation for teaching chunking. I am also considering keeping author identification and adding the use of a machine learning package to that unit, since I believe that machine learning is rapidly becoming a concept that all students should be exposed to before they graduate.

My long-term goal is to have students build an end-to-end system. A short-term goal in service of this objective would be to add a unit on text-to-speech systems.

13 Conclusions

This paper described a syllabus for teaching NLP to computer science majors with no background in the topic. Students enjoyed the course more and were more apt to participate when the course was oriented toward applications such as dialogue systems, machine translation, spelling correction and author identification. Students also learned about the architecture of these systems and the algorithms underlying them. Students implemented versions of some of the smaller applications and experimented with web versions of large fielded systems such as machine translation systems.

Acknowledgments

I thank the authors of Jurafsky and Martin (2000) and Bird, Klein and Loper (2008), whose extensive labor has made it possible to teach this course. I would also like to thank the anonymous reviewers for their suggestions.

References

Steven Bird, Ewan Klein, and Edward Loper. (2008). *Natural Language Processing in Python*. Available on the web at http://nltk.org/index.php/Book.

Wesley J. Chun. (2007). *Core Python Programming*, 2/e. Upper Saddle River, NJ: Prentice-Hall.

Reva Freedman. (2005). Concrete Assignments for Teaching NLP in an M.S. Program. In Second Workshop on Effective Tools and Methodologies for Teaching NLP and CL, 43rd Annual Meeting of the ACL.

Daniel Jurafsky and James H. Martin. (2000). *Speech and Language Processing*. Upper Saddle River, NJ: Prentice-Hall.

Mark Lutz. (2008). *Learning Python*, 3/e. Sebastopol, CA: O'Reilly.

Mark D. Kernighan, Kenneth W. Church, and William A. Gale. (1990). A spelling correction program based on a noisy channel model. In COLING '90 (Helsinki), v. 2, pp. 205–211.

Frederick and Mosteller and David L. Wallace. (1984). *Applied Bayesian and Classical Inference: The Case of* The Federalist *Papers*. New York: Springer. Originally published in 1964 as *Inference and Disputed Authorship: The Federalist*.

Brad Pascoe (2005). Webworks FSA applet. Available at http://www.cs.montana.edu/webworks/projects/theoryportal/models/fsa-exercise/appletCode/fsa_applet.html.

Roger C. Parkison, Kenneth Mark Colby, and William S. Faught. (1977). Conversational Language Comprehension Using Integrated Pattern-Matching and Parsing. *Artificial Intelligence* 9: 111–134.

Thomas W. Stewart, Jr. and Nathan Vaillette. (2001). *Language Files: Materials for an Introduction to Language and Linguistics*, 8/e. Columbus: Ohio State University Press.

Joseph Weizenbaum. (1966). Eliza—A Computer Program for the Study of Natural Language Computation between Man and Machine. Communications of the ACM 9(1): 36–45.

Psychocomputational Linguistics: A Gateway to the Computational Linguistics Curriculum

William Gregory Sakas
Department of Computer Science, Hunter College
Ph.D. Programs in Linguistics and Computer Science, The Graduate Center
City University of New York (CUNY)
695 Park Avenue, North 1008
New York, NY, USA, 10065
sakas@hunter.cuny.edu

Abstract

Computational modeling of human language processes is a small but growing subfield of computational linguistics. This paper describes a course that makes use of recent research in psychocomputational modeling as a framework to introduce a number of mainstream computational linguistics concepts to an audience of linguistics, cognitive science and computer science doctoral students. The emphasis on what I take to be the largely interdisciplinary nature of computational linguistics is particularly germane for the computer science students. Since 2002 the course has been taught three times under the auspices of the MA/PhD program in Linguistics at The City University of New York's Graduate Center. A brief description of some of the students' experiences after having taken the course is also provided.

1 Introduction

A relatively small (but growing) subfield of computational linguistics, psychocomputational modeling affords a strong foundation from which to introduce graduate students in linguistics to various computational techniques, and students in computer science[1] (*CS*) to a variety of topics in psycholinguistics, though it has rarely been incorporated into the computational linguistics curriculum.

Psychocomputational modeling involves the construction of computer models that embody one or more psycholinguistic theories of natural (human) language processing and use. Over the past decade or so, there's been renewed interest within the computational linguistics community related to the possibility of incorporating human language *strategies* into computational language *technologies*. This is evidenced by the occassional special session at computational linguistics meetings (e.g., ACL-1999 Thematic Session on Computational Psycholinguistics), several workshops (e.g., COLING-2004, ACL-2005 Psychocomputational Models of Human Language Acquisition, ACL-2004 Incremental Parsing: Bringing Engineering and Cognition Together), recent conference themes (e.g., CoNLL-2008 "... models that explain natural phenomena relating to human language") and regular invitations to psycholinguists to deliver plenary addresses at recent ACL and COLING meetings.

Unfortunately, it is too often the case that computational linguistics programs (primarily those housed in computer science departments) delay the introduction of cross-disciplinary psycholinguistic / computational linguistics approaches until either late in a student's course of study (usually as an elective) or not at all. At the City University of New York (CUNY)'s Graduate Center (the primary Ph.D.-granting school of the university) I have created a course that presents

[1] For rhetorical reasons I will often crudely partition the student makeup of the course into linguistics students and CS students. This preempts lengthy illocutions such as " … the students with a strong computational background as compared to students with a strong linguistics background." In fact there have been students from other academic disciplines in attendance bringing with them a range of technical facility in both CS and linguistics; linguistics students with an undergraduate degree in CS; and CS students with a strong undergraduate background in theoretical linguistics.

Proceedings of the Third Workshop on Issues in Teaching Computational Linguistics (TeachCL-08), pages 120–128,
Columbus, Ohio, USA, June 2008.

research in this cross-disciplinary area relatively early in the graduate curriculum. I have also run an undergraduate version of the course at Hunter College, CUNY in the interdisciplinary Thomas Hunter Honors Program.

I contend that a course developed within the mélange of psycholinguistics and computational linguistics is not only a valuable asset in a student's repertoire of graduate experience, but can effectively be used as a springboard to introduce a variety of techniques and topics central to the broader field of CL/NLP.

2 Background

The CUNY Graduate Center (hereafter, *GC*) has doctoral programs in both computer science and linguistics. The Linguistics Program also contains two master's tracks. Closely linked to both programs, but administratively independent of either, there exists a Cognitive Science Concentration.[2] In spring of 2000, I was asked by the Cognitive Science Coordinator to create an interdisciplinary course in "computing and language" that would be attractive to linguistics, speech and hearing, computer science, philosophy, mathematics, psychology and anthropology students. One might imagine how a newly-minted Ph.D. might react to this request. Well this one, not yet realizing the potential for abuse of junior faculty (a slightly more sage me later wondered if there was a last minute sabbatical-related cancellation of some course that needed to be replaced ASAP) dove in and developed *Computational Mechanisms of Syntax Acquisition.*

The course was designed to cover generative and non-generative linguistics and debates surrounding (child) first language acquisition principally focused on the question of Chomsky's Universal Grammar (*UG*), or not? Four computational models drawn from diverse paradigms – connectionist learning, statistical formal language induction, principles-and-parameters acquisition and acquisition in an optimality theory framework[3] – were presented and discussion of the UG-or-not debate was framed in the context of these models.

Over the past eight years, I've taught three variations of this course gradually molding the course away from a seminar format into a seminar/lecture format, dropping a large chunk of the UG-or-not debate, and targeting the course primarily for students who are in search of a "taste" of computational linguistics who might very well go on to take other CL-related course work.[4] What follows is a description of the design considerations, student makeup, and course content focusing on its last instantiation in Spring 2007.

3 The Course: *Computational Natural Language Learning*

Most readers will recognize the most recent title of the course which was shamelessly borrowed from the ACL's Special Interest Group on Natural Language Learning's annual meeting. Although largely an NLP-oriented meeting, the title and indeed many of the themes of the meeting's CFPs over the years accurately portray the material covered in the course.

The course is currently housed in the GC's Linguistics Program and is primarily designed to serve linguistics doctoral and masters students who want some exposure to computational linguistics but with a decidedly linguistics emphasis. Importantly though, the course often needs to serve a high percentage of students from other graduate programs.

The GC Linguistics and Computer Science Programs also offer other computational linguistics (*CL*) courses: a Natural Language Processing (*NLP*) applications survey course, a corpus analysis course, a statistical NLP course and a CL methods sequence (in addition to a small variety of electives). Although (at least until recently, see Section 7) these courses are not taught within a structured CL curriculum, they effectively serve as the "meat-and-potatoes" CL courses which require projects and assignments involving programming, a considerable math component and extensive experimentation with existing NLP/CL

[2] This is not a state-registered program, but rather an "in-house" means of allowing students to receive recognition of interdisciplinary studiy in cognitive science.

[3] Although the semester ended as we were only just getting to cover optimality theoretic acquisition.

[4] Though the details of the undergraduate version of the course are beyond the scope of this paper, it is worth noting that it did not undergo this gradual revision; it was structured much as the original Cognitive Science version of the course, actually with an increased UG-or-not discussion.

applications. The students taking these classes have already reached the point where they intend to include a substantial amount of computational linguistics in their dissertation or master's thesis.

Computational Natural Language Learning is somewhat removed from these other courses and the design considerations were purposefully directed at providing an "appetizer" that would both entice interested students into taking other courses, and prepare them with some experience in computational linguistics techniques. Over time the course has evolved to incorporate the following set of prerequisites and goals.

• *No programming prerequisite, no introduction to programming* Many of the students who take the course are first or second year linguistics students who have had little or no programming background. Students are aware that "Programming for Linguists" is part of the CL methods sequence. They come to this course looking for either an overview of CL, or for how CL concepts might be relevant to psycholinguistic or theoretical linguistics research.

Often there are students who *have* had a substantial programming background – including graduate students in computer science. This hasn't proved to be problematic since the assignments and projects are designed not to involve programming.

• *Slight math prerequisite, exposure to probabilities, and information theory* Students are expected to be comfortable with basic algebra. I dissuade students from taking the course who are intimidated by a one-line formula with a few Greek letters in it. Students are not expected to know what a conditional probability is, but will leave the course with a decent grasp of basic (undergraduate-level) concepts in probability and information theory.

This lightweight math prerequisite actually does split the class for a brief time during the semester as the probability/information theory lecture and assignment is a cinch for the CS students, and typically quite difficult for the linguistics students. But this is balanced by the implementation of the design consideration expressed in the next bullet.

• *No linguistics prerequisite, exposure to syntactic theory* Students need to know what a syntax tree is (at least in the formal language sense) but do not need to know a particular theory of human language syntax (e.g., X-bar theory or even S $\rightarrow$ NP VP). By the end of the semester students will be comfortable with elementary syntax beyond the level covered by most undergraduate "Ling 101" courses.

• *Preparation for follow-up CL courses* Students leaving this course should be comfortably prepared to enter the other GC computational linguistics offerings.[5]

• *Appreciation of the interdisciplinary nature of CL* Not all students move on to other computational linguistics courses. Perhaps the most important goal of the course is to expose CS and linguistics students (and others) to the role that computational linguistics can play in areas of theoretical linguistics and cognitive science research, and conversely to the role that cognitive science and linguistics can play in the field of computational linguistics.

3.1 Topical units

In this section I present the syllabus of the course framed in topical units. They have varied over the years; what follows is the content of the course mostly as it was taught in Spring 2007.

Janet Dean Fodor and I lead an active psychocomputational modeling research group at the City University of New York: *CUNY CoLAG* – CUNY Computational Language Acquisition Group which is primarily dedicated to the design and evaluation of computational models of first language acquisition. Most, though not all, of the topical units purposefully contain material that intersects with CUNY CoLAG's ongoing research efforts.

The depth of coverage of the units is designed to give the students some fluency in computational *issues* (e.g., use and ramifications of Markov assumptions), and a basic understanding beyond exposure to the computational *mechanisms* of CL (e.g., derivation of the standard MLE bigram

[5] The one exception in the Linguistics Program is Corpus Linguistics which has a programming prerequisite, and the occasional CL elective course in Computer Science targeted primarily for their more advanced students.

probability formula), but not designed to allow students to bypass a more computationally rigorous NLP survey course. The same is true of the breadth of coverage; a comprehensive survey is not the goal. For example, in the ngram unit, typically no more than two or at most three smoothing techniques are covered.

Note that the citations in this section are mostly required reading, but some articles are optional. It has been my experience however, that the students by and large read most of the material since the readings were highly directed (i.e., which sections and pages are most relevant to the course.) Supplemental materials that present introductory mathematics and tutorial presentations are not exhaustively listed, but included Jurafsky and Martin (2000), Goldsmith (2007, previously online) and a host of (other) online resources.

History of linguistics and computation [1 lecture] The history is framed around the question "Is computational linguistics, well uh, linguistics?" We conclude with "It was, then it wasn't, now maybe it is, or at least in part, should be." The material is tightly tied to Lee (2004); with additional discussion along the lines of Sakas (2004).

Syntax [1 lecture] This is a crash course in syntax using a context-free grammar with transformational movement. The more difficult topics include topicalization (including null-topic), Wh-movement and verb-second phenomena. We make effective use of an in-house database of abstract though linguistically viable cross-linguistic sentence patterns and tree structures – the CUNY CoLAG Domain (Sakas, 2003). The point of this lecture is to introduce non-linguistics students to the intricacies of a linguistically viable grammatical theory.

Language Acquisition [1 lecture] We discuss some of the current debates in *L1* (a child's first) language acquisition surrounding "no negative evidence" (Marcus, 1993), Poverty of the Stimulus (Pullum, 1996), and Chomsky's conceptualization of Universal Grammar. This is the least computational lecture of the semester, although it often generates some of the most energized discussion. The language acquisition unit is the central arena in which we stage most of the rest of the topics in the course.

Gold and the Subset Principle [2 lectures] During the presentation of Gold's (1967) and Angluin's (1980) proofs and discussion of how they might be used to argue (often incorrectly) for a Universal Grammar (Johnson, 2004) some core CL topics are introduced including formal language classes (the Chomsky Hierarchy) and the notions of hypothesis space and search space. The first (toy) probabilistic analyses are also presented (e.g., given a finite enumeration and a probability p that an arbitrary non-target grammar licenses a sentence in the input sample, what is the "worst case" number of sentences required to converge on the target grammar?)

Next, the Subset Principle and linguistic overgeneralization (Fodor and Sakas, 2005) is introduced. An important focus is on how keeping (statistical) track of what's *not* encountered might supply a 'retreat' mechanism to pull back from an over-general hypothesis. Although the mathematical details of how the statistics might work are omitted, this topic leads neatly into a unit on Bayesian learning later in the semester.

This is an important two lectures. It's the first unit where students are exposed to the use of computational techniques applied to theoretical issues in psycholinguistics. By this point, students often are intellectually engaged in the debates surrounding L1 acquisition. To understand the arguments presented in this unit students need to flex their computational muscles for the first time.

Connectionism [3 lectures] This unit covers the basics of Simple Recurrent Network (SRN) learning (Elman, 1990, 1993). More or less, Elman argues that language acquisition is not necessarily the acquisition of rules operating over atomic linguistic units (e.g., phrase markers) but rather the process of capturing the "dynamics" of word patterns in the input stream. He demonstrates how this can be simulated in an SRN paradigm.

The mechanics of how an SRN operates and can be used to model language acquisition phenomena is covered but more importantly core concepts common to most all supervised machine learning paradigms are emphasized. Topics include how training and testing corpora are developed and used, cross validation, hill-climbing, learning bias, linear and non-linear separation of the hypothesis space, etc. A critique of SRN learning is also covered (Marcus, 1998) which presents the important distinction between *generalization performance* and *learning within the training space* in a way that is approachable by non-CS students, but also interesting to CS-students.

Information retrieval [1 lecture] Elman (1990) uses hierarchal clustering to analyze some of his results. I use Elman's application of clustering to take a brief digression from the psycholinguistics theme of the course and present an introduction to vector space models and document clustering.

This is the most challenging technical lecture of the semester and is included only when there are a relatively high proportion of CS students in attendance. Most of the linguistics students get a decent feel for the material, but most require a second exposure it in another course to fully understand the math. That said, the linguistics students do understand how weight heuristics are used to effectively represent documents in vectors (though most linguistics students have a hard time swallowing the bag-of-words paradigm at face value), and how vectors can be nearer or farther from each other in a hypothesis space.

Ngram language models [3 lecture] In this unit we return to psycholinguistics. Reali and Christiansen, (2005) present a simple ngram language model of child-directed speech to argue against the need for innate UG-provided knowledge of hierarchal syntactic structure. Basic probability and information theory is introduced – conditional probabilities and Markov assumptions, the chain rule, Bayes Rule, maximum likelihood estimates, entropy, etc. Although relatively easy for the CS students (they had their hands full with the syntax unit), introduction of this material is invaluable to the linguistics students who need to be somewhat fluent in it before entering our other CL offerings.

We continue with a presentation of the sparse data problem, Zipf's law, corpus cross-entropy and a handful of smoothing techniques (Reali & Christiansen use a particularly impoverished version of deleted interpolation). We continue with a discussion of the pros and cons of employing Markov assumptions in computational linguistics generally, the relationship of Markov assumptions to incremental learning and psycholinguistic modeling, and the use of cross-entropy as an evaluation metric, and end with a brief discussion of the descriptional necessity (or not) of traditional generative grammars (Pereira, 2000).

"Ideal" learning, Bayesian learning and computational resources [1 lecture] Regier and Gahl (2004) in response to Lidz et al. (2003) present a Bayesian learning model that learns the correct structural referent for anaphoric "one" in English from a corpus of child-directed speech. Similarly to Reali & Christiansen (op. cit.), they argue against the need for innate knowledge of hierarchal structure since their Bayesian model starts tabula rasa and learns from linear word strings with no readily observable structure.

The fundamental mechanics of Bayesian inference is presented. Since most Bayesian models are able to retreat from overgeneral hypotheses in the absence of positive evidence, the course returns to overgeneralization errors, the Subset Principle and the alternative of using statistics as a possible retreat mechanism. Computationally heavy ("ideal") batch processing, and incremental (psychologically plausible) processing are contrasted here as is the use of heuristics (psycholinguistically-based or not) to mitigate the potentially huge computational cost of searching a large domain.

Principle and parameters [2 lectures] As the academic scheduling has worked out, the course is usually offered during years when the Linguistics Program does not offer a linguistics-based learnability course. As a result, there is a unit on acquisition within a principles-and-parameters (*P&P*) framework (Chomsky, 1981). Roughly, in the P&P framework cross-linguistic commonalities are considered principles, and language variation is standardly specified by the settings of a bank of binary parameters (i.e., UG = principles + parameters; a specific language = principles + parameters + parameter settings).

Although this unit is the furthest away from mainstream CL, it has served as a useful means to introduce deterministic learning (Sakas and Fodor, 2001), versus non-deterministic learning (Yang, 2002), the effectiveness of hill-climbing in linguistically smooth and non-smooth domains,[6] as well as the notion of computational complexity and combinatorial explosion (n binary parameters yields a search space of 2^n possible grammars). Finally, and perhaps most importantly there is extensive discussion of the difficulty of building computational systems that can efficiently and correctly learn to navigate through domains with an enormous amount of ambiguity.

In the P&P framework ambiguity stems from competition of cross-linguistic structural analyses of surface word order patterns. For example, given a (tensed) *S V O* sentence pattern, is the *V* situated under the phrase maker *I* (English), or under the phrase marker *C* (German)? Although this is a somewhat different form of ambiguity than the within-language structural ambiguity that is all too familiar to those of use working in CL, it serves as useful background material for the next unit.

Part of speech tagging and statistical parsing [3 lectures] In this unit we begin by putting aside the psycholinguistics umbrella of the course and cover introductory CL in a more traditional manner. Using Charniak (1997) as the primary reading, we cover rudimentary HMM's, and probabilistic CFG's. We use supplemental materials to introduce lexicalized statistical parsing (e.g., Jurafsky and Martin, 2000 and online materials). We then turn back to psycholinguistics and after a (somewhat condensed overview) of human sentence processing, discuss the viability of probabilistic parsing as a model of human sentence processing (Keller, 2005). This unit, more than some others, is lightweight on detailed computational mechanics; the material is presented throughout at a level similar to that of Charniak's article. For example the specifics of EM algorithms are not covered although what they do, and why they are necessary are.

The Linguistics Program at CUNY is very active in human sentence processing research and this unit is of interest to many of the linguistics students. In particular we contrast computational approaches that employ nondeterminism and parallelism to mainstream psycholinguistics models which are primarily deterministic, serial and employ a reanalysis strategy when evaluating a parse "online" (though of course there is a significant amount of research that falls outside of this mainstream). We then focus on issues of computational resources that each paradigm requires.

In some ways the last lectures of this unit best embody the goal of exposing the students to the potential of interdisciplinary research in computational linguistics. The CS students leave with an appreciation of psycholinguistic approaches to human sentence processing, and the linguistics students with a firm grasp of the effectiveness of computational approaches.

4 Assignments and Projects

Across the three most recent incarnations of the course the number and difficulty of the assignments and projects has varied quite a bit. In the last version, there were three assignments (five to ten hours of student effort each) and one project (twenty to thirty hours effort).

Due to the typically small size of the course, assignments and projects (beyond weekly readings) were often individually tailored and assessed. The goal of the assignments was to concretize the CL aspects of the primarily psycholinguistic readings with either hands-on use of the computer, mathematically-oriented problem sets, or a critical evaluation of the CL methodologies employed. A handful of examples follow.

• **Gold and the Subset Principle (Assignments)** All students are asked to formulate a Markov chain (though at this point in the course, not by that name) of a Gold-style enumeration learner operating over a small finite domain (e.g., 4 grammars, 12 sentences and a sentence to grammar mapping). The more mathematically inclined are additionally asked to calculate the expected value of the number of input sentences consumed by a learner operating over an enumeration of n grammars and given a generalized mapping of sentences to grammars, or to formally prove the learnability of any finite domain of languages given text (positive) presentation of input.

• **Connectionism (Assignments)** All students were asked to pick a language from the CUNY CoLAG domain, develop a training and test set

[6] By "smooth", I mean a correlation between the similarity of grammars, and the similarity of languages they generate.

from that language using existing software and run a predict-the-next-word SRN simulation on either a MatLab or TLearn neural network platform. Linguistics and CS students were paired on this assignment. When the assignment is given, a relatively detailed after-class lab tutorial on how to run the software is presented.

• **Ngram language models (Projects)** One CS student implemented a version of Reali and Christiansen's experiment and was asked to evaluate the effectiveness of different smoothing techniques on child-directed speech and to design a study of how to evaluate differences between child-directed speech and adult-to-adult speech in terms of language modeling. A linguistics student was asked to write a paper explaining how one could develop a computational evaluation of how a bigram learner might be evaluated longitudinally. (I.e., to answer the question, how can one measure the effectiveness of a language model after each input sentence?). Another linguistics student (with strong CS skills) created an annotation tool that semi-automatically mapped child-directed speech in French onto the CoLAG Domain tag set.

5 Students: Past and Current

As mentioned earlier, the Linguistics Doctoral Program at CUNY has just recently begun to structure their computational linguistics offerings into a cohesive course of study (described briefly in Section 7). During the past several years Computational Natural Learning has been offered on an ad hoc basis primarily in response to student demand and demographics of students' computational skills. Since the course was not originally intended to serve any specific function as part of a larger curriculum, and was not integrated into a reoccurring schedule there has been little need to carry out a systematic evaluation of the impact of the course on students' academic careers. Still a few anecdotal accounts will help give a picture of the course's effectiveness.

After the first Cognitive Science offering of the course in 2000, approximately 30 graduate students have taken one of the three subsequent incarnations. Two of the earliest linguistics students went on to take undergraduate CS courses in programming and statistics, and subsequently came back to take graduate level CL courses.[7] They have obtained their doctorates and are currently working in industry as computational linguists. One is a lead software engineer for an information retrieval startup company in New York that does email data mining. And though I've lost track of the other student, she was at one point working for a large software company on the west coast.

I am currently the advisor of one CS student, and two linguistics students who have taken the course. One linguistics student is in the throws of writing a dissertation on the plausibility of exploiting statistical regularities of various syntactic structures (contra regularities of word strings) in child-directed speech during L1 acquisition. The other is relatively early in her academic career, but is interested in working on computational semantics and discourse analysis within a categorial grammar framework. Her thoughts currently revolve around establishing (and formalizing) relationships between traditional linguistics-oriented semantics and a computational semantics paradigm. She hopes to make contributions to both linguistics and CL. The CS student, also early in his career, is interested in semi-productive multi-word expressions and how young children can come to acquire them. His idea is to employ a learning component in a machine translation system that can be trained to translate productive metaphors between a variety of languages.

These five students have chosen to pursue specific areas of study and research directly as a result of having taken Computational Natural Language Learning early in their careers.

I am also sitting on two CS students' second qualifying exam committees. One is working on machine translation of Hebrew and the other working on (relatively) mainstream word-sense disambiguation. Both of their qualifying exam papers show a sensitivity to psycholinguistics that I'm frankly quite happy to see, and am sure wouldn't have been present without their having taken the course.

The parsing unit was just added this past spring semester and I've had two recent discussions with

[7] The CL methods sequence was established only 3 years ago, previously students were encouraged to develop their basic computational skills at one of CUNY's undergraduate schools.

a second year linguistics student about incorporating a statistical component into a current psycholinguistic model of human sentence processing. Another second year student has expressed interested in doing a comprehensive study of neural network models of human sentence parsing for his first qualifying paper. It's not clear that they will ultimately pursue these directions, but I'm certain they wouldn't have thought of the possibilities if they hadn't taken the Computational Natural Language Learning.

Finally, most all of the students who have taken the course have also taken the NLP-survey course (no programming required), slightly less than a third have moved on to the CL methods sequence (includes an introduction to programming), or if they have some CS background move directly to Corpus Analysis (programming experience required as a prerequisite). We hope that eventually, especially in light of the GC's new computational linguistics program, the course will serve as the gateway for many more students to begin to pursue studies that will lead to research areas in both psychocomputational modeling and more mainstream CL.

6 Brief Discussion

It is my view that computational linguistics is by nature a cross-disciplinary endeavor. Indeed, one could argue that only after the incorporation of techniques and strategies gleaned from theoretical advances in psychocomputational modeling of language, can we achieve truly transparent (to the user) human-computer language applications.

That argument notwithstanding, a course such as the one described in this paper can effectively serve as an introduction to an assortment of concepts in computational linguistics that can broaden the intellectual horizons of both CS and linguistics students, as well providing a foundation that students can build on in the pursuit of more advanced studies in the field.

7 Postscript: The Future of the Course

The CUNY Graduate Center has recently created a structured computational linguistics program housed in the GC's Linguistics Program. The program consists of a Computational Linguistics Concentration in the Linguistics Master's subprogram, and particularly relevant to the discussion in this article, a Computational Linguistics Certificate[8] (both fall under the acronym *CLC*). Any City University of New York doctoral student can enroll in CLC concurrently with enrollment in their primary doctoral program (as one might imagine, we expect a substantial number of Linguistics and CS doctoral candidates to enroll in the CLC program).

Due to my newly-acquired duties as director of the CLC program and to scheduling constraints on CLC faculty teaching assignments, the course cannot be offered again until Fall 2009 or Spring 2010. At that time Computational Natural Language Learning will need to morph into a more technically advanced elective course in applied machine learning techniques in computational linguistics (or some such) since the CLC course of study currently posits the NLP survey course and the CL Methods sequence as the first year introductory requirements.

However, I expect that a course similar to the one described here will supplement the NLP survey course as a first year requirement in Fall 2010. The course will be billed as having broad appeal and made available to both CLC students *and* linguistics, CS and other students who might not want or require the "meat-and-potatoes" that CLC offers, but who only desire a CL "appetizer". Though if the appetizer is tasty enough, students may well hunger for the main course.

Acknowledgments

I would like to thank the three anonymous reviewers for helpful comments, and the many intellectually diverse and engaging students I've had the pleasure to introduce to the field of computational linguistics.

References

Angluin, D. (1980). Inductive inference of formal languages from positive data. *Information and Control* 45:117-135.

Charniak, E. (1997). Statistical Techniques for Natural language Parsing. *AI Magazine* 18:33-44.

Chomsky, N. (1981). *Lectures on government and binding*: Studies in generative grammar. Dordrecht: Foris.

[8] Pending state Department of Education approval, hopefully to be received in Spring 2009.

Elman, J. L. (1990). Finding structure in time. *Cognitive Science* 14:179-211.

Elman, J. L. (1993). Learning and development in neural networks: The importance of starting small. *Cognition* 48:71-99.

Fodor, J. D., and Sakas, W. G. (2005). The Subset Principle in syntax: Costs of compliance. *Journal of Linguistics* 41:513-569.

Gold, E. M. (1967). Language identification in the limit. *Information and Control* 10:447-474.

Goldsmith, J. (2007). Probability for Linguists. *Mathematics and Social Sciences* 180:5-40.

Johnson, K. (2004). Gold's Theorem and Cognitive Science. *Philosophy of Science* 71:571-592.

Jurafsky, D., and Martin, J. H. (2000). *Speech and Language Processing: An Introduction to Natural Language Processing, Computational Linguistics, and Speech Recognition*

Keller, F. (2005). Probabilistic Models of Human Sentence Processing. Presented at *Probabilistic Models of Cognition: The Mathematics of Mind*, IPAM workshop, Los Angeles.

Lee, L. (2004). "I'm sorry Dave, I'm afraid I can't do that" : Linguistics, statistics, and natural language processing circa 2001. In *Computer Science: Reflections on the Field,* 111-118. Washington:National Academies Press.

Lidz, J., Waxman, S., and Freedman, J. (2003). What infants know about syntax but couldn't have learned: Experimental evidence for syntactic structure at 18 months. *Cognition* 89:65-73.

Marcus, G. F. (1993). Negative evidence in language acquisition. *Cognition* 46:53-85.

Marcus, G. F. (1998). Can connectionism save constructivism? *Cognition* 66:153-182.

Pereira, F. (2000) Formal grammar and information theory: Together again. *Philosophical Transactions of the Royal Society* A358:1239-1253.

Pullum, G. K. (1996). Learnability, hyperlearning, and the poverty of the stimulus. *Proceedings of the 22nd Annual Meeting of the Berkley Linguistics Society: General Session and Parasession on the Role of Learnability in Grammatical Theory*, Berkeley: 498-513.

Reali, F., and Christiansen, M. H. (2005). Uncovering the richness of the stimulus: Structural dependence and indirect statistical evidence. *Cognitive Science* 29:1007-10018.

Regier, T., and Gahl, S. (2004). Learning the unlearnable: The role of missing evidence. *Cognition* 93:147-155.

Sakas, W. G., and Fodor, J. D. (2001). The Structural Triggers Learner. In *Language Acquisition and Learnability*, ed. S. Bertolo, 172-233. Cambridge: Cambridge University Press.

Sakas, W. G. (2003) A Word-Order Database for Testing Computational Models of Language Acquisition, *Proceedings of the 41st Annual Meeting of the Association for Computational Linguistics*, ACL-2003: 415-422.

Sakas, W. G. (2004) Introduction. *Proceedings of the First Workshop on Psycho-computational Models of Human Language Acquisition*, COLING-2004. Geneva: iv-vi.

Yang, C. D. (2002). *Knowledge and learning in natural language*. New York: Oxford University Press.

Support Collaboration by Teaching Fundamentals

Matthew Stone
Computer Science and Cognitive Science
Rutgers, The State University of New Jersey
110 Frelinghuysen Road, Piscataway NJ 08854-8019
Matthew.Stone@Rutgers.EDU

Abstract

This paper argues for teaching computer science to linguists through a general course at the introductory graduate level whose goal is to prepare students of all backgrounds for collaborative computational research, especially in the sciences. We describe our work over the past three years in creating a model course in the area, called *Computational Thinking*. What makes this course distinctive is its combined emphasis on the formulation and solution of computational problems, strategies for interdisciplinary communication, and critical thinking about computational explanations.

1 Introduction

The central long-term challenge of computational linguistics is *meaningfulness*. I want to build situated, embodied interactive agents that can work with people through language to achieve a shared understanding of the world. We have an increasing toolkit to approach such problems. Linguistics gives us powerful resources for representing utterance structure and interpretation, for example through the family of formalisms and models that have grown up around dynamic semantics and discourse representation theory. Supervised machine learning has proved to be a profoundly successful software engineering methodology for scaling representations and models from isolated instances to systematic wide coverage. Nevertheless, talking robots are a long way off. This is not a problem that is likely to be solved by writing down a corpus of interpretations for sentences (whatever that might mean) and training up the right kind of synchronous grammar. Nor is it likely to be solved by some one lone genius—half Aravind Joshi, half Richard Stallman—driven to learn and implement solo all of linguistics, artificial intelligence and cognitive science. Progress will come through teamwork, as groups from disparate backgrounds come together to share their discoveries, perspectives, and technical skills on concrete projects of mutual interest. In the course such collaborations, I expect research to unlock fundamental new insights about the nature of meaning, about its dependence on perception, action, linguistic knowledge and social relationships, and about the architecture of systems that can pick up on, create, and generalize meanings in their experience. This paper offers an interim summary of my reflections on preparing the next generation of scientists for this endeavor.

My efforts are anchored to the specific community where I work. Semantics at Rutgers involves a core group of eight faculty from linguistics, philosophy and computer science, with a committed group of about twice that many PhD students. That's three or four students a year: not much if you're thinking of running a class for them, but pretty big if the aim is to place graduates, as we successfully have recently, in positions where they can continue to do semantics (that is, in academic research and tenure-track faculty jobs). Interdisciplinary interaction is the norm for our group; it means that each semantics project inevitably introduces the team to questions, concepts and methodologies that lie outside the background expertise its members bring to the project as individuals. My own work is a good ex-

Proceedings of the Third Workshop on Issues in Teaching Computational Linguistics (TeachCL-08), pages 129–136,
Columbus, Ohio, USA, June 2008.

ample: papers like (DeVault et al., 2006) or (Lepore and Stone, 2007) reveal interconnections between computational ideas and philosophical analysis that my colleagues and I discovered in attempting to bridge our different perspectives on meaning and meaningfulness.

In my experience, what makes it possible for these efforts to take up sophisticated computational ideas is not getting everyone up to speed with a specific programming environment or linguistic formalism. The key step is to get outsiders to appreciate the arguments that computer scientists make, and why they make them. Jeannette Wing (2006) calls this *Computational Thinking*. Wing argues that you should have a course where you teach first-year college students to think like computer scientists. But her arguments apply just as cogently to graduate students in the sciences, and to linguists in particular. Computation as a framework for data collection, data analysis, inference, and explanation has become the norm in the physical and life sciences, and is rapidly transforming the behavioral sciences and especially now the environmental sciences. The situation is not so different in the cultural fields of media, arts and entertainment either—as video game designers are quick to remind us. A wide swath of researchers in any university are now interested in supporting exploratory and innovative interdisciplinary computing research, and specifically in training future faculty to pursue and mentor such collaborations. We decided to make common cause with them at Rutgers, since computational linguistics is such a small group. So our computer science department offers a general course called *Computational Thinking* at the introductory graduate level, aimed at preparing researchers across fields to work on collaborative projects involving computational research. You have an opportunity to do the same.

2 Overview of the Course

We hold *Computational Thinking* in three hour blocks once a week. This responds to Rutgers's quirky geography, with philosophy, linguistics and computer science each on different campuses along a five-mile stretch of the main local thoroughfare, route 18. Elsewhere, it might make more sense to meet in more frequent, shorter sessions.

Each meeting is divided so that students spend about half of each lecture session (and half of each week's work) on technical material drawn from the standard computer science curriculum. As outlined in Section 2.1, the technical material mixes programming practice, problem-solving techniques and theoretical tools, and aims to provide the key elements that are needed to appreciate the computational considerations of an interdisciplinary research project. The typical format of these sessions is live interactive literate programming. We work in Scheme, supported by the DrScheme system available at http://www.plt-scheme.org/software/drscheme/. I beam an image of the Scheme development environment in front of the class and write, run, analyze and debug short programs on the fly. Students follow along on their laptops, doing exercises, asking questions, and seeing results as they go.

The remainder of each class meeting (and the associated outside coursework) explicitly focuses on the interpretive effort and people skills required to reframe the ideas and methodologies of another field in computational terms. Partly, as outlined in Section 2.2, that involves developing a shared understanding of how computers accomplish the representation, processing and problem solving they do, so that students become comfortable at viewing computational systems abstractly as manipulating generative scientific models and knowledge. Fundamentally this understanding is what enables an interdisciplinary team to reconcile the principles of an outside field with the practice of computer science. In addition, as outlined in Section 2.3, we offer explicit discussion of the conversational strategies and interactive skills involved in bridging the different perspectives of an interdisciplinary team, and overcoming the divides of disjoint academic cultures, the stresses of work and deadlines, and the many possibilities for misunderstanding.

Homework mixes short benchmark problems, which allow students to assess their progress against objective standards, with open-ended collaborative assignments that let students apply their domain expertise and challenge their developing skills and programming, problem solving and teamwork. This year students worked individually on a set of exercises on list processing, matching of recursive structures, and interpreting programming languages designed to give some general competence in Scheme. Then they worked in teams of three to four to develop a web site using DrScheme's Scheme servlet architecture. Finally, they explored the possibilities for computational research in their home field in a brief speculative paper.

The course has been offered twice, with about a dozen students participating each session. Three or four each year—the expected number—come from linguistics and the philosophy of language. The small numbers nevertheless add up. Already more than half the students in this spring's dissertation reading group in the philosophy of language had taken *Computational Thinking*. The group's focus was context, and the related problems of common ground, presupposition, anaphora and accommodation. You could feel the difference *Computational Thinking* made for many of the students, philosophers included, who succeeded not only in framing computational arguments about context and context change, but also in synthesizing computational concerns with philosophical ones in explaining linguistic interpretation in terms of context.

2.1 Technical ideas

The technical goal of the course is to give students greater facility in stating problems in computational terms and understanding and building solutions to computational problems. The perspective aligns with the online textbook *How to Design Programs* (Felleisen et al., 2001), which accompanies the Dr Scheme distribution, but we emphasize its continuity with the general mathematical problem solving that students have been doing since elementary school (Polya, 1945). Indeed, following Wing (2006), we see computational thinking as ordinary and pervasive. "It's not just the software and hardware artifacts we produce that will be physically present everywhere and touch our lives all the time, it will be the computational concepts we use to approach and solve problems, manage our daily lives, and communicate and interact with other people" (Wing, 2006, p. 35).

On our view, the main challenge of learning to think like a computer scientist—or to argue with one—is the abstraction and flexibility you need. For example, modern machine learning techniques amount to finding a solution to a problem that is partially specified in advance but partially determined by empirical evidence that is available to the system but not to the programmer. Thus we teach computational problem solving through case studies whose input and output gets progressively more and more abstract and remote from the programmer. The progression is suggested by the following examples, which we cover either by developing solutions in in-class literate programming demonstrations or by assigning them as programming projects.

- Answer a determinate mathematical question, but one whose size or complexity invites the use of an automatic tool in obtaining the results. The sieve of Eratosthenes is a representative case: list the prime numbers less than 100.
- Answer a mathematical question parameterized by an arbitrary and potentially open-ended input. Prototypical example: given a list of numbers determine its maximum element.
- Answer a mathematical question where the input needs to be understood as a generative, compositional representation. Given the abstract syntax of a formula of propositional logic as a recursive list structure and an interpretation assigning truth values to the atomic proposition letters, determine the truth value of the whole formula.
- Answer a question where the input needs to be understood as the specification of a computation, and thus fundamentally similar in kind to the solution. Write an interpreter for a simple programming language (a functional language, like a fragment of scheme; an imperative language involving action and state; or a logical language involving the construction of answer representations as in a production rule shell).
- Answer a mathematical question where the *output* may best be understood as the specification of a computation, depending on input programs or data. A familiar case is taking the derivative of an input function, represented as a Scheme list. A richer example that helps to suggest the optimization perspective of machine learning algorithms is Huffman coding. Given a sequence of input symbols, come up with programs that encode each symbol as a sequence of bits and decode bit sequences as symbol sequences in such a way that the encoded sequence

is as short as possible.

• Answer a question where *both input and output* need to be understood as generative compositional representations with a computational interpretation. Reinforcement learning epitomizes this case. Given training data of a set of histories of action in the world including traces of perceptual inputs, outputs selected and reward achieved, compute a policy—a suitable function from perception to action—that acts to maximize expected reward if the environment continues as patterned in the training data.

We go slowly, spending a couple weeks on each case, and treat each case as an opportunity to teach a range of important ideas. Students see several useful data structures, including association lists (needed for assignments of values to variables in logical formulas and program environments), queues (as an abstraction of data-dependent control in production rules for example), and heaps (part of the infrastructure for Huffman coding). They get an introduction to classic patterns for the design of functional programs, such as mapping a function over the elements of a list, traversing a tree, accumulating results, and writing helper functions. They get some basic theoretical tools for thinking about the results, such as machine models of computation, the notion of computability, and measures of asymptotic complexity. Finally, they see lots of different kinds of representations through which Scheme programs can encode knowledge about the world, including mathematical expressions, HTML pages, logical knowledge bases, probabilistic models and of course Scheme programs themselves.

The goal is to have enough examples that students get a sense that it's useful and powerful to think about computation in a more abstract way. Nevertheless, it's clear that the abstraction involved in these cases eventually becomes very difficult. There's no getting around this. When these students are working successfully on interdisciplinary teams, we don't want them struggling across disciplines to encode specific facts on a case-by-case basis. We want them to be working collaboratively to design tools that will let team members express themselves directly in computational terms and explore their own computational questions.

2.2 Interdisciplinary Readings

There is a rich literature in cognitive science which reflects on representation and computation as explanations of complex behavior. We read extensively from this literature throughout the course. Engaging with these primary sources helps students see how their empirical expertise connects with the mathematical principles that we're covering in our technical sessions. It energizes our discussions of knowledge, representation and algorithms with provocative examples of real-world processes and a dynamic understanding of the scientific questions involved in explaining these processes as computations.

For example, we read Newell and Simon's famous discussions of knowledge and problem solving in intelligent behavior (Newell and Simon, 1976; Newell, 1982). But Todd and Gigerenzer (2007) have much better examples of heuristic problem solving from real human behavior, and much better arguments about how computational thinking and empirical investigation must be combined together to understand the problems that intelligent agents have to solve in the real world. Indeed, students should expect to do science to find out what representations and computations the brain uses—that's why interdisciplinary teamwork is so important. We read Gallistel's survey (2008) to get a sense of the increasing behavioral evidence from a range of species for powerful and general computational mechanisms in cognition. But we also read Brooks (1990) and his critics, especially Kirsh (1991), as a reminder that the final explanations may be surprising.

We also spend a fair amount of time considering how representations might be implemented in intelligent hardware—whether that hardware takes the form of silicon, neurons, or even the hydraulic pipes, tinkertoys, dominoes and legos described by Hillis (1999). Hardware examples like Agre's network models of prioritized argumentation for problem solving and decision making (1997) demystify computation, and help to show why the knowledge level or symbol level is just an abstract, functional characterization of a system. Similarly, readings from connectionism such as (Hinton et al., 1986) dramatize the particular ways that network models of parallel representation and computation anticipate possible explanations in cognitive neuroscience. However, we also explore arguments that symbolic representations, even in a finite brain, may not be best thought of as a prewired inventory of finite possibilities (Pylyshyn, 1984). Computational cognitive science like Hofstadter's (1979)—which emphasizes the creativity that inevitably accompanies compositional representations and general computational capacity—is particularly instructive. In emphasizing the paradoxes of self-reference and the generality of Turing machines, it tells a plausible but challenging story that's diametrically opposed to the "modular" Zeitgeist of domain-specific adaptive cognitive mechanisms.

2.3 Communication

Another tack to motivate course material and keep students engaged is to focus explicitly on interdisciplinary collaboration as a goal and challenge for work in the course. We read descriptions of more or less successful interdisciplinary projects, such as Simon's description of *Logic Theorist* (1996) and Cassell's account of interdisciplinary work on embodied conversational agents (2007). We try to find our own generalizations about what allowed these teams to work together as well as they did, and what we could do differently.

In tandem, we survey social science research about what allows diverse groups to succeed in bridging their perspectives and communicating effectively with one another. Our sourcebook is *Difficult Conversations* (Stone et al., 1999), a guidebook for conflict resolution developed by the Harvard Negotiation Project. It can be a bit awkward to teach such personal material in a technical class, but many students are fascinated to explore suggestions about interaction that work just as well for roommates and significant others as for interdisciplinary colleagues. Anyway, the practices of *Difficult Conversations* do fit with the broader themes of the class; they play out directly in the joint projects and collaborative discussions that students must undertake to complete the class.

I think it's crucial to take collaboration seriously. For many years, we offered a graduate computer science course on computational linguistics as a first interdisciplinary experience. We welcomed scientists from the linguistics, philosophy and library and information science departments, as well as engineers from the computer science and electrical and computer engineering departments, without expecting anyone to bring any special background to the course. Nevertheless, we encouraged both individualized projects and team projects, and worked to support interdisciplinary teams in particular.

We were unsatisfied with this model based on its results. We discovered that we hadn't empowered science students to contribute their expertise effectively to joint projects, nor had we primed computer science students to anticipate and welcome their contributions. So joint projects found computer scientists doing too much translating and not enough enabling for their linguist partners. Linguists felt like they weren't pulling their weight or engaging with the real issues in the field. Computer scientists grew frustrated with the distance of their work from specific practical problems.

Reading and reflecting on about generally-accessible examples goes a long way to bridge the divide. One case study that works well is the history of *Logic Theorist*—the first implemented software system in the history of AI, for building proofs in the propositional logic of Whitehead and Russell's *Principia Mathematica* (1910). In 1955–56, when Herb Simon, Allen Newell and Cliff Shaw wrote it, they were actually an interdisciplinary team. Simon was a social scientist trained at the University of Chicago, now a full professor of business, at what seemed like the peak of a distinguished career studying human decisions in the management of organizations. Newell and Shaw were whiz-kid hackers—Newell was a Carnegie Tech grad student interested in software; Shaw was RAND corporation staff and a builder of prototype research computers. Their work together is documented in two fun chapters of Simon's memoir *Models of My Life* (1996). The story shows how computational collaboration demands modest but real technical expertise and communication skills of all its practitioners. Reading the story early on helps students appreciate the goal of the computational thinking class from the beginning: to instill these key shared concepts, experiences, attitudes and practices, and thereby to scaffold interdisciplinary technical research.

To work together, Simon, Newell and Shaw needed to share a fairly specific understanding of the concept of a *representation* (Newell and Simon, 1976). Their work together consisted of taking knowledge about their domain and regimenting it into formal structures and manipulations that they could actually go on to implement. The framework they developed for conceptualizing this process rested on representations as symbolic structures: formal objects which they could understand as invested with meaning and encoding knowledge, but which they could also realize in computer systems and use to define concrete computational operations. In effect, then, the concept of representation defined their project together, and they all had to master it.

Simon, Newell and Shaw also needed a shared understanding of the computational methodology that would integrate their different contributions into the final program. Their work centered around the development of a high-level programming language that allowed Simon, Newell and Shaw to coordinate their efforts together in a particularly transparent way. Simon worked *in* the programming language, using its abstract resources to specify formulas and rules of inference in intuitive but precise terms; on his own, he could think through the effects of these programs. Newell and Shaw worked to *build* the programming language, by developing the underlying machinery to realize the abstract computations that Simon was working with. The programming language was a *product* of their effort together; its features were negotiated based on Simon's evolving conceptual understanding of heuristic proof search and Newell and Shaw's engagement with the practical demands of implementation. The language is in effect a fulcrum where both domain expertise and computational constraints exercise their leverage on one another. This perspective on language design comes as a surprise both to scientists, who are used to thinking of programming paradigms as remote and arcane, and to computer scientists, who are used to thinking of them solely in terms of their software engineering patterns, but it remains extremely powerful. To make it work, everyone involved in the research has to understand how their judicious collaborative exploration of new techniques for specification and programming can knit their work together.

In the course of developing their language, Simon, Newell and Shaw also came to share a set of principles for discussing the computational feasibility of alternative design decisions. Proof, like most useful computational processes, is most naturally characterized as a search problem. Inevitably, this meant that the development of *Logic Theorist* ran up against the possibility of combinatorial explosions and the need for heuristics and approximations to overcome them. The solutions Simon, Newell and Shaw developed reflected the team's combined insight in constructing representations for proof search that made the right information explicit and afforded the right symbolic manipulations. Many in the class, especially computer scientists, will have seen such ideas in introductory AI courses, so it's challenging and exciting for them to engage with Simon's presentation of these ideas in their original interdisciplinary context as new, computational principles governing psychological explanations.

Finally—and crucially—this joint effort reflected the team's social engagement with each other, not just their intellectual relationships. In their decades of work together, Simon and Newell cultivated and perfected a specific set of practices for engaging and supporting each other in collaborative work. Simon particularly emphasizes their practice of open discussion. Their talk didn't always aim directly at problem-solving or design. In the first instance, the two just worked towards understanding—distilling potential insights into mutually-satisfying formulations. They put forward vague and speculative ideas, and engaged with them constructively, not critically.

Simon's memoirs also bring out the respect the teammates had for each others' expertise and work styles, especially when different—as Newell's brash, hands-on, late-night scheming was for Simon—and the shared commitment they brought to making their work together fun. Their good relationship as people may have been just as important to their success at interdisciplinary research as the shared interests, ideas and intellectual techniques they developed together.

These kinds of case studies allow students to make sense of the goals and methods of the course in advance of the technical and interpretive details. Not much has changed since *Logic Theorist*. Effective computational teamwork still involves developing a conceptual toolbox that allows all participants on the project to formulate precise representations and engage with those representations in computational terms. And it still requires a more nuanced approach to communication, interaction and collaboration than more homogeneous efforts—one focused not just on solving problems and getting work done but on fostering teammates' learning and communication, by addressing phenomena from multiple perspectives, building shared vocabulary, and finding shared values and satisfaction. These skills are abstract and largely domain independent. The class allows students to explore them.

3 Interim Assessment

The resources for creating our *Computational Thinking* class came from the award of a training grant designed to crossfertilize vision research between psychology and computer science. The course has now become a general resource for our cognitive science community. It attracts psychologists from across the cognitive areas, linguists, philosophers, and information scientists. We also make sure that there is a critical mass of computer scientists to afford everyone meaningful collaborative experiences across disciplines. For example, participation is required for training grant participants from computer science, and other interdisciplinary projects invite their computer science students to build community.

One sign of the success of the course is that students take responsibility for shaping the course material to facilitate their own joint projects. Our initial version of the course emphasized the technical ideas and programming techniques described in Section 2.1. Students asked for more opportunities for collaboration; we added it right away in year one. Students also asked for more reading and discussion to get a sense of what computation brings to interdisciplinary research, and what it requires of it. We added that in year two, providing much of the materials now summarized in Sections 2.2 and 2.3. In general, we found concrete and creative discussions aimed at an interdisciplinary audience more helpful than the general philosophical statements that computer scientists offer of the significance of computation as a methodology. We will continue to broaden the reading list with down-to-earth materials covering rich examples.

From student feedback with the second running of the class, the course could go further to get students learning from each other and working together early on. We plan to respond by giving an initial pretest to get a sense of the skills students bring to the class and pair people with partners of differing skills for an initial project. As always this project will provide a setting where all students acquire a core proficiency in thinking precisely about processes and representations. But by connecting more experienced programmers with novices from the beginning, we hope to allow students to ramp up quickly into hands-on exploration of specification, program design and collaborative computational research. Possible initial projects include writing a production rule shell and using it to encode knowledge in an application of identifying visual objects, recognizing language structure, diagnosing causes for observed phenomena or planning goal-directed activity; or writing an interpreter to evaluate mathematical expressions and visualize the shapes of mathematical objects or probabilistic state spaces.

Anecdotally, we can point to a number of cases where *Computational Thinking* has empowered students to leverage computational methods in their own research. Students have written programs to model experimental manipulations, analyze data, or work through the consequences of a theory, where otherwise they would have counted on pencil-and-paper inference or an off-the-shelf tool. However, as yet, we have only a preliminary sense of how well the course is doing at its goal of promoting computational research and collaboration in the cognitive science community here. Next year we will get our first detailed assessment, however, with the first offering of a new follow-on course called "Interdisciplinary Methods in Perceptual Science". This course explicitly requires students to team up in extended projects that combine psychological and computational methods for visual interaction. We will be watching students' experience in the new class closely to see whether our curriculum supports them in developing the concepts, experiences, attitudes and practices they need to work together.

4 Conclusion

Teamwork in computational linguistics often starts by endowing machine learning methods with models or features informed by the principles and results of linguistic theory. Teams can also work together to formalize linguistic knowledge and interpretation for applications, through grammar development and corpus annotation, in ways that fit into larger system-building efforts. More generally, we need to bridge the science of conversation and software architecture to program interactive systems that exhibit more natural linguistic behavior. And we can even bring computation and linguistics together outside of system building: pursuing computational theories as an integral part of the explanation of human linguistic knowledge and behavior.

To work on such teams, researchers do have to master a range of specific intellectual connections. But they need the fundamentals first. They have to appreciate the exploratory nature of interdisciplinary research, and understand how such work can be fostered by sharing representational insight, designing new high-level languages and thinking critically about computation. *Computational Thinking* is our attempt to teach the fundamentals directly.

You should be find it easy to make a case for this course at your institution. In these days of declining enrollments and interdisciplinary fervor, most departments will welcome a serious effort to cultivate the place of CS as a bridge discipline for research projects across the university. *Computational Thinking* is a means to get more students taking our classes and drawing on our concepts and discoveries to work more effectively with us! As the course stabilizes, we plan to reach out to other departments with ongoing computational collaborations, especially economics and the life and environmental sciences departments. You could design the course from the start for the full spectrum of computational collaborations already underway at your university.

Acknowledgments

Supported by IGERT 0549115. Thanks to the students in 198:503 and reviewers for the workshop.

References

Philip E. Agre. 1997. *Computation and Human Experience*. Cambridge.

Rodney A. Brooks. 1990. Elephants don't play chess. *Robotics and Autonomous Systems*, 6:3–15.

Justine Cassell. 2007. Body language: Lessons from the near-human. In J. Riskin, editor, *Genesis Redux: Essays in the History and Philosophy of Artificial Intelligence*, pages 346–374. Chicago.

David DeVault, Iris Oved, and Matthew Stone. 2006. Societal grounding is essential to meaningful language use. In *Proceedings of AAAI*, pages 747–754.

Matthias Felleisen, Robert Bruce Findler, Matthew Flatt, and Shriram Krishnamurthi. 2001. *How to Design Programs: An Introduction to Computing and Programming*. MIT.

C. R. Gallistel. 2008. Learning and representation. In John H. Byrne, editor, *Learning and Memory: A Comprehensive Reference*. Elsevier.

W. Daniel Hillis. 1999. *The Pattern on the Stone*. Basic Books.

Geoffrey E. Hinton, David E. Rumelhart, and James L. McClelland. 1986. Distributed representations. In *Parallel Distributed Processing: Explorations in the Microstructure of Cognition, Volume 1: Foundations*, pages 77–109. MIT.

Douglas Hofstadter. 1979. *Gödel, Escher, Bach: An Eternal Golden Braid*. Basic Books.

David Kirsh. 1991. Today the earwig, tomorrow man? *Artificial Intelligence*, pages 161–184.

Ernest Lepore and Matthew Stone. 2007. Logic and semantic analysis. In Dale Jacquette, editor, *Handbook of the Philosophy of Logic*, pages 173–204. Elsevier.

Allen Newell and Herbert A. Simon. 1976. Computer science as empirical inquiry: Symbols and search. *Communications of the ACM*, 19(3):113–126.

Allen Newell. 1982. The knowledge level. *Artificial Intelligence*, 18:87–127.

G. Polya. 1945. *How to Solve it*. Princeton.

Zenon Pylyshyn. 1984. *Computation and Cognition: Toward a Foundation for Cognitive Science*. MIT.

Herbert A. Simon, 1996. *Models of My Life*, chapter Roots of Artificial Intelligence and Artificial Intelligence Achieved, pages 189–214. MIT.

Douglas Stone, Bruce Patton, and Sheila Heen. 1999. *Difficult Conversations: How to Discuss What Matters Most*. Penguin.

Peter M. Todd and Gerd Gigerenzer. 2007. Environments that make us smart: Ecological rationality. *Current Directions in Psych. Science*, 16(3):170–174.

Alfred North Whitehead and Bertrand Russell. 1910. *Principia Mathematica Volume 1*. Cambridge.

Jeannette M. Wing. 2006. Computational thinking. *Communications of the ACM*, 49(3):33–35.

Author Index

Baldridge, Jason, 1, 62
Bansleben, Erik, 10
Bender, Emily M., 10
Bird, Steven, 27, 62

Christian, Gwen, 80

Dorr, Bonnie J., 71

Eisner, Jason, 97
Erk, Katrin, 1

Fosler-Lussier, Eric, 36
Freedman, Reva, 114

Hockey, Beth Ann, 80

Klein, Ewan, 62

Levin, Lori, 87
Levow, Gina-Anne, 106
Lin, Jimmy, 54
Loper, Edward, 62

Madnani, Nitin, 71

Payne, Thomas E., 87

Radev, Dragomir R., 87

Sakas, William Gregory, 120
Smith, Noah A., 97
Stone, Matthew, 129

Xia, Fei, 10, 45

Zinsmeister, Heike, 19